De[...]

To

my good friends

Steve & Susan Crandall

Best wishes for the New Year

Barrie A. Mcwhot

SHARING
OWNERSHIP

SHARING OWNERSHIP

The Manager's Guide to ESOPs and Other Productivity Incentive Plans

Darien A. McWhirter

JOHN WILEY & SONS, INC.

NEW YORK • CHICHESTER • BRISBANE • TORONTO • SINGAPORE

Copyright © 1993 by Darien A. McWhirter.
Published by John Wiley & Sons, Inc.

Library of Congress Cataloging-in-Publication Data

McWhirter, Darien A. (Darien Auburn)
    Sharing ownership : the manager's guide to ESOPs and
other productivity incentive plans / Darien A. McWhirter.
        p.   cm.
    Includes index.
    ISBN 0-471-57733-2 (alk. paper)
    1. Employee stock options—United States.   2. Employee ownership—
United States.   I. Title.
HD4928.S74M35   1993
658.3'225—dc20   92-46584

Printed in the United States of America.
10 9 8 7 6 5 4 3 2 1

*This book is dedicated
to the memory of
Louis Kelso,
who dedicated his
life to the goal of
making everyone an owner*

Preface

After receiving my Ph.D. in political science from Yale University, I taught for several years at Miami University in Ohio. One course that always attracted a full house was called Modern Political Ideologies. In that course, the students and I discussed how an ideal socialist, capitalist, or anarchist economy might function. All three of these systems had, in theory, a belief that an economy would function best if the workers had an ownership stake in the companies they worked for. They differed on how that ownership stake should be structured. When students asked for more details concerning how a capitalist system could allow workers to own a stake in the companies they worked for, I could not provide a satisfactory answer.

I ultimately left Miami University to attend the University of Texas Law School in search of an answer to that question. That search led me to become a specialist in employment law and, ultimately, to work for a year and a half at the National Center for Employee Ownership.

One of the difficulties of writing a book like this is to make the information understandable to readers from a wide variety of backgrounds. For instance, students of public finance will be familiar with the use of tax incentives to change behavior, while many other readers will not. Attorneys and business executives will be familiar with the advantages and disadvantages of corporations and partnerships but may be unfamiliar with trusts and cooperatives as forms of business organization. Many lawyers who know about stock options have never encountered the term *strike price* even though it is basic to any discussion of stock options. Most business executives understand bonuses and commissions but have never studied, or thought much about, pension policy. Many government officials may be familiar with pension policy but not bonuses and commissions.

It is a fact of life in American higher education that a student can graduate from a law school without having heard the word *cooperative*, from a business school without having heard the term *stock option*, and from a graduate school of public policy without having heard a discussion of the pros and cons of dividends versus stock purchases as a way of providing money to stockholders.

It is also a fact of business life that executives reading this book will represent a broad mix of backgrounds. Some may have an MBA or a degree in engineering or some other professional field. Others may be graduates of the school of hard knocks. Each will bring his or her own perspective to the information presented. Even those readers who have studied many of the concepts discussed in this book will not have studied them all. Many readers will be surprised at what their own business education, whether formal or informal, has neglected to cover.

More than ten million U.S. workers have a significant ownership stake in the companies they work for. For most of those workers, no matter how experienced or well trained, many of the issues presented here are new. Few of these employees ask questions about the stock purchase or profit-sharing plans of a company before accepting a job even though these plans may have more impact on their long-term financial security than the size of their annual salary.

More than eight million U.S. workers own stock in the company they work for through employee stock ownership plans (ESOPs). While many companies that have ESOPs make a real effort to explain how these plans work, many others do not. In too many companies the reality is that workers do not have the basic business background needed to fully understand the hows and whys of ESOPs.

The goal of this book is to provide, in one volume, both an introduction to the business knowledge needed to understand ownership incentives and an in-depth discussion of those incentives. The book is written for executives, attorneys, government officials, and investors as well as for the average worker. Each of these readers will be familiar with some of the issues discussed and unfamiliar with others. Rather than assume knowledge that readers may not have, I will cover in Part One the basic concepts to be discussed throughout the book. Part Two will discuss the four basic types of ownership incentives—stock options, stock purchase plans, trusts, and cooperatives—and the advantages and disadvantages of each.

Part Three will focus on how the most common type of ownership incentive in the world today—ESOPs—work in the United States. ESOPs have advantages and disadvantages for employees, stockholders, managers, and taxpayers. ESOPs are the most successful experiment to date for increasing ownership among rank-and-file employees.

Throughout this book I shall make an effort to look at how other countries attempt to provide ownership incentives. While the United States is the leader in providing employees with ownership in the companies they work for, other countries are catching up. For readers outside the United States, when I refer to the "federal" government I am referring to the "national" government of the United States based in Washington, D.C. In most countries, either the national government is very weak and the state (provincial) governments are strong, or vice versa. Only in the United States are both levels of government so deeply involved in so many aspects of citizens' lives.

During the 1992 presidential campaign, a lot was heard about infrastructure. It is important to realize that the kinds of ownership that companies can and do offer to their employees is as important to the resurgence of the American economy as the amount of money spent on research or on new roads and bridges. In the long run, it may be more important. In the race for economic success, the team with the most owners is probably going to finish first.

Many people, experts in their field, have contributed short summaries dealing with particular questions of interest. You will find these inserted in the chapters or in the appendices at the end of the chapters. I will not list them here as you will see who they are as you read this book, but I want to thank them for their willingness to share their expertise with me and my readers.

I want to thank my former colleagues at the National Center for

Employee Ownership for helping me to find answers to many of my questions. I also want to thank all those who contributed, and continue to contribute, to *The Journal of Employee Ownership Law and Finance* for their willingness to share their knowledge. The 1970s and 1980s saw a tremendous growth in ownership in the United States. This could not have happened without the efforts of hundreds of lawyers, accountants, bankers, union leaders, legislators, government officials, and others interested in increasing ownership throughout the U.S. economy.

Special thanks go to Louis Kelso, who passed away recently. Louis Kelso was nice enough during what turned out to be the last two years of his life to discuss some of these issues with me. His belief that capitalism works best when everyone is a capitalist, and that this could be achieved through a combination of intelligent government policies and increased education, lives on in both the United States and around the world.

Finally, I have to say that the opinions expressed in this book are mine alone. Everyone involved in trying to increase the spread of ownership has his or her own ideas about how that can best be accomplished, and no two individuals agree on everything. Also, while I have worked diligently to verify every statement of fact contained in this book, there is always the possibility of error. This book is intended to provide a general introduction to the topics discussed, not a technical manual for performing complex legal tasks. Persons wishing to follow through on any of the schemes discussed in this book must consult an attorney expert in this field who can provide them with advice concerning their unique situation. Also, the law in this area has changed a great deal in the past 10 years and will continue to change. Any statement of what the law is may be out of date by the time you read this. While I do not expect the general thrust of the law to change much in the 1990s, the details certainly will change over time.

DARIEN A. McWHIRTER

Austin, Texas
  and San Jose, California
July 1993

Contents

ONE
THE BASICS

TWO
FORMS OF OWNERSHIP

THREE
EMPLOYEE STOCK OWNERSHIP PLANS

1

Introduction

Throughout most of the twentieth century, the productive wealth of the world has been in the hands of a very small group. Whether they called themselves the 400 (400 families were estimated to own over half the productive wealth in the United States in the 1940s) or the Politburo (an equal number of families controlled the productive wealth of the Soviet Union during the days of Communist party rule), ownership of what Marx called the "means of production" was restricted to a very small group. Beginning in the 1940s in the United States, later in other countries, productive wealth began to be divided more generally among the population. There were many reasons for this, but the most important were government policies that encouraged the expansion of wealth ownership. The United States government encouraged people to buy their own homes by guaranteeing long-term mortgages and allowing people to deduct the amount paid for mortgage interest from their income taxes. The other major incentive for spreading ownership among a larger group in the United States came about almost by accident. It was the creation of employee pension and benefit plans.

During World War II, wages in the United States were frozen for the duration of the war. Labor unions negotiated promises of later compensation for the work done during the war in the form of private pension and benefit plans. Many of these pension plans were originally

1

pay as you go. This meant that the company did not put any money in a fund to pay future pensions but simply promised to pay retired workers out of the company's future revenue. Over time, spurred by accounting rules and federal legislation, more and more pension funds actually placed money into a trust account for the workers. This modest beginning had turned into a major economic force by the end of the twentieth century. In 1980, 18 percent of all the common stock of American companies was owned by American employee pension and benefit funds. In 1990, the figure had grown to 28 percent according to the Columbia University Institutional Investor Project. If trends continue, soon after the year 2000 American employee pension and benefit funds will own over half the common stock in America and that stock will have a value of over $3 trillion.

During the 1970s and 1980s, more and more executives found that they could increase their wealth significantly if they participated in the ownership of the companies that they managed. By the early 1990s, over half the executives in America had an ownership stake in the companies they worked for. Millions of rank-and-file employees also found themselves owning a significant stake in the companies they worked for through a variety of mechanisms.

The purpose of this book is to explain to managers, workers, and stockholders how these various ownership incentives work. What are the advantages and disadvantages of ownership incentives from these three points of view, and from the point of view of the average citizen in America and around the world? When is one type of incentive more appropriate than another? What are the tax and accounting consequences as well as the potential managerial and financial consequences of each type of ownership incentive? We begin with the supposition that having more people owning more companies is good and that having them own more of the company they work for is potentially even better.

The issue of spreading ownership is of interest to more than just Americans. Leaders of dozens of countries around the world from Argentina to Australia and from Poland to Trinidad are asking how they can structure a capitalist economy that "works" and at the same time allows ownership to be divided among a large segment of the population. These same leaders are asking if spreading ownership can contribute to economic growth and political stability and how it can be structured to best achieve those results.

We heard much during the 1992 presidential campaign about the "vision thing." Americans, having won the Cold War, wanted to know what was in it for them. The ancestors of many of these Americans did not have a problem with the "vision thing." They had a very clear vision of what they wanted when they came to America or when they were freed from slavery. They wanted *ownership*. No one had to explain to them what ownership meant. Ownership meant control, and ownership of your own home and business meant control over your own life. In New England in the beginning of the nineteenth century, it was considered a disgrace if someone had to stoop to working for "wages." By the end of the nineteenth century and into the twentieth, the desire for ownership had been replaced with the desire for a job. In 1946, with passage of the Full Employment Act, it became the major policy of the United States government to do everything possible to make sure that every adult American had a "job." Ownership was moved to the back burner of government policy except to encourage as many people as possible to own their own homes.

While everyone, liberal and conservative, Democrat and Republican, recognized that sharing ownership was, at least in theory, a good idea, no one could figure out in the 1940s how a large number of people could share the ownership of America's productive wealth in any meaningful way.

By the 1990s, U.S. companies had created for their executives, and in some cases for their rank-and-file employees, dozens of ways for them to share in the ownership of the company. An executive might have a compensation package that included stock options, restricted stock, regular stock, preferred stock, phantom stock, and stock appreciation rights. He or she might have the opportunity to participate in a profit-sharing plan, a 401(k) plan, or an employee stock-ownership plan, all of which owned or intended to purchase stock in the company the executive worked for.

During the late 1980s and early 1990s, more and more college graduates found job offers coming from smaller, newer companies rather than from Fortune 500 companies. Some viewed that state of affairs with disappointment, but for many it could mean the chance to participate in the creation of a major new company in the twenty-first century as both an employee and an owner. Thousands of young executives and programmers who grew the Microsoft Corporation from a start-up venture to a multibillion dollar company in less than a decade became millionaires at very young ages (Bill Gates, the founder, became a billionaire).

During the 1980s, more and more rank-and-file employees were also given a chance to participate in the game of capitalism through everything from stock option plans (PepsiCo instituted a stock option plan for every employee) to employee stock ownership plans (some 10,000 such plans were in place in the United States by the early 1990s). Many of these employees greatly increased their net worth in a relatively short time. Today no one, from the chief executive officer (CEO) to the janitor, from the stockholders to the managers, from the union president to the members of the board of directors, can afford not to understand how all this works and "what's in it for them."

Restructuring America and the World

Early in the 1950s, America sat on top of the world. It is hard to imagine today, but the gross national product of the United States was 80 percent of the gross national product of the entire world! The productive capacity of the rest of the world had been destroyed by World War II. Through the Marshall Plan in Europe and massive rebuilding efforts in Japan, the European and Japanese economies began to seriously compete in the world market for manufactured goods by the 1960s. During the 1950s and 1960s, many American companies became fat and inefficient. Many American companies did not care about quality because they had no real competition in the world market. Companies in countries like Germany and Japan took advantage of this complacency and gained larger and larger shares of the world markets for manufactured goods by building better quality goods for a lower price. This caused the United States economy to require a massive restructuring unlike any seen in the history of the world. As this book is written, this restructuring is about half way through to completion. America's place in the twenty-first century depends on how that restructuring is completed.

Other countries also entered the decade of the 1990s in need of major change. The former Communist countries of Eastern Europe and the Soviet Union were faced with changing to a capitalist economy. Australia, a country that once boasted the highest standard of living in the world, had slipped out of the top 20 in terms of real living standards because of low productivity and lower product quality. All of this restructuring is, of course, being watched by the developing countries, who would like to have as many of the advantages of a free enterprise system as possible without so many of the disadvantages.

By the end of the 1980s, many lamented the state of the U.S. economy. As Mark Twain would say, the reports of the death of the American economy are greatly exaggerated. However, the restructuring is only half over. More layoffs and more downsizing can be expected in the 1990s. The pain from this restructuring will be felt by the managerial sector most of all. The average Japanese company has 5 percent of its work force engaged in management, compared with about 10 percent in the average American company. In the 1990s, more and more American companies will have to learn to live with fewer managers. Ownership incentives for rank-and-file employees may be part of that de-management strategy.

In two dozen "new" countries in Eastern Europe and the former Soviet Union, the question of how to share ownership is one of the key questions surrounding privatization. How can thousands of formerly state-owned enterprises be sold in a way that does not result in "foreigners" owning most of the productive assets of the country? Leaders in these countries wonder how they can use tax and pension policy to increase the level of ownership in their society the same way that the United States has done.

Running a Capitalist Society

During the twentieth century, the United States and other western countries have been experimenting with different ways of running a capitalist society. Problems from the Great Depression to the recession of

1990–1992 demonstrate that they have not perfected it yet. Economists may worship at the altar of the "market," but no market is perfect and all markets experience some degree of "failure." Whereas it was generally believed at the end of the nineteenth century that the best government policy was laissez-faire, it is now believed that markets need government intervention, but intervention of the right kind. Government intervention that protects inefficient producers or tries to control prices is believed to be counterproductive in the long run. Government intervention that tries to increase competition or consumer information or to cause the "true cost" of a product to be reflected in its price is believed to further the cause of an efficient free market economy.

When discussing the "dismal science" of economics, something is often forgotten. The basic purpose of an economic system is not to make the rich richer or the poor richer, but to create and distribute as many goods and services as possible. The Communist system of the Soviet Union created few goods and services and distributed them as unequally as any other system. While the system of secret police and state terror was unpleasant, it was the collapse of the economy that brought about the downfall of the Soviet Union. Communists talked about the "ownership of the means of production," but critics pointed out that the means of production in the Soviet Union were really owned by a small group of Communist party officials who used their ownership to live very well while most people in the society stood in line for bread and toilet paper. After the revolution of 1991, the citizens of the former Soviet Union suddenly found themselves the actual owners of the means of production, but this was a hollow victory given the obsolete state of most of the factories and farms. These countries want foreign investment, but they do not want to give up "ownership." Foreign investors are not willing to invest in Eastern Europe without ownership any more than they were willing to do so in the nineteenth century when they invested in the United States.

Stages of Capitalism

When immigrants came to the United States in the eighteenth and nineteenth centuries, they came hoping to become owners of farms, shops, and small businesses. During the first stage of capitalism, a skilled farmer or craftsperson, with nothing but hand tools, created finished products with little or no help from anyone else. Then came capitalism, stage two—the Industrial Revolution. Between the 1870s and the 1970s, uneducated, unskilled, and relatively unmotivated workers could produce a vast amount of wealth using machines. Beginning in the 1970s, the industrialized nations began moving into the third stage of capitalism. In this third stage, the skilled and educated workers of stage one are being combined with the advanced machines of stage two to produce goods and services of unheard of quality and quantity. Early in the twenty-first century all workers, from the janitor to the CEO, will have a personal computer to aid them in doing their job.

Will these highly educated workers, working with computerized machines, be content to receive only "wages" for their work or will they want something more? The skilled workers of two centuries ago expected to become owners of their own business. Will the skilled workers of the twenty-first century expect anything less?

Three Mind-Sets

Workers at the end of the twentieth century can be viewed as having one of three mind-sets. The first could be called the *bureaucratic mind-set*. The worker with a bureaucratic mind-set is trying to work as little as possible without being fired. One of the factors that led to the collapse of the Soviet Union was the fact that millions of workers had a bureaucratic mind-set in a system in which it was almost impossible to be fired. If workers are trying to see how little they can do without being fired and no one is ever fired, very little work gets done. Visitors to the Soviet Union came back with stories of restaurants where the waiters simply sat at the side of the room and waited until the customers got tired of not being waited on and left. This bureaucratic mind-set is not limited just to government agencies. There are millions of workers in private corporations around the world who fit this description.

The second mind-set is best called the *professional mind-set*. The worker with the professional mind-set is motivated by a desire to live up to the standards of his or her profession. The quantity and quality of the work done by people in different professions is dictated largely by the standards of that profession. A well-trained lawyer, doctor, accountant, or scientist is going to try to do a good job whether he or she works for government or private industry. It is funny to hear that this or that job would be done better by private enterprise when the actual person who would do the job in either case is a professional and would be bound more by professional standards than by any other motivator.

A third mind-set is the *entrepreneurial mind-set*. Persons with an entrepreneurial mind-set are motivated to do what is in the long-term best interest of the enterprise they work for, regardless of the short-term consequences for themselves personally in terms of longer hours or lower pay. A person who begins a business usually has an entrepreneurial mind-set, and this accounts for the ability of many new enterprises to weather the storms that inevitably come. One of the key questions of the 1990s and beyond is how we can give an entrepreneurial mind-set to a large number of workers.

The Sole Proprietor Model

During the twentieth century, much of what passed for management science was an attempt to create in a large organization with many employees the same type of structure that exists in a sole proprietorship. A sole proprietor is one person owning and running a small business. When sole proprietors tell themselves to do something, they know why they are being told to do that, and what effect it will probably have on them personally and on the organization as a whole. Also, because the proprietor is both the person giving the orders and the person taking the orders, proprietors know that their opinions were taken into account when it was decided to take a particular course of action and they agree that this is the course of action the business should take under the circumstances.

In an attempt to model the sole proprietor, management science has instituted elaborate communication systems in even the largest organizations. Employees are brought into the decision-making process in an effort to make them "feel" that their opinion counts (whether it really counts or not is considered of secondary importance by much of modern management science). The idea is that if employees "feel" that they were consulted about a decision, they will be more likely to support the final decision and work to make it a success.

Recently, a new copy center opened near my home. During the first year the owner, a sole proprietor, was there to help me. He always went out of his way to help me meet my deadlines, even if it meant staying late at the shop or letting me use a machine normally reserved for himself. Needless to say, I became a steady customer. He was so successful that he soon hired two assistants who did not go out of their way to help me and did not care if I came back the next day with more business or not. I began to try to time my visits to the shop to coincide with the presence of the owner. After a year the shop expanded, more employees were hired, and the sole proprietor went on to start another location. I no longer have any special incentive to take my business to this particular copy shop. While it is no worse than others I could frequent, it is no longer any better. The employees do not care whether I am a satisfied customer or not. If I don't come back tomorrow that is just one less piece of work for them to do. The owner is gone and with him has gone the entrepreneurial mind-set.

Could modern management science, with its expanded communication and decision-making procedures, be combined with something that would give even the lowest level employee an entrepreneurial mind-set? If that could be accomplished, would that be advantageous for the long-term health of the enterprise? Many people think so. However, there is probably no way to give employees an entrepreneurial mind-set without giving them some form of ownership in the enterprise.

Sharing Ownership

That leads us to the subject of this book. How can ownership be shared with employees? Should it be shared with all employees in the same way or should higher level employees receive one type of ownership incentive and rank-and-file employees another? What are the tax and financial consequences of each type of ownership incentive?

PART
ONE

THE BASICS

2

The Tax Man Cometh

One of the main differences between decision making at the end of the twentieth century and decision making at the end of the nineteenth century is the fact that every decision has to be made today with the tax consequences taken into account.

Taxing Individuals

Two centuries ago, taxes on individuals were basically of two types—tariffs and property taxes. Both were relatively easy to collect. Tariffs were simply collected as goods crossed the border, and property taxes were collected once a year on the value of a person's property. Because most property was in the form of real estate and animals, property was fairly easy to observe and value. Property taxes were progressive (fell more heavily on the wealthy) because most wealth was held in the form of observable property. In other words, the wealthier a person was, the more taxable property the person had and, therefore, the more property taxes the person paid. It is ironic that in many countries today, because most wealth is no longer in the form of real or personal property, property taxes are no longer progressive; in some cases, they are actually regressive (fall more heavily on the poorest citizens in the society).

Sales taxes were introduced as a way to raise revenue for the government on goods made and sold inside the country. The value-added tax popular in Europe today is in reality nothing more than a complex sales tax. The ultimate customer for a product or service ends up paying a higher price, and the money is given to the government.

The great innovation of the twentieth century was the income tax. As wealth became more portable and easier to hide from the tax collector, the idea of taxing income became more fashionable and more practical. Over time, tax codes made distinctions between different kinds of income with basically five types of income recognized for income tax purposes in most countries: wages, interest, dividends, bonuses, and capital gains. Wages are the money paid to employees for work done. Interest is the income made when money is loaned from one person to another. Dividends are the income made on an investment of money in an enterprise. When someone buys stock in a corporation and receives money each year in return, that is a dividend. A bonus is money paid to an employee because the employee has done a particularly good job or the enterprise has done particularly well. It might be paid in the form of cash, property, or stock in the company. Finally, capital gain is the money made when a piece of property is sold for more than its purchase price. If someone buys an ounce of gold for $300 one year and sells it for $400 another year, they have made $100 on the transaction and this income is called a capital gain.

One of the major discoveries of the twentieth century is that taxes affect behavior. If people have to pay sales taxes on some products and not on others, this discourages them from buying the taxed products and encourages them to buy the untaxed or lower taxed products. If different forms of income are taxed differently, people, over time, will try to increase the form of income that is taxed at a lower rate.

In the 1980s, the United States and Canada conducted one of the largest experiments in history on the ability of taxes to discourage behavior. During this decade, both governments taxed tobacco products heavily while at the same time providing information to the general population on the dangers of smoking cigarettes. During the 1980s, the percentage of adults in the United States that smoked cigarettes declined from almost 70 percent to less than 30 percent.

Smoking by teenagers was reduced by two-thirds in Canada. At the same time, during the same decade, the governments of the United States and Canada attempted to discourage the use of a variety of recreational drugs by making them illegal. This strategy was not nearly as successful as the "tax and educate" strategy used to reduce cigarette smoking.

The "tax and educate" policy also had other benefits. While making certain popular drugs illegal had little or no effect on the consumption of those drugs, governments were forced to spend billions of dollars in an ineffective attempt to force people to stop doing something that they wanted to do. At the same time, these governments made billions of dollars on tobacco taxes. Canada raised more revenue because the average tax on a pack of cigarettes in Canada as of the summer of 1992 was $3.25 compared with 51¢ in the United States. In summary, when trying to change the behavior of citizens, taxing and regulating the behavior discourages it and raises revenue; criminalizing the behavior is a less effective discouragement and costs money.

Encouraging Home Ownership

During the twentieth century, many countries decided that they would be better off if a high percentage of their population owned the houses in which they lived. Homeowners take better care of their property, take an active part in community affairs, and generally are considered an asset in most societies. In the United States in the 1930s, the federal government put in place two policies that proved very effective. First, people were allowed to deduct from their income taxes the cost of interest payments made on a home mortgage. Second, agencies were set up to guarantee the payment of these mortgages, allowing banks to offer lower interest rates than would otherwise have been the case.

This experiment in tax policy turned out to be one of the great success stories of the twentieth century. Millions of American citizens, who would otherwise have spent their lives renting, came to own equity in their homes. Home ownership in the United States increased every decade from the 1940s onward. According to the U.S. Census

Bureau, in the 1980s the level of home ownership in the United States leveled off at approximately 65 percent, meaning that 65 percent of all American households own the homes they live in.

It is ironic that what was throughout most of the twentieth century a great success story in encouraging middle-class people to obtain wealth by buying a home has become mainly an encouragement only for the richest Americans. It has also encouraged homeowners to increase the mortgage on their homes to pay for other expenses, putting that home ownership in jeopardy. This occurred because, in the 1980s, the federal government of the United States tried to close various tax loopholes (one person's tax incentive is another person's tax loophole). Individuals at one time had been able to deduct from their personal income money spent on interest for consumer purchases. By the late 1980s, they no longer could. However, they could still deduct the interest paid on a home mortgage. What millions of Americans did was to increase the debt on their home to pay for a variety of purchases, ranging from cars, to boats and vacations. This allowed them to have a lower interest rate on these consumer loans and to deduct the interest payment from their income, thus further reducing their income taxes. It also meant that the debt on their homes increased, making it more likely that they would lose their home if the economy turned sour and they lost their job. Of course, in the recession of 1990–1992, that is exactly what happened to thousands of Americans. Government tax policy had encouraged them to gamble their homes away.

Also, in the 1990s, what had been a progressive tax policy that helped mainly middle-class people to buy a home that they could not otherwise afford became mainly a tax break for the rich. A study by James B. Poterba of the Massachusetts Institute of Technology, using Internal Revenue Service data, came up with some interesting results (reported in the *San Francisco Examiner*, 20 May 1992, A-4). Poterba found that in the year prior to the major tax reform of 1986, 28.1 million households took advantage of the home mortgage interest deduction. In 1991, only 24.1 million households did so, in spite of the fact that three million more households owned their homes in 1991. Why? Because the federal government also increased the "standard deduction" (the amount people could deduct if they did not want to itemize their individual deductions such as mortgage interest). This meant that, for many lower-income households, it was just as advantageous to take the standard deduction and not the mortgage interest deduction. In 1988, Poterba estimates, 52 percent of the mortgage interest deduction went to the top 8.5 percent of American income earners. How much tax revenue is being lost to provide the richest Americans with an incentive to buy a home (something most of them would do anyway)? In 1991, the mortgage interest deduction cost the national treasury $40.6 billion, and estimates are that it will cost $42.9 billion in 1992. If fewer people are taking advantage of the mortgage interest deduction, why is the cost so high and going up? Because high-income households are increasing the level of their home loans to pay for other purchases in order to take advantage of the mortgage interest deduction. Home mortgage debt has gone from $1.44 trillion in 1985 to $2.69 trillion in 1991.

The result of the Tax Reform Act of 1986 is that the United States government is spending over $40 billion a year to encourage the rich to buy homes and load up those homes with as much mortgage debt as possible. What was once a progressive tax incentive, encouraging the middle class to do something that they would not otherwise do, had become regressive and a destabilizing force in the society. Could this be remedied? Of course, tax policy can always be reformed. If what we want to do is encourage lower-income people (people who would not otherwise buy a home) to buy a home rather than rent, we could say that every taxpayer who owns a home gets a $6,000-a-year deduction for owning that home, regardless of whether the home is mortgaged, and regardless of how high the interest payments are. Where the current interest payment deduction encourages the wealthy to load up their homes with higher levels of mortgage debt, this new type of deduction would discourage increased debt and might actually encourage more people to pay off their mortgage debt because they would still get the home ownership deduction. How much would this cost in lost revenue? If there are 30 million homeowners in America, 30 million times $6,000 adds up to $180 billion. If we assume that 20 percent of income is actually paid to the federal government as income tax, then deducting $180 billion from income would mean the loss of $36 billion in tax revenue. Considering that the federal government is currently losing more than $40 billion a year in tax revenue, this would mean increased revenue. Rich people would no longer be encouraged to increase mortgage debt, everyone would have an incentive to pay off their mortgages, and lower-income households would have a real incentive to buy a home.

Ireland dealt with this problem of the mortgage interest deduction being an incentive only for the rich by limiting the amount that can be deducted (in 1991 the limit was £1,600 for a single person, £2,320 for a widowed person, and £3,200 for a married couple). While this prevents the home mortgage interest deduction from being mainly a tax break for the rich, it still encourages people to mortgage their homes rather than pay off the mortgage debt.

There are other ways to encourage home ownership. In Ireland, all but the most expensive homes are exempt from property taxes (in 1990, homes valued below £91,000 were exempt). Again, by not taxing an activity—in this case, home ownership—Ireland encourages that activity. In the United States, many states have home ownership exemptions from property taxes, but these exemptions have not kept up with inflation so most homeowners have to pay significant property taxes. If these home ownership property tax exemptions were raised to reasonable levels, it would encourage lower-income households to own their own homes.

Encouraging Stock Ownership

It is the announced policy of many countries not only to encourage individual home ownership but also to encourage individual citizens to own shares of stock in local companies. This provides those local companies with funds for investment and provides the citizens with a second source of income from dividends and the sale of stock. In the United States, the major incentive to buy stock has been an employee pension and benefit system that encourages individuals and companies to place funds in pension accounts where the money can be used to buy stock. When the individual retires, the income from those stock purchases can be used to provide a retirement income.

Outside of employee pension and benefit funds, the major incentive to buy stock in most countries has been lower taxes on capital gains. In the early 1990s in the United States, capital gains were taxed for all intents and purposes like other income. That was not the case in many other countries. In Great Britain and Ireland, capital gains were tax free up to a maximum amount each year. In Ireland in the early 1990s, the amount was £2,000 a year; in Great Britain, the amount was between £5,000 and £6,000 a year. In Canada in the early 1990s, an individual enjoyed a lifetime exemption from capital gains tax of $100,000. While the reason given for these tax exemptions was to encourage investment in local companies, none of these three countries actually accomplished that goal. That is because all capital gains, from whatever source, were included in the definition of capital gains. If someone speculated in the gold market and made money, that was included. In Canada, much of the capital gains were made by investing in the U.S. stock market. This provided investment capital for the United States; however, it is difficult to understand why the Canadian government would want to subsidize that investment when the United States government did not provide the same incentive for its own citizens.

How could capital gains taxes be levied in a way that would encourage citizens to invest in their local economy? Suppose the United States government wanted to do just that. It could exempt from income tax the first $6,000 in capital gains or dividends made in a year, and it could define a capital gain to be money made buying and selling stock in U.S. companies if that stock had been owned for at least five years. In other words, average citizens would be encouraged to "make a long-term investment" in the American economy. Allowing dividend income to also count would further encourage people to hold on to their stock rather than sell it. This could conceivably do as much to encourage average citizens to increase their wealth as the mortgage interest deduction did in the 1950s and 1960s.

Throughout the late 1980s and early 1990s, President George Bush asked for lower capital gains taxes. Congress refused because Congress could see no reason to give someone who purchased gold or an old painting a tax incentive to do so.

There are five basic types of individual income—wages, bonuses, interest, dividends, and capital gains—and each can be taxed at a different level to achieve specific goals. One of the most successful uses of differential tax policy in history occurred in Japan after World War II. The Japanese economy was crippled after the war. The Japanese government decided that income on interest and bonuses would be taxed at half the level of other income. This encouraged Japanese workers to negotiate with their employers to receive money in the form of bonuses, not wages. This tied their income to the profitability of the companies they worked for, giving them a strong incentive to work for the long-term profitability of those companies. It also encouraged them to place money in savings accounts where the interest income was taxed at a lower rate. These savings were then lent to Japanese companies at low interest rates. The entire world has witnessed the result of this tax policy. Japanese companies have a higher level of investment per worker than any other country. The availability of low-interest loans has meant that investment has continued, even in the face of recession. The fact that much of the personnel expense of Japanese companies is in the form of bonuses tied to profits has meant that if profits shrink, bonuses shrink, but people are not laid off and they continue to receive their basic wage. Other countries, such as the Netherlands, allow employees to receive up to a maximum amount of profit-sharing bonus money tax free each year. Again, this encourages companies to give a profit-sharing cash bonus, not turn employees into stockholders.

It was not the goal of the Japanese government to increase the distribution of wealth in the society. The same 1,000 families that owned most of the wealth in Japan at the beginning of the twentieth century still owned most of the wealth at the end of the twentieth century. What if the Japanese government had wanted to encourage average citizens to attain wealth by owning stock in Japanese companies? Instead of taxing interest at a lower rate, it could have taxed dividends paid by Japanese companies to Japanese stockholders at a lower rate. This would have encouraged citizens to buy stock instead of putting money into savings accounts. The money would have been used for the same purpose, to increase the productivity of Japanese companies, but the increased wealth that productivity created would have gone to average citizens rather than to a handful of very wealthy families.

Exhibit 2.1 United States and Ireland Basic Income Tax Rates for 1992

	Ireland		United States	
	Tax Rate (%)	Income Level (£)	Tax Rate (%)	Income Level ($)
Low	30	First 6,500	15	First 21,450
Medium	48	Next 3,100	28	Next 30,500
High	53	Above 9,600	31	Above 51,900

What if a country wanted to encourage its citizens to invest in their local economy and to encourage its companies to keep jobs at home instead of exporting them? It might, for example, exempt from tax the first $6,000 made in a year on capital gains from the sale of local company stock (held for the required length of time) and on dividend payments from local companies. It would define a "local company" as a company that spent more than half of its payroll inside the country.

The United States used to have a progressive income tax system. Today it is a system that falls most heavily on the middle-income taxpayer. This is because Social Security taxes amount to 15.3 percent of the tax bite, and these taxes fall only on wages below a fixed level (approximately the first $55,000 of wages in the early 1990s). Americans making below approximately $25,000 a year are in the 15 percent tax bracket (plus 15 percent for Social Security). If they earn between $25,000 and $55,000, they are in the 28 percent bracket (plus 15 percent for Social Security). After that, they are in the 31 percent tax bracket without any Social Security tax liability (see Exhibit 2.1). That means that middle-income Americans who earn between approximately $25,000 and $55,000 are paying more than 40 percent of their income to the federal government, while the rich who earn wages and other income above that level pay only 31 percent. Because Social Security taxes fall only on wages, the wealthy who have a higher proportion of their income in the form of interest, dividends, and capital gains pay a lower tax (in a very real sense in the United States, interest, dividends, and capital gains are already taxed at a lower level because they are not subject to Social Security taxes). Over time this tax structure should encourage people to shift income away from wages and toward dividends, interest, and capital gains. The United States tax system does not make a distinction between "regular wages" and "bonuses" like the Japanese system does. Both are considered wages and subject to Social Security taxes.

Taxing Corporations

While usually unmentioned in discussions of tax policy, the major reason European kings invented corporations half a millennium ago was to provide themselves with tax revenue that they could not otherwise acquire. From time to time some economist suggests that corporations should not be taxed. These people miss the whole point of having corporations. As you will see in the next chapter, corporations are essentially criminal organizations. If they did not generate tax revenue, there would be no reason to have them at all from the point of view of most governments.

Once we decide we are going to tax corporations, the question becomes how and how much? The general answer has been to tax corporate income. In the early 1990s, U.S. corporations are supposed to pay approximately one-third of their profits to the federal government in the form of income taxes. While many thought this would bring in more than $300 billion a year in tax revenue, it has never brought in more than $150 billion a year. Why? The answer has to do with how "profits" are calculated. Profit is the money left over after deductible expenses. The key is what expenses are deductible. In the United States during most of the twentieth century, interest payments have been deductible while dividends paid to investors have not been deductible. This fact caused U.S. corporations to raise capital by borrowing rather than selling stock to investors. Again, this practice concentrated wealth in the hands of a small group of corporate owners. The average citizen made a little money in interest and the owners of the corporations made a lot of money using that money. The risk that some of these loans would not be paid off was shifted from the corporation to the American taxpayer because the federal government insured these savings accounts. As a result, the federal government will pay out $200 billion during the 1990s to compensate people who had savings accounts in failed banks and savings and loan associations.

The United States government could raise more money in corporate income taxes if it allowed corporations to deduct dividends along with interest payments. How would allowing dividend payments to be a deductible expense result in an increase in income tax revenue from American corporations? The people who manage corporations play a game called capitalism, and they win the game to the extent that there is money in the corporate bank account at the end of each year. The more money there is, the more management feels it has won the game. Let's imagine a corporation that is going to go into the business of making widgets, and it needs $100 million to buy land and machinery. It can either sell stock to investors to raise the $100 million or it can borrow $100 million. Let's suppose investors would expect to receive $10 million a year as a dividend on their stock and the bank would expect to receive $12 million a year as interest on a loan. Let's also suppose that the corporate income tax rate is 50 percent. If the corporation sells stock and makes a profit of $20 million a year making widgets, the government will take half of that ($10 million) as corporate income taxes; investors will take the rest ($10 million) as dividends; and corporate management will be left with nothing in the corporate bank account at the end of the year. Now suppose the corporation borrows the $100 million instead. Now it must pay $12 million in interest, but this is tax deductible. Only the $8 million that is left is subject to income tax. Of that $8 million, $4 million is sent to the government as taxes and $4 million is left in the corporate bank account at the end of the year (see Exhibit 2.2). The government thought the corporation would raise money by selling stock and the government would end up with $10 million a year in income taxes. Instead the corporation borrowed the money and the government ended up with only $4 million. Now suppose that dividends are also tax deductible and that the corporation sells $100 million in stock instead of borrowing the money. The investors would get $10 million a year as dividend payments, which leaves $10 million. The government would get $5 million as income taxes, and the corporation would have $5 million left over in the bank account at the end of the year. By allowing

Exhibit 2.2   Should Dividends Be Deductible for Corporations?

Assume 50 percent corporate income tax rate.
Assume $20 million operating income.

Assuming dividends are not tax deductible for corporations:
If $100 million raised by selling stock:
   $20 million income − $10 million taxes − $10 million dividends =
   $0 left for corporation.

If $100 million raised by borrowing at 12 percent interest:
   $20 million income − $12 million interest − $4 million taxes =
   $4 million left for corporation.

Assuming dividends are also tax deductible for corporations:
If $100 million raised by selling stock:
   $20 million income − $10 million dividends − $5 million taxes =
   $5 million left for corporation.

---

dividends to be tax deductible, the government has increased its tax revenue.

But, wait a minute, you say, what if the corporation pays out all $20 million as dividends? That's fine too. Assuming a 30-percent tax bracket, $20 million paid out in dividends provides $6 million in income taxes to the government. When the corporation was borrowing the money, the government received only $4 million. Of course the government might also receive some tax money from the $12 million paid out in interest, but it is doubtful whether the government would receive more than $2 million of that as income taxes given the realities of corporate finance and the way banks are taxed.

Allowing dividends to be tax deductible would have other advantages for both a nation and its corporations. Currently, if wages are deductible and dividends are not, corporations and their workers have little or no incentive to place stock in the hands of workers. If dividends were also deductible, then corporations would encourage their workers to own stock and receive income in the form of dividends, which would be deductible to the corporation. Why would workers want to receive dividends instead of wages? Because dividends are not subject to Social Security taxes, which currently amount to 15.3 percent of wages in the United States. If workers owned stock in the companies they worked for, they might work harder and smarter, increasing the value of that stock for themselves and for the other stockholders, keeping in mind that half of those other stockholders are the workers of America investing through their pension, benefit, and mutual funds.

Not allowing dividends to be deductible has encouraged business to make use of a variety of "forms" of doing business to avoid this problem. It is entirely possible, if dividends were tax deductible for corporations, that the government would raise more money simply because it would no longer be worth while to spend a fortune on legal fees to create elaborate business structures to get around this rule.

APPENDIX

Taxing Dividends and Interest Payments Equally

There are two basic choices that meet this goal of tax neutrality. First, we could make both dividends and interest payments equally deductible from corporate income. There would, of course, be a loss of corporate tax revenue, if that were the only change. To avoid a loss of revenue, Congress could either increase the tax rate, which I don't suggest, or it could limit both the interest and dividend deduction, for example, to 80 percent of the amount of the payment (or whatever other proportion would be revenue-neutral). This 80-20 proposal is sometimes called the hybrid solution. In addition to being revenue-neutral, it would also be essentially neutral as between debt and equity. But not perfectly so. Interest is deductible as it accrues, regardless of when it is in fact paid out, whereas the earnings that accrue on common stock would be deductible only when paid. There would be pressure, therefore, for payouts, which may be a good thing or bad, but the arrangement is not wholly neutral.

Louis Lowenstein, Simon H. Rifkind Professor of Finance and Law at Columbia University, and author of *Sense & Nonsense in Corporate Finance* (Addison-Wesley, 1991) testified in May 1989 before the House Ways and Means Committee. He recommended that dividends and interest paid out by corporations be treated equally by the Internal Revenue Code. This is an excerpt of his testimony (edited by Professor Lowenstein).

The second choice is to make neither interest nor dividends deductible at all. Relying on data in a January 1989 study prepared by the staff of the Joint Committee on Taxation, it appears that eliminating the interest deduction would roughly double the amount of taxable corporate income. The tax rate therefore could be cut in half, to about 16 or 18 percent, thus making this proposal also neutral as to the amount of revenue collected. This second proposal may well be more attractive as a conceptual matter. The corporate business would be taxed, but the tax would not be affected by purely financial decisions. The tax would be the same regardless of the choice between debt and equity and regardless of the payout ratio on the common stock.

I regard both proposals as attractive, with a mild preference for the second one. Under that proposal, the corporate income tax would be measured solely by operating income. We would not be able to use debt/equity choices to jiggle the result. In addition, the no-deduction proposal also solves the problem that, at present, some U.S.-source income escapes taxation here altogether, that is, in those cases where the debt is held by foreign investors. On the other hand, I recognize that the loss of any tax incentive to pay out income would be regarded by some as a disadvantage.

In either case, it would be necessary to phase in the changes over a period of several years. The second choice, in particular, would otherwise prejudice companies that are capital-intensive, such as finance companies and public utilities. Those problems are not insuperable, but they do need to be dealt with. (For utilities, the phase-in period might be stretched out. The finance company problem could be solved by a rule of general application that would tax interest income on a "net" basis, that is, tax it only to the extent that it exceeds interest expense.) A rule would be needed to deal with leases and other debt alternatives. Similarly, we might elect to exempt small companies entirely from the double tax, much as if they had all elected to be taxed as partnerships, as many of them now do.

In conclusion, let me urge you not to fall into the trap of so many other committees that have addressed these issues: lots of hearings, lots of bills, lots of inertia.

[Professor Lowenstein reports that so far there have been lots of hearings, lots of bills, and lots of inertia.]

3

Creating Artificial People

This chapter is entitled "Creating Artificial People" because the ability to do just that was one of the great legal innovations of the modern era. While societies down through history have experimented with creating artificial people (and I don't mean robots), it was the kings and queens of Europe (and their lawyers) during the Middle Ages who began to do just that in a big way. To understand what they did and why they did it, we need to travel back in time.

European monarchs lived in a world of "real people" and personal relationships. If they wanted to reward someone for service, they gave that person a title and an estate. Over the generations that estate passed from father to son to grandson, but there was no guarantee that the grandson would be as loyal to the king as his grandfather had been. If a section of territory on the border needed guarding, the king gave that estate to someone he believed would do a good job repelling invasion. There was always the danger that the person would be bribed to go over to the other side, which happened frequently. Messy business dealing with real people! If a region needed public services performed, the king sent in an administrator and paid for the services out of the national treasury. Expensive business providing public services! If some conquered territory or colony needed exploiting, the king sent in soldiers to subdue the native population. Of course the neighboring king might not take kindly to having troops next to his territory; in fact, he might even start a war because of it. Costly business exploiting colonies! During the Middle Ages, many wealthy citizens died and left their land to the Roman Catholic Church. They did this to such an extent (everyone wanted to buy their way into heaven) that kings had to confiscate church property every few generations even though it meant excommunication for them and near rebellion in the kingdom. Risky business dealing with the Pope!

To help take care of all this, kings and their lawyers hit upon the idea of creating artificial people. For the border that needed guarding, they granted a town charter to the residents, who were allowed to elect a town council to govern themselves and were exempted from paying some national taxes. In return, the town promised to defend the border, and every able-bodied man had to be a member of the militia. An artificial person called a "town" had been created. It was much more difficult for this artificial person to go over to the enemy the way a duke might do. This town could also raise money to pay for its own public services. No more traitors on the border; no more drain on the national treasury. Instead of allowing citizens to give their land to the Pope, the kings chartered monasteries. These artificial people owed allegiance to the king, not the Pope; and if they became too wealthy for the good of the kingdom, their charter could be revoked. Under the most ancient law of Europe, once property had no legal owner it became the property of the king, and this property no longer had a legal owner because its former owner no longer existed. Who could object when the king simply performed his ancient legal duty and took possession?

What about exploiting the colonies? For that purpose the first corporations were formed. What a brilliant idea. Here is a new territory that needs exploiting. Who knows if it will pay in the long run to spend money exploiting it. Instead of spending money out of the national treasury, the king allows a group of private investors to spend their money. If they go broke, no skin off the king's nose. If they make a profit, the king gets part of it in the form of a corporation tax. Who could ask for a better deal? England's Queen Elizabeth I sent corporations in the form of armed ships of war (privately owned, of course) into the Caribbean for the express purpose of stealing Spanish gold. It is ironic when people get upset upon learning that a corporation has broken the law. That was the express reason why early corporations were formed! They were criminal enterprises, with the king or queen as a silent partner.

During the seventeenth and eighteenth centuries, European monarchs learned a lesson that the Soviet Union had to relearn in the twentieth century. Given a choice between having the government go into a business itself and allowing "artificial people" to come into being to conduct the business, the government is usually better off if it lets the artificial people handle it. Government can control the artificial people through regulation and ultimately can "kill" them, if they get out of line, by revoking their charters. To the extent that these artificial people are successful, the government gets a piece of the action in the form of taxes. During the twentieth century, the governments of Western Europe made significantly more money taxing corporations than the governments of Eastern Europe made owning corporations!

Suppose we want to go into business. What form will our business take? There are five basic forms we can use: sole proprietorship, partnership, corporation, cooperative, and trust.

Sole Proprietorships

The sole proprietorship is the simplest form of business ownership. A real live individual simply goes into business. Because there is no artificial person, there is no need for a charter from the government. If the person plans to operate the business under a fictional name, he or she may have to file a DBA (doing business as) certificate with the local government. There is no need for a bunch of lawyers and accountants. Sole proprietors can operate their businesses right out of their individual bank accounts if they want to. If sole proprietors want to extend their businesses into other states or nations, they can usually do so with a minimum of legal fuss. A business being operated as a sole proprietorship does not "live on" after the death of the owner, but the owner can leave the business to someone else who then becomes the new sole proprietor. The key issues in deciding whether or not to operate a business as a sole proprietor are control, liability, and taxes.

In a sole proprietorship, the control of the business is in the hands of one person. This has the advantage of allowing decisions to be made quickly and with a limited amount of procedure. No meetings have to be called, no opinions solicited; the owner simply decides, and that's that. Of course, if the owner makes the wrong decision, that could mean the end of the business. If those decisions turn out to be illegal, the police know whom to arrest and put in jail—the sole proprietor.

The major disadvantage of the sole proprietorship form of ownership is the problem of unlimited personal liability. Because the owner and the business are one and the same, there is no difference between the debts of the business and the debts of the owner. If the business owes money, the owner owes money. If the business hurts someone, the owner gets sued and has to pay for the damages.

Taxes are another factor. For sole proprietors, their business accounts and their personal accounts are all in one book. If the business makes money, the owner pays personal income taxes on that profit. If the business doesn't make money, the owner has no income to tax. The advantage is that the business is not taxed separately from the individual. The business does not pay an income tax, followed by the owner paying an income tax again on the profits received from the business.

Partnerships

A partnership is just about as easy to form as a sole proprietorship in most countries. Two people shaking hands and saying, "Let's go into business together" is enough. Of course, they would be wise to consult an attorney and have a partnership agreement drawn up to avoid confusion in the long run about who is responsible for what. Suppose five people form a partnership. Their agreement can say that decisions will be made by majority rule, or require unanimous consent. They can distribute the profits equally, or some other way. They can each put up the same amount of money, or different amounts. They can each be active in the business, or only a few can take an active part.

In most countries, a partnership is not viewed as an artificial person. It is a collection of very real people who have banded together to pool their money and their talent to make a successful business. The partnership is considered to be at an end if one of the partners dies, resigns, is thrown out, or goes bankrupt. Of course the remaining partners can form a new partnership or some other form of business with their share of the partnership assets. What happens to the assets that belonged to the departed partner depends on the partnership agreement.

A partnership has many disadvantages. If the partners cannot agree on major decisions, this can cause delays or worse. Also, every partner is individually liable for all the debts of the partnership. If one of the partners buys a lot of material, more than the partnership can pay for, all of the partners are liable for the bill. If one of the partners hurts someone and the partnership gets sued, all of the personal assets of the various partners can be taken to pay for the damages. Where a sole proprietorship had one person in control and one person personally liable for the debts and damages, a partnership has many people in control and many people liable for the debts and damages.

On the other hand, there is taxation at only one level. The partnership does not pay an income tax, followed by the partners paying another personal income tax on their share of the profits. Whether the profits are distributed to the partners or reinvested in the business, the income is taxed to the individual partners as if they had personally received it.

What if the partnership loses money? Then the individual partners can show a loss on their individual tax returns. If a business is expected to lose money for the first few years and the partners have income from other investments, this ability to pass through the loss to the individual partners can be considered an advantage.

What if a partner wants out? This can be difficult. The other partners do not have to accept the person the departing partner might choose to buy his or her partnership interest; or no one may want to buy such an interest. In many cases, the other partners buy the share of the departing partner, but is the departing partner really getting a fair payment for his or her share?

There is a special kind of partner called a limited partner. In many states and countries, a group of partners (who are called general partners) can take on limited partners. These limited partners invest money in the business, but their liability is "limited" to the amount of money they invest. Their influence on decision making is also limited. Because a limited partnership is a kind of artificial person, the law in most countries requires the partners to have a written agreement and a charter from the government recognizing the special nature of that partnership agreement. The limited partner has a certificate much like a share of stock in a corporation. While a limited partner can sell that certificate, the agreement may require the approval of any new limited partner by the general partners, thus restricting to whom the limited partner can sell his or her interest.

Corporations

A corporation is a true artificial person. It does not exist until someone goes to the appropriate government agency, files the necessary papers, pays the necessary fees, and receives a corporate charter. The charter (or certificate of incorporation or articles of incorporation) means that the government has created a new artificial person. This new artificial person can sue and be sued, own property, and do everything else necessary to carry on a business. However, artificial people cannot act for themselves (because they do not really exist). They cannot go to court except through an attorney. They cannot make decisions except through a board of directors and corporate officers chosen by that board. They cannot do anything that the corporate bylaws do not allow them to do.

There are a lot of advantages to having an artificial person instead of a real one. Artificial people do not die. While sole proprietors and partners do die (causing a lot of problems), corporations go on and on, in theory, forever. Stockholders can come and go, employees can be hired and fired, new managers and directors can rise and fall, but the corporation goes on.

For the owners (that is, the stockholders), the major advantage is limited liability. Where a sole proprietor or a partner is personally liable for the debts of the business, stockholders can lose only what they have invested in buying the stock. Their personal bank account is safe from the corporation's creditors. Also, it is usually much easier for stockholders to sell their interest in the corporation than it is for a sole proprietor or a partner to sell his or her interest in a business. In many cases if the sole proprietor or a key partner is not going to be working for the business any longer, the business may not be worth very much. A corporation, on the other hand, is structured so that stockholders can come and go with little effect on the operation of the corporation.

While government has been willing to give the owners of corporations a major advantage—namely, limited personal liability—there is a price for that in most countries. The corporation, being an artificial person, must pay taxes on its profits before it can distribute any of those profits to the stockholders. Suppose the corporation pays a 40-percent corporate income tax, the stockholders pay a 30-percent individual income tax, and the business makes a $100,000 profit. If the business is a sole proprietorship or a partnership, the government receives $30,000 in taxes while the sole proprietor or the partners make $70,000. If the business is a corporation $40,000 is paid to the government as corporate income taxes. If the remaining $60,000 is then distributed as a dividend, 30 percent of that ($18,000) is paid as individual income taxes. The government has gotten $58,000 in taxes and the stockholders have only $42,000 for themselves. This difference, an extra $28,000 of taxes in our example, is the price government extracts in exchange for the right of limited liability, unlimited life, and the other advantages of using the corporate form.

The fact that corporations pay taxes at the corporate level and the stockholders pay taxes again at the personal level is called *double taxation*. Many people have called for an end to double taxation by allowing corporations to deduct dividend payments. In that way, if the corporation wanted to keep the profits, they could pay a corporate income tax; if they distributed the profits in the form of dividends, the individual stockholders would pay a personal income tax.

In the United States, stockholders can achieve this advantage if they form a Subchapter S corporation. A Subchapter S corporation pays taxes as if it were a partnership and continues to enjoy all of the advantages of a corporation. However, a Subchapter S corporation cannot have more than 35 stockholders and must meet other restrictions. This is simply another tax break for the wealthy. If 35 wealthy people want to form a corporation, they can do so and meet the Subchapter S test. If small investors want to form or invest in a corporation, it takes more of them to raise the capital, so they are out of luck.

Cooperatives

There is another kind of artificial person that can be formed under the laws of many countries, namely, a cooperative. A cooperative is like a corporation in that it is an artificial person chartered by the government. It must have a set of bylaws and a board of directors to set policy. It can only act through attorneys and agents because it does not have a life of its own. It can live forever. It combines the main advantage of the corporation—limited personal liability—with the main advantage of a partnership—taxation only at the personal level. Historically, three types of cooperatives have been popular.

The consumer cooperative has a long history in both the United States and Great Britain. In a classic consumer cooperative, the owners are the people who will be buying the goods or services of the cooperative (many consumer cooperatives are retail stores). The consumers will be the owners and, if there are any profits, they will be distributed to the cooperative members at the end of the year, usually as a percentage of the money each member spent during that year (the more money you spend, the more money you get back). The most popular consumer cooperatives in the United States today are credit unions. Instead of making a profit for investors, most credit unions pay higher interest rates on the savings accounts of their members. Of course the members pay income tax on this interest income, but there is no "corporate" income tax paid at the level of the credit union (there is no double taxation as there would be with a regular bank).

The second type of cooperative is a producer cooperative. A producer cooperative is usually formed when a group of farmers feels that they are not getting a good price for their product. Instead of selling to a middleman who then markets the product to retail outlets, the farmers form a cooperative to perform that middleman's function. Because the cooperative cuts out the middleman, it is able to pay higher prices to the farmers for their products. The producer cooperative does not make a "profit" as such. The profit is passed on to the cooperative members in the form of higher prices for their products. There is no "corporate income tax."

The third major type of cooperative is the worker cooperative. The owners and the workers are one and the same. If there are any "profits," they are passed on to the workers in the form of higher wages. In this way, there really are no "profits" in the usual sense and thus there are no taxes to be paid at the corporate level.

If a cooperative does make a profit, that is, if the cooperative makes money and keeps it to reinvest in the business, it is treated like the profit of a partnership and taxed at the level of the individual cooperative members. This can cause a problem because cooperative members have to pay income taxes on money they did not actually receive.

If cooperatives have the dual advantages of limited liability for the members and single taxation of profits, why aren't there more cooperatives? There are many reasons, but the most important is a lack of capital. Any business needs money to get started and to grow. Generally, people who would become members of a cooperative do not have enough money to start a business. While they could borrow that money under ideal conditions, in most of the world the banks and other financial institutions that might lend the money have not been interested in financing cooperatives.

Cooperatives usually operate (and are required by law in most countries to operate) on the one-member, one-vote principle. Also, while technically run by a board of directors just like other corporations, many cooperatives have members who feel entitled to more of a voice in the day-to-day running of the organization than just a vote once a year for the board of directors. This can be an advantage or a disadvantage to the smooth running of the organization, depending on the circumstances. While decisions may take longer to make, once made they are better understood by all of the members.

In some cooperatives, members pay little for their membership and are entitled to no more than their money back when they leave. In other words, if the business is worth a lot more when they leave than it was when they joined, that value is an advantage to them as long as they belong, but they can't take it to the bank when they leave. How-

---

Sign Above the Desk of a Bank Trust Officer

There are three rules when holding other people's money:

Don't lose any money.

Don't lose any money.

Don't lose any money.

---

ever, a cooperative can be set up so that departing members receive the "market value" of their ownership interest when they leave. While this gives them the same financial interest that investors have in a corporation (their shares go up in value as the corporation itself increases in value), it can make it difficult for new members to join the cooperative because of the high cost of buying a membership.

Trusts

Finally, a business can be "owned" by a trust. A trust is not exactly an artificial person, and not exactly a real one. Trusts became popular in the Middle Ages during the Crusades. Departing crusaders, particularly in England, would transfer the title to their property to a "trusted" friend. The deed and other documents would make it clear that the friend was to own the property only as a trustee and use the profits from the land to support the crusader's wife and children while he was away. If the crusader died, the trustee could continue to look after the property until the male heir was old enough to run things, at which time the trustee would hand the property over to the heir. The trust property is owned by a real person, the trustee; however, if the trustee is incompetent or corrupt, the trust beneficiaries could go to court and ask the judge to name a new trustee. Over time, many trusts came to look more and more like privately created artificial people.

In countries that have trusts, the legal system has developed rules that trustees must live by. Basically, trustees are charged with using the utmost care to make sure that the value of the trust property does not decline. While it would be nice if the value went up, that is less important. The problem with that philosophy is that trustees

Exhibit 3.1 Comparing Control, Liability, and Taxation

Sole Proprietorship	Partnership	Limited Partnership	Trust	Corporation	Cooperative
		Control			
Full	Full	Limited	None	Elected board	Elected board
		Liability			
Full	Full	Limited	Limited	Limited	Limited
		Taxation			
One level	One level	One level	One or two levels	Two levels	One level

are therefore very conservative investors. Where individual investors might be willing to take a risk in exchange for a substantial potential reward, most trustees are not. Therefore, money placed in trust does not shrink, but it often does not grow very much either.

Many states in the United States allow special trusts to be created, just as corporations are created, to engage in particular kinds of investment activities. For example, real estate investment trusts (REITs) sell certificates (much like shares), and the money is invested in real estate. The income from that investment (rent income minus operating expenses) is then passed on to the certificate holders without having to pay a "business or corporate" level income tax. REITs allowed the small investor to take part in the real estate speculation that was popular in the United States during the 1970s and 1980s (in many cases, this meant that these small investors had the pleasure of losing a significant portion of their money as property values first shot way up, and then came crashing down).

In the world of business, we have real people (sole proprietors and partners), partially artificial people (limited partnerships and trusts), and totally artificial people (corporations and cooperatives). As Exhibit 3.1 illustrates, each has its advantages and disadvantages. Questions of control, liability, and taxation usually decide which form will be used under a particular set of circumstances. Only a cooperative (or a special corporation such as the Subchapter S in the United States) allows the investor-owners to control the business, have limited personal liability, and avoid double taxation.

4

Stocks, Bonds, and Options

This chapter is about securities. Presumably they are called *securities* in an effort to make people who buy them feel secure. Any discussion of securities must begin with an explanation of stocks, bonds, options, and the difference between the three.

Stocks

One attorney is fond of telling about the day he attempted to explain how employee stock ownership plans (ESOPs) work to several hundred blue-collar workers. He began by telling them that the company would issue stock; that the ESOP would borrow money and use it to buy the stock; that the ESOP would pay off the loan over time with money paid to it by the company and, as it did so, stock would be placed in the individual accounts of the workers so that when they left the company they would have a lot of stock. When he had finished his hour-long explanation, he asked if there were any questions. For a long moment there was only silence. The attorney thought he must have done a wonderful job explaining how it all works when he saw a lone hand go up in the crowd. "Yes?" he asked. "What's *stock?*" inquired the worker.

Let's begin to answer that question by talking about cars. Many people own a car and have a car "title" issued by the government that says they own the car. The title is a *certificate of ownership*. Suppose 10 people wanted to own a car together. The title would have 10 names on it. If one of the car owners wants to sell her interest to someone else, that will be difficult. All 10 owners will have to agree to sell the car to a new set of 10 owners that excludes the seller and includes the buyer. A new title will have to be prepared with the new names on it. Suppose 10 people own a corporation. Could we arrange the legal paperwork so that if one person wanted to sell, the sale would not be such a hassle? That is where stock comes in. Each of our 10 owners could have one share of stock representing one-tenth ownership of the corporation. If one of them wanted to sell, that person could simply sell his or her share (it's called a *share* because it represents a share of ownership).

Bonds

If shares of stock are certificates of ownership, a bond is a *certificate of debt*. If a business wants to borrow money, it can go to a bank like anyone else and take out a loan. The banker acts as a middleman who pays people who deposit money in the bank interest on their money and then lends that money out at a higher interest rate to people who want to borrow it. For doing this work of taking in deposits and lending out money, the banker makes a profit by charging more interest on the money he lends out than he pays on the money deposited in his bank.

Suppose a business wanted to cut out this middleman, allowing it to borrow the money at a lower interest rate and, in turn, to pay the would-be "depositors" more for the use of their money. The common way to do this is by selling *bonds*. If the bank was willing to pay depositors 6 percent for their money and lend it out to a business at 10 percent, the business might be able to sell bonds that pay 8 percent. The business gets the money at a lower price than it would get from a bank, and the people doing the lending get a higher return on their money.

Just as a banker wants to know what collateral is going to back up the loan (what hard assets the business has that can be sold if the business defaults on the loan), bond buyers want to know what backs up their bonds. Usually, the bonds have the first right to receive money if the business goes bankrupt. In other words, if the corporation goes out of business, its assets will be sold off and the money will go first to the bondholders and other creditors. Only after they have been paid will there be anything for the stockholders. Because of this, stocks are generally considered a riskier investment than bonds.

Options

If stocks are certificates of ownership and bonds are certificates of debt, an option is a *contract* in which one person promises to do something for another person if that person wants him to over some period of time. A person could buy an option on a house, on shares of stock, or on anything imaginable.

Suppose Fred does not have enough money to buy the house of his dreams now, but he has enough to rent it. Suppose he goes to the current owner and says that he will rent the house but he also wants an option to buy it at a fixed price over the next three years. The current owner agrees but only if Fred will pay extra for this "option to buy." If the house goes down in value during the three years, Fred can decide not to "exercise" his option and either offer to buy the house at a lower price or buy another house. If the house goes up in value, Fred can exercise his option and buy the house. The current owner of the house has the extra money he received by selling the option, but he cannot sell the house to someone else as long as the option is in force, in this case for three years.

People can also buy an option on stock. Buying a stock option allows the buyer to realize a bigger payoff if he or she is right and the stock does go up in a short period of time. Time is the crucial element. In the United States, people buy and sell stock options every day on the Chicago Board of Trade. There are two basic kinds, "put" options and "call" options. With a *put option*, the person holding the option has the right to force the other party (called the option-writer) to buy the option-holder's shares at the agreed price (the right to put the shares to the option-writer). With a *call option*, the person holding the option has the right to force the option-writer to sell shares to the option-holder at the agreed price (to call in the shares that currently belong to the option-writer).

Options traded in Chicago are usually for a maximum of six months. For example, if it is February and you want to buy an option, you would buy an August option (Chicago stock options expire on the Saturday after the third Friday of the month, so an August option in 1993 expires on August 21, 1993). The date the option expires is called the *expiration date*, and the price at which the option can be exercised is called the *strike price*. For example, an option to buy 100 shares of Ishtar stock at $50 a share until August means a strike price of $50 a share and an expiration date of August 21, 1993. The amount of money needed to purchase the option is called the *premium*. How much a stock option costs depends on what the buyer and seller of the option think the price of the stock is going to do over the next six months.

To see why Sandra, our call option buyer, wants an option instead of the stock, let's imagine the following: Sandra buys 1,000 shares of Ishtar stock at $50 a share on February 15, 1993, for a total of $50,000 (plus a small commission for the stockbroker). At the same time, Sandra also buys options entitling her to buy another 1,000 shares of Ishtar at any time before August 21, 1993, at a strike price of $50 a share and pays a premium of $3 a share ($3,000 dollars) for this stock option. Suppose on August 20, 1993, Ishtar is selling for $60 a share. Sandra sells her option for $10,000 (the right to buy 1,000 shares at $50 share and sell them immediately for $60 a share can usually be sold without having to actually buy and sell the shares yourself). She also sells the 1,000 shares she had purchased for $50,000. Sandra made $10,000 profit on the shares she purchased for $50,000. She tied up $50,000 for six months and made $10,000 in return, which comes to 40 percent interest on the money. Not bad. She invested $3,000 in a stock option for six months and got back $10,000 for a profit of $7,000, which comes to 466 percent interest. Even better.

Of course things might not have turned out so well. Suppose the stock price did not change. She sells her 1,000 shares and gets back her $50,000 (minus commissions paid to the stockbroker). She can't sell her option so she is out the entire $3,000 she spent buying it. By buying stock options, investors can maximize their gain on the up side, but they can also lose all the money if the shares do not go up in price during the option period.

The Attributes of Ownership

When someone owns something, anything, they have certain rights over that thing. There are basically five rights of ownership: the right to control it, the right to receive income from it (if it makes any), the right to receive any increased value from it (if it goes up in value while you own it), the right to sell it (and receive any money from the sale), and the right to know everything there is to know about it. Suppose you buy a car for $10,000. Because you own it, you are the one who drives it or decides who else can drive it. If you rent the car out for antique shows, you receive the income. If the car goes up in value, that value belongs to you and, if you sell it, that money belongs to you. It is your car and you have the right to look under the hood.

The same is true of a corporation. The owners of a corporation have five basic rights: voting rights, dividend rights, appreciation rights, liquidation rights, and information rights. Corporations are run by a board of directors. The owners vote on who will sit on that board of directors (voting rights). If the corporation makes money, the owners may get a yearly dividend as their share of the profits (dividend rights). If the assets of the corporation increase in value, that should be reflected in the value of the owners' stock (appreciation rights). If the corporation goes bankrupt and the assets are sold off, the owners have a right to the money after the corporation's debts are paid (liquidation rights). Also, the owners have a right to know how the corporation is doing, to receive regular reports on the corporation from the board of directors and the corporate officers and, if necessary, to look at the corporate books (information rights).

Government also shares some of these rights. Governments control corporations by regulating what they can do. Governments share in the profits through corporate income taxes and share in the liquidation rights if the corporation goes bankrupt owing taxes. Governments also have the right to demand information from a corporation in order to regulate it and collect taxes.

While stockholders usually have all five rights, different kinds of stock can be created that have different combinations of ownership rights. The best example of this is *preferred stock*. Preferred stock is not exactly normal stock (usually called *common stock*) and not exactly a bond. A preferred stockholder usually has the right to a fixed dividend if the corporation has made enough money to pay a dividend. If the corporation has not made enough money, the preferred stockholder does not get paid, but neither does the common stockholder. If there is a profit, it goes first to pay the bondholders their interest, then to pay the promised dividend to the preferred stockholders, and then to pay the common stockholders, if there is anything left. The preferred stockholders usually do not vote for the board of directors (although there is such a thing as voting preferred stock), and they do not participate in increases in the value of the assets.

There can be many types of preferred stock, but two common varieties are "cumulative" and "convertible." Cumulative preferred stock is entitled to a special dividend. Suppose the stock sells for $100 a share and each share of preferred stock is entitled to receive a $10-a-year dividend if there is any money left after taxes (before any dividend can be paid to the common stockholders). If there is no profit, then the preferred shareholders are out of luck, unless the stock is cumulative preferred, which means that the dividends owed accumulate. If the corporation cannot pay any dividend this year, it owes $20 next year, assuming it has the money.

Convertible preferred stock means that the holder of a preferred share has the right to convert the share of preferred stock into common stock. Suppose the preferred shares are selling for $100 and the common stock is selling for $80. Five years later, the common stock is selling for $200 a share. The holder of a convertible preferred share can convert the share into common stock and then sell it for a $100 profit on top of the high dividends the preferred stock paid while the shareholder held onto it. As a general rule, dividends on preferred

Exhibit 4.1 Comparing Return, Risk, and Control

	Bonds	Preferred Stock	Common Stock	Options
Return	Interest only	Dividends only	Dividends plus appreciation	Only if exercised
Bankruptcy	Paid first	Paid second	Paid last	Not paid
Control	No	No	Yes	No

stock are not tax deductible for the corporation while interest paid on bonds is, so most corporations prefer to issue bonds rather than preferred stock.

To review, bonds are usually more secure then preferred stock, which is more secure than common stock, which is more secure than options (see Exhibit 4.1). Bonds usually have a lower total return than preferred stock, which has a lower total return (dividends plus appreciation) than common stock, which has a lower total return than a "guessed right" stock option (of course a "guessed wrong" stock option has the lowest return of all). If a corporation goes bankrupt, the assets will be sold off and bondholders will be paid first, along with other creditors; preferred stockholders, second; common stockholders, third; and anyone holding a stock option issued by the corporation will generally be out of luck. Unless the corporation is in bankruptcy, the common stockholders will control the corporation and elect the board of directors. People holding bonds, options, and preferred stock will have little or no say in how the corporation is run.

Doing a Leveraged Buyout

Before we can do a leveraged buyout, we have to understand what *leverage* means. When someone wants to lift a heavy object, they use leverage to help lift it. When someone wants to buy something they cannot pay cash for, they use borrowed money to make up the difference. Most people who buy houses use leverage. In some cases, home buyers may put down only 5 or 10 percent of the actual cost of a house. A bank will lend the rest and take a mortgage back in return.

A mortgage is a promise to pay and, if the payments are not made, the bank has the right to take the house and sell it to pay off the debt.

Suppose Bill and his friends want to buy a corporation that is worth $100 million and they have only $10 million to spend. Bill might be able to borrow $60 million and secure that debt with the hard assets of the company: the land, buildings, and machines. This borrowed money might come from a bank or perhaps from the sale of bonds. These bonds will be called "senior secured" bonds. They are senior because they get paid before anyone else if the corporation goes bankrupt, and they are secured by the hard assets of the corporation. If the corporation goes bankrupt and these assets are sold, all the money will go to the bondholders.

Bill and his friends now have to come up with another $40 million. Of course they could sell shares of common stock. If they did that, however, they would be able to buy only $10 million worth of stock while others would buy $30 million worth, and Bill and his friends would end up owning only 25 percent of the company. They want to own more than that if they can.

They might sell *junk bonds*. A junk bond pays a much higher rate of interest than other bonds but carries a much higher risk. If the corporation is successful, the junk bondholders get more money for their investment. If the corporation goes bankrupt, they get nothing. Before the 1980s, people who purchased such bonds expected some kind of "equity" participation in exchange for their higher risk. For example, they might ask for common stock along with the bonds. The junk bond buyers might have gotten junk bonds plus 10 million shares of common stock (valued at $1 a share). Bill and his friends would get the other 10 million shares and own half of the company. That is better than 25 percent, but Bill was hoping for more. The junk bondholders might ask for options to buy stock in the future if the company is successful and the value of the stock rises. These kinds of stock options are commonly called *warrants*. Or they might want cumulative, convertible preferred stock instead of junk bonds. This would give them the right to receive a high dividend and to also make money if the value of the common stock increased over time.

A strange bird appeared in the United States at the beginning of the 1980s and disappeared at the end of the 1980s. This bird was willing to buy junk bonds without getting any stock in the company or any options to acquire stock in the future. This was a golden age for Bill and his friends. They could buy the $100 million corporation, spend only $10 million of their own money, and own 100 percent of the common stock. Of course they were taking a risk, but so were the people who purchased the $30 million in junk bonds. The junk bond purchasers were taking the same risk—that the corporation would go bankrupt—only they were risking three times as much money. If the corporation was a success, the junk bondholders got a high interest rate; but when the bonds were paid off, they got nothing more. Bill and his friends owned the corporation. Their $10 million investment would be worth $100 million or more. Of course, unlike some fairy tales, this one had an unhappy ending for many junk bondholders. The corporation could not pay the interest on all that debt once the recession came at the end of the 1980s, and the junk bondholders lost their money.

Starting a New Company

Suppose Bill and his friends wanted a high return for their money and decided to invest in new companies instead of using leverage to buy old ones. Let's take the case of Susan and Steve in California. Susan and Steve always dreamed of having their own little technology company someday. Steve, the engineer, worked in the garage on weekends perfecting a new invention. Susan kept books for the new company when she wasn't working at her regular job. After a year of experimentation, they had a product that worked, but they needed money to go into production. They turned to an expert in such things who put them together with Bill and his friends, who had decided to become *venture capitalists*. Bill and his friends agreed to invest $10 million in the corporation, but they wanted 50 percent of the stock in return. Susan and Steve decided 50 percent of a successful corporation was better than 100 percent of nothing, so they agreed.

The new company, SuperStuff, was a big success. Within five years the company was taking in over $50 million in revenues and making $10 million a year in earnings (profits minus taxes). At this point, Bill and his friends wanted to take their profit and get out. They figured

---

Exhibit 4.2   Advantages and Disadvantages of Going Public

Advantages
- Easier access to permanent, noninterest-bearing capital.
- Easier for owners to cash out their investment with high return.
- Increased public awareness of the company.
- Enhanced credibility with suppliers, banks, and customers.
- Easier to attract and retain key employees by using stock and stock options.
- Easier access to debt, possibly borrowed at lower cost.
- Easier to complete a merger or acquisition in the future.

Disadvantages
- Cost of completing the initial public offering, and fulfilling the reporting obligations of a public company.
- Requirement that company operations be open to the public.
- Possible dilution of ownership and control of current owners.
- Possible loss of flexibility as procedures become more formal.
- Pressure to improve short-term performance as quarterly earnings reports become a part of company routine.
- Restrictions as a result of SEC and other government regulations.
- More susceptible to hostile takeover.

Source: Compiled from Paul G. Joubert, "Going Public," in *The Portable MBA in Finance and Accounting*, ed. John Leslie Livingstone (New York: John Wiley & Sons, 1992), chap. 12.

that the company was worth $80 million and they wanted their $40 million (not bad for five years of investing—$10 million in, $40 million back). Steve and Susan wanted to issue bonds and buy out Bill and his friends. But as a small, relatively new company, SuperStuff was still considered too risky. No one would buy the bonds. After weighing the pros and cons, Susan and Steve decided to go public (see Exhibit 4.2). Bill and his friends would sell their shares; the company would also issue additional shares and use the money to expand the company even more.

Going Public

To sell shares to the general public, Susan and Steve needed the help of an investment bank. The investment bank charges a fee and also hopes to make money buying stock from the SuperStuff corporation and selling it to the public at a higher price. The investment bank will *underwrite* the *initial public offering* (IPO). That means the investment bank agrees to buy all of the shares at a fixed price, whether it can sell all of the shares to the general public right away or not. It is called an initial public offering because SuperStuff has never sold stock to the general public before. Once it sells this stock and has thousands of stockholders, it will become a *public company* under U.S. law. As a public company, SuperStuff will become subject to a whole set of regulations by the government, particularly the Securities and Exchange Commission (SEC). It will have to send out an annual report to all of its shareholders, and it will have to conduct an annual meeting for shareholders and elect a board of directors following the rules of the SEC.

Before selling this initial stock to the public, SuperStuff will have to prepare a *prospectus* and register the stock with the SEC. The prospectus will have a great deal of information about the company, including its history and the fact that the new shares will serve two purposes: buy out the venture capitalists and provide additional capital for the company to expand its operation. The prospectus will contain audited financial statements setting out the last five years of the company's operations. The purpose of the prospectus is to give the buyers a good idea of the potential risks and rewards that might come from buying this stock. Lawyers who specialize in writing prospectuses and accountants who specialize in auditing companies for an initial public offering will be called in and paid handsomely for their services. The lawyers will also have to comply with the securities laws in all 50 states, another significant expense. The SEC will review the prospectus and changes will be made at their request. Finally, the prospectus will be ready for distribution.

When it is all over, Susan and Steve will own 40 percent of the company, down from the 50 percent they owned with Bill and his friends. While they will have a lower percentage of ownership, they will have much more control over the corporation. Before, as equal owners with Bill and his fellow venture capitalists, Susan and Steve had to get Bill's permission for every major change. Now, although they own only 40 percent of the stock, the other 60 percent is divided among thousands of people. At the next stockholder's meeting, only 70 percent of the shares are present to vote for the board of directors. Because Susan and Steve own 40 percent of the stock, they pick the new board, giving them much more "control" over the corporation than they had before.

A Better Way to Go Public

The prospectus for an IPO is probably the most expensive unread document in the United States. Almost no one reads them because they often run to hundreds of pages of fine print. Any country considering a move into the world of capitalism would do well not to copy this feature of American capitalism. Suppose you wanted a more realistic system, or you were an American who wanted to reform the U.S. system to cut down the expense without really decreasing the safety of selling shares to the public. You might decide to set up three categories of stock sold directly to the public: Very Risky, Risky, and Regular.

Anyone who sells stock that has "Very Risky" printed on its face and who puts the Very Risky mark in every advertisement can sell stock without a prospectus or registration or anything else. The public would be warned that if they buy Very Risky stock, they are taking a chance. They cannot sue the sellers of Very Risky stock for anything except fraud and, to sue for fraud, stockholders must have statements in writing from the stock sellers. In other words, sellers of Very Risky stock can pass out any kind of information they want to, including no information at all.

To move up to the Risky category, a stock must have a short prospectus that includes audited financial statements covering the last two years and a "brief" history of the company; the company must have shown a profit for one of the last three years. The prospectus would be less than four pages long and provide basic information in a question-answer format.

To qualify for the Regular category, the company must have been under SEC regulation as a public company for at least two years. It must have filed at least two annual reports to the stockholders that contain all the information those reports are required by the govern-

ment to contain. There must also be a short prospectus, no more than
two pages, that provides basic answers to questions like: What will
the money raised by the sale of these shares be used for? and What
have shares of this company been selling for over the last two years?
This system would be cheaper for the companies selling stock and
better for the people trying to buy the stock. Requiring companies to
spend a fortune writing a prospectus that no one ever reads is the
stupidest thing the United States government does.

Further Expansion

After three years as a public company, Susan and Steve are ready to
expand again. They do not want to sell more shares because they do
not want to *dilute* their ownership any further. The company is now
worth $200 million and needs $200 million more for expansion. If
they sell stock to raise the additional $200 million, Susan and Steve
will own only 20 percent of the company after the new shares are sold.
Because they have been a public company for several years, they are
now in a position to sell bonds and raise the same amount. Of course
the bonds will require interest payments, and the company books will
show that the company is in debt. However, it is not unusual for a
public corporation to have debt equal to the equity of the stockholders,
and they can get a low-interest rate because of the good record of the
company.

Susan and Steve decide to sell senior secured bonds (secured by the
assets of the company) that will pay 8 percent interest. They will be
10-year bonds that can be called in by the company at any time
(bonds that can be called in are called "callable" bonds; most bonds are
callable). At the end of the 10 years, the SuperStuff corporation must
pay back the $200 million. It will either do that with the extra profits
it will be making by then or it can borrow more money (or sell more
stock).

The Benefits of Merger

At the end of the 10 years, the bonds are paid off with the excess
profits and Susan and Steve are thinking about retirement. Their shares

of SuperStuff are now worth $400 million. Susan and Steve could sell their stock but, if they do, they will have to pay income tax on the profit (at the capital gains rate). In the United States, income taxes will take over a third of the profit they make on the sale. But they want to get out of the SuperStuff business and they do not want to have all of their assets tied up in SuperStuff stock. Under United States law, they can merge SuperStuff with a larger corporation, BIG corporation, that is involved in a lot of businesses (commonly called a conglomerate).

Because BIG corporation is a conglomerate involved in a lot of businesses, Susan and Steve consider this a safe place for their $400 million. They can sell a few shares of BIG each year or live off the dividends that they will receive from BIG corporation. Many of the other SuperStuff shareholders are unhappy. They want to own shares in SuperStuff, not BIG. Susan and Steve tell them that they can always sell their new BIG shares. The deal goes through as a stock trade. BIG shares are currently selling for $20 a share and SuperStuff shares are selling for $40 a share, so every shareholder of SuperStuff gets two shares of BIG for every SuperStuff share they own. Susan and Steve owned 10 million shares of SuperStuff so they now own 20 million shares of BIG. Because BIG is a large company, their 20 million shares represent only 2 percent of the shares outstanding. Susan and Steve will obviously not have a controlling interest of BIG. Unhappy shareholders of SuperStuff stock can now sell their BIG shares and invest them somewhere else. Of course, when they do, they will have to pay capital gains tax on the increase in value over what they originally paid for their SuperStuff shares.

Susan and Steve merged with BIG rather than sell their shares for tax purposes. The United States government considers this a "stock swap," not a sale. Susan and Steve do not have to pay any income tax until they sell their newly acquired shares in BIG corporation.

Each year in the United States hundreds of major companies either go public or merge. In each case, the shareholders are trying to maximize the money they will make and minimize the income taxes they will have to pay.

5

What Is It Worth?

The answer to the question, What is it worth? is both very simple and very complicated. At the simplest level, anything is worth what someone is willing to pay for it, no more and no less. During the first half of the twentieth century, gold was generally not worth more than $50 an ounce. At one point in the 1980s, it was selling for almost $1,000 an ounce. So far in the 1990s, it has generally sold for between $300 and $400 an ounce. People like to talk about such things as "intrinsic value" or "base value" or "assured value," but all of that is really nonsense. Nothing has intrinsic, base, or assured value. Everything is subject to the forces of the market.

Valuing Shares

If someone owns shares in a large public company and those shares are traded on a major stock exchange, we can figure out how much the shares are worth by simply looking in the newspaper. If a share sold for $10 yesterday it is probably worth about $10 today. The free market has set the value. The shares may go up or down in price, but at any given moment they are "worth" what someone is willing to pay, no more and no less. Now, suppose Carol owns 10,000 shares in the QED corporation. The company does not have many stockhold-

52

ers and its shares are not traded on a stock exchange. There are one million shares outstanding, so Carol owns 1 percent of the company. How can we find out how much her shares are worth?

First, we should look at the market. Have any QED shares sold recently? No. Are there companies like QED, about the same size and in the same business, whose shares are traded on stock exchanges? If there are, this will give us a rough idea of how much QED is worth. We find that while several companies like QED are traded on stock exchanges, they are each different from QED in significant ways. Some have a lot of debt; QED does not. Some are new companies; QED has been in business for a long time. Some are limited to selling in a small region; QED sells all over the world. It seems there really is no "comparable" company. Using the "comparable companies with similar shares selling in the open market approach" (called the *market approach*, for short), we arrive at a rough guess of $10 a share. We are not very confident of the accuracy of this price.

Next we look at the hard assets of QED. If the company went bankrupt and all of its assets were sold off, how much would they bring? While most companies are worth significantly more than their liquidation value, this gives us a baseline to work from. Let's suppose that QED's assets would sell for $6 million after company debts are paid off. This would give the shares a $6-a-share value using this *asset approach*. While most companies sell for more than this, sometimes two, three, or even four times more, they seldom sell for less. We will accept $6 a share as a minimum value for Carol's shares.

We can use a third approach to set a value for Carol's shares, the *income approach*. This approach looks at the earnings of the company (the money left over after all the expenses and taxes have been paid), and we find that this company earns about $1 million a year. Companies generally sell at a multiple of earnings that is called the *price/ earnings ratio*. The price/earnings ratio is calculated by putting the price of the shares over the line and the per-share earnings of the company under the line to come up with a number. For example, if a company's shares were selling for $10 a share and the company earned $1 per share, we would say it had a price/earnings ratio of 10 (10 divided by 1). During the second half of the twentieth century, the average P/E ratio in the United States has been approximately 14.

Except for companies on the verge of bankruptcy or a great technological breakthrough, the P/E ratio is seldom below 6 or above 40.

These numbers give us some idea of what the ballpark P/E ratio for Carol's company might be. At the same time, we know that different industries traditionally have different ratios. During the early 1990s, competition in the airline industry was very difficult, causing the ratios in that industry to fall below the usual 14 average. At the same time, biotechnology companies and some computer software companies were expected to have significant growth in value, and their shares were selling with a P/E ratio of near 40 in some cases. Carol's company is not on the verge of bankruptcy and it is not expected to have significant growth in the years ahead. Companies competing against it in the same business had an average P/E ratio of 12, which looks reasonable given historical levels. Using this income approach, we would multiply the earnings (in this case the company is earning $1 per share per year) times the price/earnings ratio for the industry of 12 and decide that Carol's shares are worth $12 a share.

However, we are not through with this analysis because interest rates also affect P/E ratios. To see how, let's suppose that we own a very secure corporate bond that pays 8 percent interest. It cost $100 and is a 10-year bond. This means that every year we will receive $8 in interest and, at the end of 10 years, we will get our $100 back (the bond has a face value of $100 and a term of 10 years). We might say that the bond has a price-to-earnings ratio of 12½. That is, the bond earns $8 a year and sells for $100 so its P/E ratio is 100/8 or 12½.

Stock of a company that is not expected to grow much and is not expected to go out of business is a lot like a bond. If bonds are selling at a P/E ratio of 12½, then the stock of this kind of company will probably have a similar P/E ratio. We would put Carol's company in this category. Now suppose the interest rates paid on quality bonds go up to 12 percent. A $100 bond would earn $12 and its P/E ratio would be 100/12 or 8⅓. For companies whose stock is similar to bonds, their P/E ratio would also go down, meaning that, if earnings stayed the same, a company earning $1 a share would be worth only about $8 a share.

What if interest rates go down? Suppose our quality bond is paying 4 percent interest. The bond's P/E ratio would be 100/4 or 25. If our stock is still earning $1 a share and we use a P/E ratio of 25, we get a value of $25 per share. This is why when interest rates go down, the value of stocks (all other things being equal) go up.

Our valuation has led us to three values for Carol's stock: $6 by the asset approach, $10 by the market approach, and $12 by the income approach. Another factor that must be taken into account is the marketability of her shares. Shares in the company Carol owns are not traded on a stock exchange. This means that shares, once bought, are not easy to sell. We came up with our income-approach value by looking at companies that are sold on stock exchanges. We have to discount the value we arrived at, $12 a share, to take this into account. We know from past experience that shares that cannot be freely sold on the open market sell at a discount of between 35 and 50 percent compared with publicly traded shares. A discount of one-third seems reasonable under the circumstances. The income approach combined with a consideration of the marketability of the shares leaves us with a value of $8 a share.

Several other factors should also be considered. What nation or state provided the corporate charter? Why do we care? Because any corporation chartered by a state or nation is subject to its controls. Many states in the United States passed laws in the 1980s to make it more difficult for corporate raiders to take over companies chartered in those states. Corporate raiders have traditionally been willing to pay high prices for stock. If Carol's company is chartered by a state that has passed laws making "takeover" more difficult, we will value the shares at a lower value. Carol's company is chartered by Delaware, which has passed such laws. Too bad! Georgia, Illinois, Kansas, Massachusetts, Pennsylvania, New York, New Jersey, and South Dakota have also passed similar laws designed to make it harder for a takeover artist to buy out the shareholders of a company (thus making the shares of companies incorporated in these states worth less than would otherwise be the case).

We would also like to know if the corporation's bylaws call for cumulative voting. What's cumulative voting? Generally, when stockholders elect the board of directors, the state law or the corporate bylaws call for either straight voting or cumulative voting. With straight voting, stockholders can cast a vote for each candidate equal to the number of shares they own. With cumulative voting, they can cast all their votes for one person.

Suppose there are 10 seats on the board of directors. A stockholder owns 10,000 shares and there are 100,000 shares outstanding. With cumulative voting, this stockholder can cast 100,000 votes (10,000 shares times 10 seats on the board equals 100,000 votes) for one person, guaranteeing that the stockholder will be able to elect at least one candidate to the board of directors to look out for his or her interest. If Carol's company has cumulative voting, her shares will be worth more. Why? Because rich people do not like to buy shares in a company unless they can put someone on the board of directors. Why do we care what rich people want to do? Because they buy and sell stock. If Carol's shares are not attractive to rich people, then some of the people who might buy her shares are not going to be interested. Because everything is a question of supply and demand, and the demand for these shares will be less because of the lack of cumulative voting, Carol's shares are worth less because of this.

At the end of the 1980s, T. Boone Pickens purchased almost a third of the shares in a large Japanese company. Even with such a large stake he was unable to place even one representative on the board of directors. Is it just a coincidence that when the world of investors realized that this was the case, the price of stock in Japanese companies fell dramatically?

The final factor to look at is the country in which the company is located and the countries in which it does business. The stock of a company in the United State is worth a great deal more than the stock of a similar company in war-torn Lebanon. Many factors go into this "country value." Is there a good local market for goods of this type? Does the country provide a supply of educated workers? Does the government provide public services efficiently?

One of the things that brought down the value of companies in the United States at the beginning of the 1990s was the high cost of health care in the United States coupled with the fact that U.S. companies were expected to pay that cost for their employees (in 1991, General Motors paid $3.7 billion for health insurance for its work force, just under $1,000 a car). The fact that American automobile companies had to pay twice as much per car for health care costs compared with their Japanese competitors made them less competitive, less profitable and, therefore, worth less than their Japanese competitors. Companies in countries with socialized medicine are generally worth more than

Eliminating the Control Premium with a Corporate Senate

Investors are willing to pay a "control premium" because by buying significantly less than all the shares of a corporation they are able to select all the members of the board of directors and thereby "control" the whole company. This allows them to engage in transactions with the corporation that will be to their special advantage.

The "control premium" and the opportunity to engage in self-serving actions with the corporation could be reduced by the election of a corporate senate. While the board of directors is elected by the stockholders on the basis of one vote for each share, the corporate senate would be elected on the basis of one vote for each shareholder. The senate would have the power to veto any action by the board of directors that involved a possible conflict of interest for any of its members or the major stockholders. The senate would take over the functions currently performed by special board of director committees such as the remuneration, audit, and nominations committees. The board of directors would still have the power to run the corporation.

Shann Turnbull
ESOP Advisers
Sidney, Australia

companies in primitive countries such as the United States that have been unable to solve the medical cost problem.

Carol's company is in the United States, and does most of its business in the United States. We have compared it with other American companies, so we do not need to figure that in. Given all the factors, we think that Carol's stock is worth $8 a share for a total of $80,000 ($8 times 10,000). But Carol says that the founder of the company just sold his 48 percent stake in the company (480,000 shares) for $16 a share. Why are her shares worth less than his? Because he enjoyed what we call a *control premium*. The control premium recognizes that if someone can buy a controlling interest in a corporation, that person is willing to pay more for the stock. As a rule of thumb, we can assume that if these shares were freely traded on the stock markets, they would be worth $12 a share. We often see a control premium increasing a stock's value by from 35 to 50 percent ($16 is what the founder received, which sounds reasonable to us). As noted earlier, when shares cannot be marketed easily because they are not traded on stock exchanges, their value is discounted from 35 to 50 percent. We think Carol's shares are worth $8, which fits in with this assumption. The founder, with his control premium, got $16 a share; if the shares were freely traded, they might be worth $12 a share; they are not freely traded, so Carol's shares are worth $8 a share.

No Accounting for Taste

In evaluating any company, we want to see three financial statements: the cash flow statement, the income statement, and the balance sheet. Exhibit 5.1 shows what these statements might look like for the imaginary WAWAWA corporation. The *cash flow statement* is the simplest for most people to understand because it looks a lot like a household budget. The cash flow statement for a year simply shows how much "cash" came into the company during the year and how much cash went out. WAWAWA makes and sells personal computers around the world. During the last fiscal year, it took in $110 million in revenues from the sale of computers. It also borrowed $20 million and sold some land for $10 million. It took in $140 million in cash. It spent $40 million for supplies, along with $30 million for wages and employee benefits. It paid out dividends of $10 million and paid $10 million in taxes to states, the United States, and foreign countries. It spent $10 million renovating the factory and buying new machines to help improve productivity and paid another $10 million as interest on its debts. This left it with $30 million at the end of the year to add to the bank account. The cash flow statement tells us how something real—cash—behaved in this company. This statement tells us that at the end of the year the company had $30 million more in cash than when it started, but it also borrowed $20 million and sold land worth $10 million.

The *income statement* is, in some ways, one step away from reality. Money that comes in from borrowing or from the sale of stock is not considered income. While $10 million came into the company from the sale of land, the company had paid $10 million for the land in the first place so there was no profit, no income, on the deal. The only

Exhibit 5.1 Accounting Statements for WAWAWA
(in millions of dollars)

Cash Flow Statement

Cash In

$110	revenue from sales
20	borrowed
10	sale of land
$140	

Cash Out

$ 40	supplies
30	wages and benefits
10	dividend
10	taxes
10	buildings and machines
10	interest on debt
$110	

$140 − $110 = $30 added to bank account at end of year.

Income Statement

Revenues

$110 revenue from sales

Costs

$40	supplies
30	wages and benefits
10	depreciation
10	interest on debt
$90	

$110 − $90 = $20 profit before taxes
− 10 taxes
$10 earnings for year.

Balance Sheet

Assets

$ 40	cash
40	inventory
40	accounts receivable
50	land
50	buildings and machines
$220	

Liabilities

$ 40	accounts payable
80	debt
$120	

$220 − $120 = $100 stockholders' equity.
(10 million shares with book value of $10 per share)

thing from our cash flow statement that counts as income on the income statement is the $110 million taken in because of the sale of computers. On the cost side, we first put the costs of materials, labor, and depreciation. Accountants consider buildings and machinery to be "wasting assets," meaning that they are worth something when they are first purchased but they lose their value over time as they wear out. Accountants feel it is better to "depreciate" these assets over time to present a more realistic picture of how much this year's computers actually cost. Interest paid is also an expense. Revenues minus expenses shows a profit for the company this year of $20 million. On that profit the company had to pay $10 million in taxes of various kinds, so the $10 million left is what the company actually *earned* at the end of the year. We know from the cash flow statement that all of that money was paid out to the stockholders as a dividend.

The third financial statement, the *balance sheet*, gives us an idea of what the assets of the company are worth. We see by looking at this balance sheet that this company had $40 million in the bank at the end of the year ($10 million to start plus the $30 million it added at the end of this year). It also had computers in inventory worth $40 million and it was owed another $40 million by people who had purchased computers and not yet paid for them (called accounts receivable). It also had $50 million worth of land and $50 million worth of buildings and machinery (after depreciation for this year). The assets add up to $220 million. Liabilities are what the company owes. It owes $40 million in accounts payable, meaning it has received materials and supplies that it has not yet paid for. It owes $80 million in debt on bonds that it has sold to raise money for total liabilities of $120 million. Assets minus liabilities give us $100 million, which is the equity that the stockholders have in the company. Just as a homeowner who lives in a home worth $200,000 with $100,000 still owed on the mortgage has equity in the home of $100,000, so the stockholders have equity in the assets of a corporation. During this year, this company earned $10 million on stockholders' equity of $100 million for a 10 percent return on equity.

A 10 percent return on equity is considered low. After all, if people can get 8 percent on a very safe bond, they should expect to get significantly more investing in the stock of a business that is riskier than most bonds.

There is still much about the WAWAWA corporation we would like to know. What are they planning to do with the $40 million in cash that they have built up in the corporation's bank account? Why did they declare a dividend of $10 million when they had to borrow that amount and more? If the answer to these questions is that the management has gone crazy, we would not want to buy this stock. If the answer is that the company is preparing to move into a new market where it has good reason to believe it will be successful and thus be able to significantly improve earnings for the future, then we might want to buy this stock.

Reinvestment, Dividends, and Stock Repurchase

Let's suppose we manage a corporation that has earned $100 million this year. What should we do with the money? We have basically four choices. First, we can reinvest in the business we are in, buying new buildings and machinery or even buying other companies. Second, we can put the money into a bank account to earn interest until we see a good reinvestment opportunity. Third, we can give it to the stockholders in the form of dividends. Fourth, we can use it to buy shares of our own stock on the open market.

How much of a return do we think we can get by reinvesting in the business we are currently in? Our stockholders purchased their stock because they felt that this business was a good investment. It is our duty to use the money in that business as best we can to make money for the stockholders, but the return we can expect will be a factor. If we do not think we can make more than 10 percent on the money, then, given that our stockholders can make 8 percent buying very safe bonds, perhaps we should give the money to them and let them invest it themselves.

If we decide to give the money to the stockholders, we can go about it in two ways: by sending out a dividend or by repurchasing some of our shares on the open market. Which one we choose has more to do with the tax consequences for our stockholders than anything else. If our stockholders are in a low tax bracket, then they would probably prefer to receive the money in the form of a dividend. Some companies know that their stock is owned by a lot of widows who depend on their dividend checks to make ends meet. These widows are in low tax brackets so they would like to receive the cash.

Some companies know that their stockholders are mainly in high tax brackets, where a dividend would result in a large percentage of the money going to the government in the form of income taxes. If the company uses its earnings to repurchase shares on the open market, this brings the price of the shares up. Why? Suppose 10 million shares are outstanding and the share price is $50. The company uses its $100 million to buy back as many shares as it can, which would be 2 million shares. The company has the same assets and value after this stock repurchase, but the number of outstanding shares has gone from 10 million to 8 million. If the company was worth $500 million before and $500 million after, then the shares that were worth $50 a share before ($500 million divided by 10 million) are worth $62.50 a share after ($500 million divided by 8 million). Our rich shareholders can now sell their shares when it is most advantageous to them and, if they meet the requirements of the country involved, they will pay only capital gains taxes on the sale (in many countries, rich people are going to be better off receiving capital gains income rather than dividend income). This strategy will also be to the advantage of any shareholders who purchased their shares planning to hold on to them and sell them after they retire and are in a lower income tax bracket. To the extent that our shareholders are planning to use their shares for income at a later time, they are going to want us to repurchase our shares, not declare a dividend. The decision to reinvest, declare a dividend, or make a stock repurchase will depend on the prospects for making money in the industry and the income and tax effects such a move will have on the stockholders.

In the United States, employee pension and benefit funds own a large percentage of the common stock in U.S. companies. Because these funds do not pay income taxes, they do not care whether the company reinvests the money, pays a dividend, or repurchases its shares as long as the fund can realize a reasonable return on its investment. Most pension fund managers do not like to see a company place a large amount of cash in a bank account to earn a low level of interest. Because the company will pay income taxes on that interest income, the pension fund managers would rather have the money in the form of higher stock prices or a dividend so they can invest it themselves.

6

Pensions and Employee
Benefit Plans

A discussion of sharing ownership cannot begin without a basic understanding of employee pensions and benefit plans. Any discussion of
pension plans must begin with a discussion of social security.

Social Security

The first major national system of social security retirement benefits
appeared in Germany at the end of the nineteenth century. Legend
has it that Bismarck instituted social security as a way to neutralize the
Socialists and Communists who threatened to bring about a revolution. He chose 65 as the retirement age because studies at the time
found that almost no one lived past the age of 65. Needless to say, the
idea caught on. Today every industrialized country has some form of
government pension plan and in many countries it is called social
security.

Social Security in the United States today includes a medical insurance program for the elderly called Medicare, a disability insurance
program for workers, and a government pension system. In 1992,
the Social Security tax in the United States was 15.3 percent. The

government likes to pretend that the worker pays 7.65 percent out of wages and the employer matches this amount. From the point of view of the employer, however, it is all part of "payroll expenses" and it doesn't matter what the pay stub says. In the United States, Social Security taxes are paid only on wages, not on other kinds of income such as dividends, capital gains, or interest. In the United States, there is a maximum in wages beyond which no more Social Security taxes are due (except for a small percentage used to pay for Medicare). In 1992, the first $55,500 in wages were subject to full Social Security taxes.

The Social Security Administration in the United States used to talk about the Social Security Trust Fund. There really is no trust fund. In the United States, as in most other countries, the Social Security taxes paid in a year are used to pay retirement (and other) benefits during that same year. It is a pay-as-you-go system.

Is it a good deal? In the United States, it was a good deal for people who worked during the first half century of Social Security's existence. They received significantly more from the Social Security system than they would have received from a private pension fund. The same is not true for those paying into the system after the mid-1980s. To see why, let's imagine that a worker earning the national average wage of $20,000 a year puts 15 percent of that, or $3,000, into a fund every year for 30 years. Let's also imagine that the money in this fund earns 10 percent a year. This is not an unreasonable assumption given that bonds over the long run have earned 8 percent while stocks over the long run have earned 12 percent, and most pension/benefit funds invest in a combination of stocks and bonds. Exhibit 6.1 (on page 69) shows the simple calculations. After 30 years, our fund would have $544,828 in it. Thus more than half a million dollars would be available to pay a retirement income during the remaining life of the worker. Assuming the fund continued to earn 10 percent, this worker would receive $54,000 a year to live on. Also this worker would have more than half a million dollars to leave to his or her heirs when the time came. It is highly unlikely that anyone paying into Social Security in the 1990s is ever going to see yearly payments like that and, of course, there will be no half a million dollars to leave to heirs at the end of the road.

It is unlikely that Social Security will be able to pay such handsome benefits in the twenty-first century. During the 1990s, some three U.S. workers were paying into the Social Security system for every retired worker receiving benefits. This ratio will fall to less than two workers for every retired worker by the 2020s.

There is another factor to consider. The Social Security system in the United States is "weighted" to favor lower paid workers. This means that the lowest paid workers receive 60 percent of their preretirement wages when they retire, while the highest paid workers receive only 26 percent of their preretirement wages when they retire. For people making less than the average in wages, the system is a better deal than for people making more than the average.

People in some European countries live fairly well on their government social security pension check. In the United States, Social Security is expected to pay only the most basic living expenses for a retired worker. Anyone without a private pension plan in the United States can expect to be living in poverty in the twenty-first century. About half of all the workers in the United States were covered by some other retirement plan in the 1990s. This was not always the case.

Until the 1930s, most workers had no pension plan whatsoever. In 1935, the U.S. Social Security system was established. In the 1940s, World War II helped to create a whole new set of private pension and benefit plans. That is because during the war real wages were frozen. Unions representing workers negotiated pension plans as a way to receive pay in future years for work done during the war. While these plans were called "pension plans," they were really delayed-wage-payment plans. They were generally pay-as-you-go, meaning that, in future years, these companies were planning to pay the promised pension benefits out of corporate revenues. There was no trust fund with money in it to pay these benefits. By the 1960s, it became clear that older corporations would be at a major disadvantage because of this pay-as-you-go system. Their payroll expenses would continue to go up as more and more workers retired, while their new competitors would not have this expense and would eventually be able to sell their products at a lower price. This would eventually put the older corporations out of business, leaving the retired workers with nothing.

In 1974, the United States Congress passed the Employee Retirement Income Security Act (ERISA) to deal with this problem. This law required companies offering pension plans to actually put money into a trust fund each year while the workers were working. This money would be invested so that when the workers retired there would be money in a fund to pay for retirement, and the corporation would not have to go out of business because of the cost of paying these retirement benefits out of current revenue. This law also required pension funds to pay into an insurance fund to help pay the cost of pension funds that could not pay their promised retirement benefits. The Pension Benefit Guaranty Corporation (PBGC) was set up to collect these premiums and to pay out benefits if necessary. It is reasonable to believe that by the end of the twentieth century, most private pension funds in the United States will be solvent and able to actually pay their retirement obligations.

Pensions and Defined-Benefit Plans

By a pension plan, we mean a *defined-benefit plan* where an employer places money in a trust fund to pay out benefits to future retirees. The amount of money a particular retired worker will receive will be determined by the amount of wages the worker earned while under the particular plan and the number of years the worker worked under the plan. In a true pension plan, the benefit is defined. That means there is no individual account for each worker. There is simply a large pool of invested money that earns interest and dividends each year with which to pay out benefits.

Whether this is a good deal depends on how generous the system has promised to be. During the 1980s and 1990s, more and more of these pension plans in the United States were modified to "integrate" their benefits with Social Security. This means that they promise to pay only enough to make up the difference between what Social Security pays and what the worker is entitled to under the pension plan.

During the 1980s and into the 1990s, few corporations set up defined-benefit pension funds and many eliminated them. Why? First, because they were now forced to live under the pension regulations of the United States government. Complying with regulations is always an expensive proposition. Second, they were forced to pay insurance premiums to the PBGC. This also added to the expense. Third, many companies realized that they had more money in their pension trust fund than they needed to pay out promised benefits. Many companies closed out their pension funds and took back this excess money. The United States government eventually passed laws imposing taxes to make this an expensive thing to do but, by the time the government acted, many pension funds had stopped functioning.

During the 1970s, 1980s, and early 1990s, most workers would have been better off with a defined-contribution fund rather than a defined-benefit pension fund. If the money supposedly placed in the defined-benefit pension fund for their benefit had been put in an account with their name on it, and reasonable interest and dividends from the purchase of stocks and bonds had been reinvested, most workers would have found that their account had increased significantly during that time period.

Defined-Contribution Plans

With a *defined-contribution plan*, the contribution is definite but the actual benefit to be paid out at retirement is not. With a defined-benefit plan, money is placed in a large pool; when the worker meets the requirements of the system, he or she begins to draw out benefits. Those benefits will be determined by looking at a table showing years in the system and average wages or wages during the final years of employment. With a defined-benefit plan, the worker cannot take "her money" out because there is no special account with her name on it. With a defined-contribution plan, there is an individual account with the worker's name on it. The employer places money in that account every year, and the account grows as it earns interest and dividends, which are reinvested. A defined-contribution plan could provide a worker with that half a million dollars shown in Exhibit 6.1.

There are three major types of defined-contribution plans in the United States: profit-sharing plans, employee stock ownership plans (ESOPs), and thrift plans.

Profit-Sharing Plans

The two basic types of profit-sharing plans are cash plans and trust fund plans. In a cash profit-sharing plan, an employer simply pays a cash bonus to employees if the company makes a profit. This is not what most profit-sharing plans do; so in the remainder of this book, when we talk about profit-sharing plans, we will be talking about trust fund plans. French law requires any company with more than 100 employees to have some kind of profit-sharing scheme. This scheme can be either a profit-sharing bonus or payment into a profit-sharing trust fund.

An employer with a trust fund profit-sharing plan places money into the individual account of each worker. Each year more money is added, and the account also grows as interest and dividends are reinvested. Each worker has an individual account that can be used for retirement and other purposes according to the limits of the law and the specifics of the plan. The employees do not pay any taxes (either Social Security or income taxes) on the money placed in their individual accounts. Until recently in the United States, an employer could not place money into a profit-sharing trust fund unless the company actually made a profit. That restriction was removed in the 1980s so that, as this book is being written, a company in the United States can make contributions to a profit-sharing plan whether or not the company makes a profit in a particular year. A profit-sharing plan in the United States can be written so that any amount of the funds, up to 100 percent, may be used to buy the company's own stock.

One of the significant advantages of a defined-contribution plan over simply paying the money out to the employees in the form of wages and letting the employees invest the money as they see fit is illustrated by Exhibits 6.1, 6.2, and 6.3. Exhibit 6.1 shows that if $3,000 is placed in a fund every year, earning 10 percent a year, and the money earned is also reinvested each year, at the end of 30 years the fund would have $544,828.

What if the worker had to pay Social Security and income taxes on the money before it was invested? Exhibit 6.2 supposes that taxes will take a third of the money so that instead of placing $3,000 a year into the fund, the worker can invest only $2,000 a year. Assuming that the interest earned is not taxed, we arrive at $361,882 at the end of 30

Exhibit 6.1 Deposits and Interest Untaxed

Year	Put In	New Total	10% Interest	End-of-Year Total
1	$3,000	$ 3,000	$ 300	$ 3,300
2	3,000	6,300	630	6,930
3	3,000	9,930	993	10,923
4	3,000	13,923	1,392	15,315
5	3,000	18,315	1,831	29,146
6	3,000	23,146	2,315	25,461
7	3,000	28,461	2,846	31,307
8	3,000	34,307	3,431	37,738
9	3,000	40,738	4,074	44,812
10	3,000	47,812	4,781	52,593
11	3,000	55,593	5,559	61,152
12	3,000	64,152	6,415	70,567
13	3,000	73,567	7,357	80,924
14	3,000	83,924	8,392	92,316
15	3,000	95,316	9,532	104,848
16	3,000	107,848	10,785	118,633
17	3,000	121,633	12,163	133,796
18	3,000	136,796	13,680	150,476
19	3,000	153,476	15,348	168,824
20	3,000	171,824	17,182	189,006
21	3,000	192,006	19,201	211,207
22	3,000	214,207	21,421	235,628
23	3,000	238,628	23,863	262,491
24	3,000	265,491	26,549	292,040
25	3,000	295,040	29,504	324,544
26	3,000	327,544	32,754	360,298
27	3,000	363,298	36,330	399,628
28	3,000	402,628	40,263	442,891
29	3,000	445,891	44,589	490,480
30	3,000	493,480	49,348	544,828

years. While this is a significant sum, having to pay taxes on the money before investing it has cost this worker $182,946.

What if the worker paid Social Security and income taxes on the money and then invested it in a fund paying 10 percent a year, but the income from this fund was also subject to taxes every year as the money was earned? If we suppose a 30 percent tax on this interest and dividend income, the worker ends up making only 7 percent on the

Exhibit 6.2 Deposits Taxed, Interest Untaxed

Year	Put In	New Total	10% Interest	End-of-Year Total
1	$2,000	$ 2,000	$ 200	$ 2,200
2	2,000	4,200	420	4,620
3	2,000	6,620	662	7,282
4	2,000	9,282	928	10,210
5	2,000	12,210	1,221	13,431
6	2,000	15,431	1,543	16,974
7	2,000	18,974	1,897	20,871
8	2,000	22,871	2,287	25,158
9	2,000	27,158	2,716	29,874
10	2,000	31,874	3,187	35,061
11	2,000	37,061	3,706	40,767
12	2,000	42,767	4,277	47,044
13	2,000	49,044	4,904	53,948
14	2,000	55,948	5,595	61,543
15	2,000	63,543	6,354	69,897
16	2,000	71,897	7,190	79,087
17	2,000	81,087	8,109	89,196
18	2,000	91,196	9,120	100,316
19	2,000	102,316	10,232	112,548
20	2,000	114,548	11,455	126,003
21	2,000	128,003	12,800	140,803
22	2,000	142,803	14,280	157,083
23	2,000	159,083	15,908	174,991
24	2,000	176,991	17,699	194,690
25	2,000	196,690	19,670	216,360
26	2,000	218,360	21,836	240,196
27	2,000	242,196	24,220	266,416
28	2,000	268,416	26,842	295,258
29	2,000	297,258	29,726	326,984
30	2,000	328,984	32,898	361,882

money each year after paying taxes. Exhibit 6.3 shows that this worker would have $202,145 at the end of 30 years. Taxes have cost the worker another $159,737 over the course of the 30 years because less money was available for reinvestment each year.

A fund of money that is not subject to any taxes when the money is put in and is not subject to any taxes as long as it stays in the fund

Exhibit 6.3 Deposits and Interest Taxed

Year	Put In	New Total	7% Interest	End-of-Year Total
1	$2,000	$ 2,000	$ 140	$ 2,140
2	2,000	4,140	290	4,430
3	2,000	6,430	450	6,880
4	2,000	8,880	622	9,502
5	2,000	11,502	805	12,307
6	2,000	14,307	1,001	15,308
7	2,000	17,308	1,212	18,520
8	2,000	20,520	1,436	21,956
9	2,000	23,956	1,677	25,633
10	2,000	27,633	1,934	29,567
11	2,000	31,567	2,210	33,777
12	2,000	35,777	2,504	38,281
13	2,000	40,281	2,820	43,101
14	2,000	45,101	3,157	48,258
15	2,000	50,258	3,518	53,776
16	2,000	55,776	3,904	59,680
17	2,000	61,680	4,318	65,998
18	2,000	67,998	4,760	72,758
19	2,000	74,758	5,233	79,991
20	2,000	81,991	5,739	87,730
21	2,000	89,730	6,281	96,011
22	2,000	98,011	6,861	104,872
23	2,000	106,872	7,481	114,353
24	2,000	116,353	8,145	124,498
25	2,000	126,498	8,854	135,352
26	2,000	137,352	9,615	146,967
27	2,000	148,967	10,428	159,395
28	2,000	161,395	11,298	172,693
29	2,000	174,693	12,228	186,921
30	2,000	188,921	13,224	202,145

creates a great deal more money for the worker than a fund that is subject to tax before the money is placed in the fund and again when money is earned by the fund. The difference between $544,828 and $202,145 is $342,683. The double tax benefit enjoyed by a profit-sharing plan in the United States accounts for more than half the growth in value over the 30-year life of the plan in this example.

Employee Stock Ownership Plans

An ESOP is similar in many ways to a profit-sharing plan except that the money is used mainly to buy shares of stock in the company for which the employee works instead of a group of different stocks and bonds. The company can also simply issue new shares and place them in the individual employee accounts. Because a profit-sharing plan can also buy stock in the company for which the employees work and because contributions are no longer limited by the amount of "profit" the company makes in a particular year, the major difference between profit-sharing plans and ESOPs in the 1990s in the United States is the ability of ESOPs to borrow money with a loan guaranteed by the company.

As a general rule, pension or benefit trust funds can borrow money; but the loan cannot be from, or guaranteed by, a "party-in-interest," meaning any of the people involved in the fund such as the company that set up the fund or the employees. Because no one else would be interested in lending money to such a fund, or guaranteeing a loan to such a fund, these funds generally do not borrow money. In the United States, an ESOP is different. It can borrow money from a party-in-interest or it can borrow money from someone else, such as a bank, and have the loan guaranteed by a party-in-interest. This means that a company can borrow a lot of money to buy its own shares, hold those shares in an ESOP and, as the loan is paid off, place the shares in the accounts of the individual employees. (I will discuss this in much greater detail in Part Three).

Why would a company ever want to do this? Many reasons. The stock might be undervalued at the moment and it would be a good deal to buy it for the employees; also it would provide the employees with an incentive to help increase the value of those shares. Or a large shareholder might want to sell all of her shares, and the company would like those shares to go to the employees instead of to the person who is trying to buy them. This ability to "leverage" the purchase of stock, particularly stock that is undervalued, allows a company with an ESOP to provide its employees with a potentially greater amount in their individual accounts.

Thrift Plans

The third major type of defined-contribution plan in the United States is the thrift plan. In a thrift plan, the employees put some of their wages into the plan each month. In most cases, the employer provides some kind of match. For example, the employer may promise to contribute a dollar for every dollar the employees put in up to some limit. This provides employees with an extra incentive to place money in these funds. Generally the money placed in these funds by the employees is first taxed for Social Security. The most common thrift plan in the United States is called a 401(k) plan (because Section 401(k) of the Internal Revenue Code controls these plans).

The Rules

Pension and benefit plans in most countries are subject to a series of complex laws and regulations. The United States may have the most complex in part because of the variety of plans recognized by law, and in part because the United States government has decided that these plans should not be simply a tax-advantaged benefit for only the most "highly compensated employees." These rules provide significant headaches for plan administrators and attorneys but are not of interest to most people. These rules require that most employees participate in a plan before the employer can deduct the contributions made to the plan.

Most countries control *vesting*. Someone *vests* in a plan when the money placed in the plan by the employer belongs to the employee. In other words, when the employee has a legal right to receive a benefit, we say that employee is vested. The basic vesting rules in the United States allow for two types of vesting: gradual or cliff.

If an employer wants employees to vest gradually, the employer can allow the employee to be vested 20 percent after 3 years and 20 percent each year thereafter until the employee is 100 percent vested after he or she has been with the plan for 7 years. In cliff vesting, the employee is not vested at all for 5 years but is 100 percent vested after that. In the United States, employees who participate in multi-employer plans (usually tied to a union) can cliff vest after 10 years. This means that if the employee stops working after 9 years, he or she gets nothing from the plan, but if the employee works more than 10 years, he or she is entitled to some kind of benefits from the plan upon retirement.

Employers in the United States are free to allow employees to vest faster than required by law. It is important to remember that vesting refers only to "employer" contributions. If the employee is making contributions to the plan, for example with a 401(k) plan, those funds belong to the employee 100 percent from the moment they are placed in the fund.

In the United States, these funds are placed in a trust. A trustee controls the funds and is bound by law to act only in the best interest of the employees covered by the fund. This is true even if the trustee is paid by the employer; it is the employees who are the beneficiaries of the trust. In countries without the concept of "trust" in their law, this function may be handled by a special nonprofit corporation that will act very much like a trust would act in countries that inherited their law from Great Britain.

There are maximum limits on how much money may be placed in these funds (or paid out if they are defined-benefit funds). In the United States, the Tax Reform Act of 1986 set a limit of $90,000 a year that can be paid out by a defined-benefit plan. This amount is indexed for inflation and was $102,582 in 1990, for example. The amount that can be contributed by the employer to defined-contribution plans is limited to $30,000 a year per employee. When inflation causes the defined-benefit limit to reach $120,000, then this limit on defined-contribution payments will also go up to match inflation (maintaining the four-to-one ratio).

The amount employees can contribute to thrift plans is also limited (and adjusted for inflation). For example, in 1990 an employee could not contribute more than $7,979 using pre-income-tax dollars. The amount an employer can contribute to defined-contribution plans is generally limited to 15 percent of payroll (special rules apply if an employer has both a defined-benefit and a defined-contribution plan). The major exception to this rule is for leveraged ESOPs. If an ESOP is leveraged, the employer may contribute up to 25 percent of payroll. This allows employers with leveraged ESOPs to contribute significantly more to their employees' defined-contribution and pension plans than would otherwise be the case.

There are, of course, rules on when the money in any of these funds can be distributed to the employee. The general rule is that the money is not distributed until the employee retires, dies, or is too disabled to work. There are, of course, exceptions to the general rule. In some situations, employees may be able to borrow from the plan or receive an early distribution. As a general rule, in the United States anyone receiving money from a plan before death, disability, or retirement must either roll over the funds into an Individual Retirement Account (IRA) or pay a penalty tax on the money. Also, as a general rule, in the United States employees may not receive benefits until age 59 and must begin to receive retirement benefits after they reach the age of 70.

The Problem with Benefits

The twentieth century has seen more and more benefit plans receive tax-favored status in the United States. In 1921, the United States government first provided tax incentives for employer-sponsored pension plans. In 1954, employer health plans became tax deductible. By the 1990s, a wide variety of employee benefits are tax deductible to employers. If the employers paid the wages to the employees who then paid for these benefits themselves, a significant amount of money in the form of Social Security and income taxes would be collected. Because of this, employers have a strong incentive to provide benefits (tax free to employees) rather than increase wages. This is one of the reasons average wages in the United States did not increase during the 1970s and 1980s (the other major reason being the significant increase in both Social Security taxes and the cost of providing health insurance to employees). Besides the pension and benefit plans already discussed in this chapter, an American employer might provide every worker with health insurance, life insurance, disability insurance, dental insurance, tuition reimbursement, legal fee reimbursement, and child care. All of these benefits act as a drag on hiring during recessions. This was particularly true during the recession of 1990–1992.

Imagine an employer in the United States in 1992 who paid $6 an hour to entry-level employees. The company had increased demand for its product and had to decide whether to pay overtime wages to its employees or to hire new workers. Overtime pay is 1½ times the usual wage; if already-hired workers work 40 hours extra each week, this employer would have to pay 40 times $9 or $360 for that work. If the employer hired a new worker, it would cost 40 times $6 or $240. Overtime would cost this employer $120 a week. If there were no benefits involved, this employer would probably hire a new worker rather than ask its employees to work overtime.

In 1992, there were lots of benefits. Some of these benefits, such as pension payments or payments to a defined-contribution plan, are usually a percentage of payroll and do not effect the decision to hire a new worker. Other benefits, such as child care, disability insurance, and life insurance, are per worker not per dollar. These expenses will go up only if new workers are hired.

The biggest per-worker expense in the United States in 1992 was the cost of health insurance. An employer with a full set of these per-worker benefits may well spend $120 a week just on these expenses. Add the cost of hiring the new worker, with the risk that the new worker might have to be fired if the increase in new orders does not continue, and you have a very strong incentive not to hire new workers. In 1992, therefore, the high cost of health insurance was a drag on recovery in two ways: first, because it discouraged the hiring of new workers, which would have brought down unemployment; and, second, because money that would have been spent on buying goods and services was spent instead on paying inflated health care bills.

Sharing the Wealth

The United States government has done two things to drastically change the wealth equation in the United States over the course of the twentieth century. First, it encouraged people to own their own homes through tax incentives and mortgage-guarantee programs. The significant increase in the value of residential real estate in the United States in the 1980s, combined with the long-term effect of these tax incentives, has turned the average American into a "wealthy" person by world standards. Where the average American "owned" little or nothing at the depths of the Great Depression in the 1930s, today the average American at retirement age has a paid-for house worth close to $100,000. This particular wealth-distribution scheme was quite intentional. The government believed that homeowners make better citizens and set out to make as many people homeowners as possible.

The other program that has changed the wealth equation just as dramatically is the pension/benefit plan laws passed to grant tax incentives to employers who provide private pension or benefit plans for their employees. The Institutional Investor Project at Columbia University estimated that pension/benefit plans owned 18 percent of all the common stock in the United States in 1981 and 28 percent by 1990. This does not include all the other securities such as bonds and real estate that these plans also own. Where 90 percent of the productive wealth (common stock and real estate) in the United States was owned by less than 5 percent of its population at the beginning of the twentieth century, more than half of the productive wealth will be owned by average citizens by the end of the century. A significant portion of this wealth will be held in trust for these average citizens by thousands of employee pension and benefit funds.

While this is certainly good news for anyone who believes that a society is better off when wealth is more evenly distributed, there are some problems. For example, during the 1980s and continuing into the 1990s, more and more pension/benefit funds in the United States began investing in the stock of foreign companies. This practice makes excellent sense from the point of view of a pension fund trustee, who is charged by law with diversifying the securities in the portfolio to decrease the risk of loss and possibly to increase the potential for growth. However, it also has the effect of taking investment capital that would have made the United States stronger economically and exporting it to foreign countries.

Early in the twenty-first century, pension/benefit fund trustees will own a controlling interest in every major corporation in the United States. Whether you call it trustee-capitalism or trustee-socialism, the United States will clearly have entered a new type of economic system. It is difficult to imagine the effects this will have on the social, economic, and political realities of the twenty-first century.

7

Why Ownership?

Employers in the United States and around the world are interested in providing some kind of ownership stake in the company for both executives and rank-and-file employees. Why should they? Or rather, why ownership? Why not simply give employees what they have always been given as an incentive to work harder in the past: commissions, bonuses, and various types of incentive plans? Let's look first at the pros and cons of the various nonownership options available to the average employer around the world. Then we will examine why giving employees some form of ownership in the company might offer advantages over these conventional methods of inspiring more and better quality work.

Commissions, Bonuses, and Incentive Plans

Suppose Bill, Fred, and John all work for MayDay's, a large department store chain in the United States. Bill works selling clothes in the men's department; Fred is a buyer of men's clothes for the whole chain; and John is in charge of advertising of men's clothes for the whole chain. At present, none of these three gentlemen has a long-term commitment to MayDay's department store. In fact, all three of these workers assume that they will work at MayDay's for a few years and then move on to a competitor who will pay them more money for the experience they have gained at MayDay's.

Bill is paid a small salary and commissions. He is one of four salespeople in his department, and each makes a commission only on what he or she rings up at the cash register. Bill spots a large man entering the men's department. His first thought is that this man will never fit into any of MayDay's suits because he is too big. He should be shopping at a specialty store that specializes in sizes for large men. The customer might buy other products at MayDay's, but MayDay's suits are not for him. However, Bill gets a large commission if he sells a suit, much more than if he sells a shirt or a tie; and, of course, if this big man buys something in another department, Bill gets nothing at all.

Bill smiles broadly and tells the customer he has just the suit for him. The sleeves are too short, but Bill says they will "ride down with wear." The chest is snug, but Bill says it will "stretch out over time"; and besides, "snug" is all the fashion this year. Bill sells the man a suit for $500. When the man gets home, his wife first laughs and then cries when she finds out how much the suit cost. She drags her husband down to the store the next day where they go through the usual hassle of trying to get their money back. The store will not refund the money but will give them credit with which to purchase other items at the store.

The customer and his wife devote the rest of the day to spending the $500 on everything under the sun. Bill loses his commission because the item was returned, and other clerks get a commission on the items they sell to this customer with his store credit. Bill is unhappy and MayDay's has lost a customer. The man and his wife vow never to set foot in MayDay's again!

Fred is in Europe on a buying trip. Fred gets a bonus based on the sales of men's clothes in MayDay's. The more sales exceed a "target," the larger his bonus. In Italy he discovers a new line of men's Italian suits. The fabric is of inferior quality but the cut is good and the design is great. Fred places a large order. The suits sell very well over the next year, and Fred gets a big bonus and an offer he can't refuse to move to another store. The suits are fine for about a year, then the zippers begin coming apart and the sleeves begin to show excessive wear.

Thousands of men decide, you guessed it, never to shop at MayDay's again!

John is in advertising. He does not get a commission or a bonus based on sales. He is eligible to win a "prize" given out each month for the best advertising campaign. The head of the department gives out the prizes, which has caused a lot of resentment in the department because everyone feels that he gives them mainly to his "favorites." Some of the staff have noticed that most of the awards go to white men, so they sue MayDay's for race discrimination. In the middle of the lawsuit, you guessed it, MayDay's files for bankruptcy!

Let's move from the world of the hypothetical to actual cases. Mr. Lessley was recruited out of college by a promise made during the job interview to provide a bonus plan so wonderful that the employer called it the "golden handcuffs" bonus plan (727 P.2d 440 (Kan. 1986)). The plan called for 10 percent of the income from each project to be set aside and distributed to key employees based on their contribution to the success of the project, but Mr. Lessley became dissatisfied with the plan. He felt that the employer was not distributing the bonus money fairly given what Mr. Lessley believed to be his contribution to the success of the enterprise. The Kansas Supreme Court said he could sue and that it would be up to a jury to decide what a fair and honest employer would have done under the circumstances.

When John Scott, a brick mason, began making suggestions concerning how the brick pits at the Lone Star Steel Company could be rebuilt to increase efficiency, he got nowhere for several years (759 S.W.2d 144 (Tex. App. 1988)). Brick pits are used to cool the steel. Slag falls off the steel as it soaks, causing the brick soaking pits to have to be rebuilt on a regular basis. Finally, at the end of 1979, John Scott got the chance to try out his idea. He eventually rebuilt all of the brick pits. The number of brick pit cleanouts fell from 212 in 1979 to 62 in 1980. Lone Star Steel had an employee suggestion plan that promised employees a reward of at least 5 percent of the money saved in a year from using the employee's suggestion. Experts said that John Scott's suggestion had saved the company $60 million in one year. The company committee in charge of suggestion plans decided to award John Scott nothing even though he had worked on his own time in the beginning to demonstrate how his new design could save the company money. John Scott sued and a Texas jury awarded him $3 million.

During the 1980s, one section of the United States Army based promotions in part on the number of "performance awards" that civilian employees had received over the years (897 F.2d 1435 (8th Cir. 1990)). Black employees sued, proving that these performance awards were given mainly to white employees, while the army failed to prove that people who received promotions based on these performance awards actually performed better in the higher ranks. The federal judge ruled that performance awards can no longer be used and that the army was guilty of illegal discrimination.

These three lawsuits represent only the tip of the iceberg. For every case that is actually brought into court, hundreds are not brought but the damage to morale and performance is just as great. People who feel they are not being treated fairly do not work hard to provide quality goods and service, and they do not think about the long-term health of the organization.

What's wrong with individual commissions, bonuses, and awards? They cause employees to focus on the short term and to view their fellow employees as competitors. Would MayDay's have been better off if Bill had not sold the man a suit? Yes. Would MayDay's have been better off if Fred had not purchased that new line of badly made Italian men's clothes? Yes. Did either of these men have any incentive to think about the long-term health of the business as a whole? No.

What about Ownership?

Now let's imagine that all of these employees, real and imagined, did not receive commissions, bonuses, or awards. Imagine that they each owned a significant amount of stock in the business and that they expected to become the owners of even more stock in the course of time. Imagine Bill telling the large customer about the special store for him around the corner and that he could sell him shirts and ties but not suits. Imagine Fred not buying the cheap suits in Italy. Imagine John not quitting after deciding that the boss was a racial bigot.

In Chapter 1 we discussed the entrepreneurial mind-set and the ideal of the sole proprietor. Imagine a large company in which every employee thinks like an entrepreneur—always looking for ways to improve the productivity and efficiency of the business; always looking for new products or services that might improve profitability.

The one thing an entrepreneur has that most employees do not have is a long-term perspective. The entrepreneur is trying to build a business and is in it for the long haul. The fact that most American employees, even American executives, are not in it for the long haul puts American companies at a major disadvantage. The Japanese worker has made a lifetime commitment to the company and is not concerned about today so much as tomorrow.

If employees owned stock and planned (or were forced) to own that stock over the long term, perhaps even until they retired, they would have a strong incentive to work to increase the value of that stock over time. They would want to see their company expand, become more profitable, and repurchase shares of stock to increase the share price rather than give out a bonus.

Let's say that again. A company in which the workers own significant amounts of stock would find the workers asking not to receive a bonus in the short run if the money could be spent to improve the value of their stock in the long run. Why? If they get a bonus now, they have to pay Social Security and income taxes on it. In most countries, the average worker expects to see between 30 and 60 percent of any money paid in wages lost in taxes. If the money is used to significantly increase the value of their stock, that would usually be to their advantage. This would be particularly true in countries such as Great Britain and Canada where capital gains receive a significant tax break. A smart British worker would rather be able to sell some stock each year for a nice tax-free capital gain rather than pay a large tax bill on wage income.

In many countries, the worker would be better off with a dividend rather than wages because the dividend will not be subject to social security taxes. In the Netherlands, for example, dividends and capital gains are not subject to either social security or income tax. In many countries, such as the United States, dividends are subject to double taxation, meaning the company must pay corporate income taxes on the money before it is paid out as a dividend. If dividends were tax deductible to the corporation, this would not be a problem and would give both corporations and their workers an even greater incentive to see workers owning stock. This double taxation can be avoided in the United States if employee stock ownership plans are used, as will be seen in Part Three.

Can average workers be educated to understand these advantages? Of course, but it requires effort on the part of management to make them understand the potential advantages from both a business and a tax perspective. This can be done. Take the Springfield Remanufacturing Company in Springfield, Missouri. This company was once a subsidiary of International Harvester, which decided to sell it. The employees used an employee stock ownership plan to borrow the money and buy the company. (We will discuss in Part Three how this is done.)

After many years of making payments on the loan, the company at the end of the 1980s was faced with a choice. It could either pay the employees the "usual" Christmas bonus or use that money to pay the loan off early. If the company paid off the loan, its stock would go up significantly in value because investors view companies with no debt very differently from companies with any debt. Companies with no debt are considered to be healthier and a safer investment because if something goes wrong they can always borrow money. A company that has borrowed all the money that anyone would lend it is in the opposite category. It has no safety margin left and is considered a much riskier (and, therefore, less valuable) investment. Springfield Remanufacturing decided that this was too important a decision for management to make so they put it to a vote of the employees: receive the usual Christmas bonus (subject to Social Security and income taxes) or pay off the company debt and see a significant increase in the value of the shares owned by the employees as part of their plan for long-term financial security. The employees voted to forgo the bonus and pay off the debt.

Would other employees make a similar decision? In 1990, the Gallop Organization asked average Americans if they would be willing to trade their next pay increase for stock in the company; 44 percent said they would, 44 percent said they would not, and 12 percent did not know. In other words, even without an explanation concerning the particular advantages of stock over cash, half of those with an opinion would take stock.

During the second half of the twentieth century, Japanese employees were willing to literally work themselves to death to see the companies they worked for prosper. In most countries, however, that kind of loyalty will not be forthcoming without some kind of ownership stake in the company. It will probably not be forthcoming from the next generation of Japanese workers either without some kind of ownership stake. After World War II, millions of Japanese were willing to invest their money in savings accounts that were used to make a handful of people very rich. They were also willing to work very hard over the long term with only a paycheck in return. Will Japanese workers who did not suffer the deprivations of World War II be willing to make similar sacrifices so that a few very rich Japanese can become even richer? Will they continue to accept the idea that their money and their work are used to provide a few wealthy owners with wealth that will forever be out of reach for them?

Why ownership? Because it offers the best incentive for employees and investors and managers to work together for the long-term success of the company; because government has provided tax incentives to bring about a greater distribution of wealth in society; because it will be cheaper in the long run than providing bonuses and wages; and because in the future more sophisticated workers will demand it before they work harder and smarter just to make someone else richer.

PART
TWO

FORMS OF OWNERSHIP

Stock Options

The granting of stock options is the most common way executives in corporations around the world are given an ownership stake in the companies they work for. A stock option is a contract between two parties, in this case a corporation and its employee. Just like a stock option that can be purchased by anyone on the Chicago Board of Trade (discussed in Chapter 4), an employee stock option has a *current price* (the price the stock is currently selling for on the open market), a *strike price* (the price the employee may buy the stock for during the life of the option), and an *expiration date* after which the option will have expired and the employee will no longer have the right to exercise it and purchase shares. All employee stock options are *call options* that give the employee the right to buy stock from the company.

Employee Stock Option Plans

Some obvious differences exist between the kind of stock options traded on the Chicago Board of Trade and the kind usually given to employees. First of all, most employee stock options are personal. Only the employee can exercise it and force the company to sell shares at the strike price. In most cases, the employee cannot sell the option to someone else the way that an option on the Chicago Board of Trade can be bought and sold. Second, stock options on the Chicago Board of Trade expire after a six-month period. Someone buying a call option on the Chicago Board of Trade is betting that the stock price will go up significantly in less than six months. Employee stock options are usually for a period of several years.

Finally, unlike stock options traded on the Chicago Board of Trade, many corporate stock option plans have a kind of vesting scheme. This simply means that the employee cannot exercise all of the option at one time. Instead, the employee can exercise the option only as the employee "vests," usually over a period of years. For example, an option to buy 1,000 shares over a five-year period may state that only up to 200 shares may be purchased at the strike price in any one year. The employee may purchase up to 1,000 shares with this option, but he or she must do a little each year instead of waiting until the fifth year and buying the shares all at once. The vesting feature may be cumulative, meaning that the employee can buy up to 200 shares in the first year, or wait and buy 400 the second year, and so on, allowing the employee to save up and buy all 1,000 shares in the fifth year if that is what the employee wishes to do.

To see how this works, let's look at the PepsiCo "SharePower" stock option plan. PepsiCo makes Pepsi Cola and owns several food chains, including Kentucky Fried Chicken (KFC) and Taco Bell. In 1989, PepsiCo instituted a stock option plan for all of its employees. Every July 1, employees are given the option to buy a number of shares, depending on the amount of their compensation during the year. The higher the pay the employee earned during the year, the more shares the employee has the option to buy. The employee has the right to buy that number of shares, at the July 1 selling price, for the next 10 years.,The option vests 20 percent a year. This means that the employee can buy only 20 percent of the shares the first year, 20 percent more the next year, and so on; or the employee can hold onto the option and wait several years before exercising the option, allowing the vesting to add up. PepsiCo is not the first large company to grant stock options to all of its employees. In the late 1980s, Kroger granted stock options to all of its employees, resulting in 35 percent of the company's stock being owned by employees by the end of 1990.

Tax Consequences in the United States

One of the major factors in the choice of stock options for either executives or rank-and-file employees is the tax consequences. In many countries, stock options can be issued in a tax-favored way. These tax-favored stock options are called incentive stock options (ISOs) in the United States. Stock options that do not qualify for special tax breaks are called nonqualified stock options (NSOs). How is a nonqualified stock option generally taxed? First of all, the employee does not pay any income tax when the option is issued. Because the employee cannot sell the stock option, it is treated simply as a right to purchase shares, not as a security in its own right. At the same time, the company does not receive any tax deduction for simply issuing the stock option. It is viewed by the Internal Revenue Service for what it is, an offer to sell shares in the future if certain things occur.

When the employee exercises the nonqualified stock option, the company is selling a share of stock, let's say for $20. If the company could have sold that share for $25 on the open market, two things have happened. First, the company has simply sold a share for money and this money is put into the capital account of the company. Money received from the sale of stock is not income to the corporation and is not subject to income tax. Second, the company has provided the employee with a benefit worth $5 in that the stock is worth $5 more than the employee paid for it. This is an expense of the company and is deductible by the company as any other payroll expense would be deductible. The employee has, in turn, received a benefit in that the employee has received a share of stock worth $25 and paid only $20 for it. The employee must pay income taxes on the difference, in this case $5, at the time the option is exercised (when the employee actually buys the shares).

Most stock options granted in the United States are NSOs, nonqual-ified for any special tax benefit. If the employee has to pay income tax on the difference between the strike price and the market price at the time the shares are purchased, the employee is probably going to sell the shares soon after exercising the option. To avoid this "instant sale" consequence, some countries provide a tax break to employees if the plan meets certain requirements. The United States currently has two special stock option provisions known by the number of the Internal Revenue Code sections in which they are discussed: Section 422 stock option plans and Section 423 stock option plans.

Generally, in the United States, when people refer to ISOs they are talking about Section 422 stock options. To qualify under Section 422, the option must be exercised no more than 10 years from the date the option is first granted to the employee; the strike price must be at least 100 percent of the current market price of the stock when the option is granted; the employee may not own at the time of the grant more than 10 percent of the corporation's stock (this does not apply if the strike price is at least 110 percent of the market price at the time the option is granted); the plan must be approved by the shareholders and must specify a maximum number of shares that can be issued under the plan; the option must not be transferable except to the employee's heirs upon the employee's death; and the value (at the time the option is first granted) must not be more than $100,000 during any one year (meaning if shares were selling for $10 a share when the option was granted, an employee may not have the option to buy more than 10,000 shares in any one year). Also, at the time the option is exercised, the person must actually still be an employee or have been an employee within the last three months (unless the person has stopped being an employee because of death or disability, in which case the person or the person's estate has 12 months after the death or disability to exercise the option).

If all of the Section 422 rules are followed, then the employee does not have to pay income tax when the option is exercised. Also, if the employee keeps the stock for at least one year after the shares are purchased (and at least two years after the option itself was first granted), the employee will pay only long-term capital gains taxes when the shares are finally sold (on the difference between the price the employee paid for the shares and the price the shares are ultimately sold for).

One problem with NSOs is that while the employee has an incentive to work harder to improve share price performance before exercising the option to buy the shares, the employee has no incentive to keep the shares. Indeed the employee would generally be considered stupid not to sell them right away. After all, the employee has to pay income tax on the difference between the purchase price and the market price at the time the shares are actually purchased, whether the employee keeps the shares or sells them.

With Section 422 ISOs, the employee has an incentive to hold onto the shares. Employees who hold the shares for at least a year receive long-term capital gains tax treatment. Employees may choose to hold the shares for many years into the future in anticipation of a further increase in share price or in expectation of being in a lower income tax bracket upon retirement.

Under Section 422, the strike price must be at least 100 percent of the market price on the day the option is granted to the employee. Under Section 423, the option price may be as low as 85 percent of the market price when the option is granted (or as low as 85 percent of the market price when the option is exercised, if that is lower still).

Section 422 options can be given to any group or subgroup of employees. Section 423 options must be given to all the employees (except new employees, part-time employees, and highly compensated employees); all the employees must be granted options bearing a similar ratio to their compensation (if higher paid employees get options to buy 10 percent of compensation, then lower paid employees must receive the same deal); no single employee may be given an option to purchase more than $25,000 worth of stock in any one year (based on the value of the stock at the time the option is granted); the plan must be approved by the shareholders; employees who own 5 percent or more of the company's stock cannot participate in the plan; the options cannot be transferred except to heirs upon the employee's death; the option period cannot be for more than 27 months (if the strike price is 85 percent of the price at the date the option is granted) or five years (if the strike price is 85 percent of the price at the time the option is exercised).

An employee buying stock under Section 423 does not pay tax until the stock is sold; any profit is treated as long-term capital gains if the stock is held for six months (as opposed to one year under Section 422). Also, if the option offers the stock at a discount below what the stock was selling for when the option was granted, the employee must pay income tax on this difference as if it were ordinary income (not long-term capital gains) at the time the shares are sold. Again, if the requirements of Section 423 are met, the employee can avoid paying taxes until the stock is sold, giving the employee an incentive to hold onto the stock.

To illustrate, suppose XYZ stock is selling for $100 a share on the day the option is granted to the employee. If it is a Section 422 option, the employee may be given the option of purchasing the shares at $100 a share at any time over the next 10 years, and the employee cannot buy more than 1,000 shares in any one year ($100,000 worth at the time the option is granted). If the employee is given a Section 423 option, the employee may be given the option of buying shares at $85 a share at any time during a period of 27 months and may not purchase more than 250 shares ($25,000 worth based on the price at the time the option is granted) in any one year. In both cases, if the holding period is met, the employee does not pay any income tax until the shares are sold. Because long-term capital gains are currently taxed at almost the same rate as ordinary income in the United States, this is not much of an incentive to use Sections 422 and 423. However, if the employer wants the employees to hold onto their shares after exercising the option and begin to think and act like stockholders, Sections 422 and 423 are attractive alternatives to the nonqualified stock option.

Although not commonly done, companies can give employees another kind of stock option called a "transferable" stock option. The employee can sell a transferable option just like anyone else who buys a stock option on the Chicago Board of Trade. Say the company gives an employee a transferable option to buy 1,000 shares of stock at the current market price of $100 a share during the next five years, and the employee sells that option, then the company is viewed by the Internal Revenue Service as having given the employee a "security" as part of his pay package. The company can deduct the value of that security at the time it is awarded to the employee, and the employee has to pay income tax on the value of the option at the same time. While the employee has only a piece of paper, the "readily ascertainable value" of that piece of paper is not much, particularly if the strike price is equal to or greater than the current market price at the time the option is granted to the employee. The Internal Revenue Service does

Exhibit 8.1 Tax Consequences for Different Types of Stock Option Plans in the United States

Type of Option	Implications For	Tax Consequences When		
		Option Granted	Option Exercised	Shares Sold
Option with readily ascertainable value	Employee	Ordinary income tax	No tax	Capital gains tax
	Employer	Deduction	No deduction	No deduction
Nonqualified stock option plan	Employee	No tax	Ordinary income tax	Capital gains tax
	Employer	No deduction	Deduction	No deduction
Incentive stock option plans				
Section 422	Employee	No tax	No tax	Capital gains tax
	Employer	No deduction	No deduction	No deduction
Section 423*	Employee	No tax	No tax	Ordinary income plus capital gains taxes
	Employer	No deduction	No deduction	Deduction to extent employee pays ordinary income tax

* Stock purchased below market value when option granted.

not like to tax employee stock options this way, and there is no special tax break for the company, so most companies do not give their employees "transferable" stock options.

Exhibit 8.1 illustrates the tax consequences to both the employee and the company if the employee receives one of the four types of stock options. With an ISO, the company does not receive any tax deduction even though it has given the employee something of value. The employee does not pay taxes until the stock is sold and then pays a capital gains tax on the difference between the price the shares were purchased for and the price they were finally sold for (however, the difference between the strike price and market price at the time of exercise may be subject to the alternative minimum tax).

With an NSO, the employee pays ordinary income tax when the option is exercised on the difference between the strike price and the market price (and the employer is responsible for withholding a percentage of the gain for income tax purposes). If the employee holds onto the shares and sells them for a profit later, the difference between the market price when purchased and the price when the shares are sold is taxed as capital gains. The company takes a tax deduction on the difference between the strike price and the market price when they are purchased by the employee.

With transferable stock options, which have a readily ascertainable value, the employee pays ordinary income tax on the value of the option when it is first granted and a capital gains tax when the stock is finally sold by the employee. The company takes a deduction when the option is granted, based on its readily ascertainable value at that time.

The fact that ISOs do not show up on the company books has bothered accountants in the United States, and early in the 1990s they vowed to make changes so that this would not be the case. However, as this book is being written, these rules have not been changed. If the ISO restrictions are followed, ISOs do not show up as an expense on the company books and the company, in turn, does not get any kind of tax deduction even though clearly the company has given the employees "something of value." It is difficult to see how this fact could be changed by the accountants as long as the corporate income tax laws allow and even encourage this effect.

Tax Consequences in Foreign Countries

Many European countries have statutes that provide various tax advantages for stock purchased through employee stock options if the rules are followed. In France, for example, if the stock is not sold until five years after the option was granted and one year after the option was exercised, the employee receives a tax benefit.

In the Netherlands, the employee pays a small tax when the option is granted (7.5 percent of the value of the shares at the time the option is granted). The employee does not pay a tax when the option is exercised or when the stock is finally sold because there are no taxes on capital gains made by individuals in the Netherlands. For many years the Netherlands Parliament has debated whether or not to allow stock options to be exempt from even this small tax if certain conditions are met. These conditions would include a requirement that most employees receive similar options and that the value of the stock covered by the option not be more than a certain amount. As yet, this has not become law in the Netherlands. If this law is ever passed, given current Dutch income tax laws, this would allow employees to receive some of their income tax-free if they received it in the form of stock options that meet all the legal requirements.

In Great Britain, the law recognizes the difference between NSOs and ISOs just as it does in the United States. Nonqualified stock option plans have basically the same tax results as in the United States. The employee pays ordinary income tax on the difference between the strike price and the market price when the option is exercised, and the company takes a deduction for the same amount. If the British rules for ISOs are followed, an employee does not pay income tax until the shares are sold, and then the increase in price is treated as a capital gain. Because of the very real tax advantages enjoyed by capital gains in Great Britain, both employees and companies have a real incentive to follow the rules. These advantages include exempting the first several thousand pounds of capital gains income in any one year and not counting as taxable gain any increase in value that is the result of inflation. This tax treatment allows employees to hold onto their shares after they purchase them. The British ISO rules require that the option not be exercised until three years after the option was granted and three years after exercising another ISO. In 1991, the British Parliament passed legislation allowing stock options similar to Section 423 options in the United States. Shares may be sold at a percent discount to the current fair market price, but a number of complex restrictions must be met.

Incentive Stock Options in Great Britain

The British equivalent of an incentive stock option plan is a share option scheme approved by Inland Revenue. This scheme enables a corporation to grant 10-year stock options to selected full-time employees. If the employee exercises an approved option more than three years after the date of grant and more than three years after the last occasion on which he or she exercised an approved option under the same scheme, the optionholder will escape income tax on exercise and incur capital gains tax on actual disposal of the shares. The advantage of these schemes is that they enable the employee to claim capital gains tax treatment. Although most income is taxed at the same rates in Great Britain, capital gains tax treatment normally is preferable because each individual has a £5,000 annual exemption from capital gains tax. Approved share options are usually limited to four times the employee's taxable pay.

A share option scheme that is not approved by Inland Revenue is similar to the approved share option scheme, except that there is no statutory limit on the value of the options. The employee realizes taxable income equal to the value of the "spread" (the difference between the strike price and the market price) when he or she exercises the option. The advantage of these schemes is that no Inland Revenue approval is required; therefore, they can be structured more flexibly than approved schemes.

The major difference in stock option schemes between the United States and Great Britain is that in the United States an employer can obtain an income tax deduction for the "spread" upon the exercise of a nonqualified stock option. In Great Britain, however, the employer normally does not get a corporate tax deduction with respect to benefits provided to employees through a stock option scheme.

John R. Cornell, Attorney at Law
Jones, Day, Reavis & Pogue
Cleveland, Ohio, and London, England

Stock Appreciation Rights

The major reason for granting stock options is to encourage employees to do whatever is necessary to help the stock price rise during the term of the option. If the stock price does not go up, then the employees will not get anything from a stock option. If they do work harder and smarter and the price of the stock does go up, many employees are simply going to sell the shares on the open market the same day they purchase them from the company (unless the special requirements of the tax laws have been met allowing the employees to delay paying income taxes until the shares are sold). If the employees are simply going to sell the shares the same day they exercise the option, why go through all of this? Why not simply give the employee a promise to pay a bonus based on the increase in the value of the shares during a particular period of time? That is what stock appreciation rights are. They are a promise (a contract between the employer and the employee) that if the stock of the company goes up, the employee will receive a bonus based on the amount of the increase in the stock price.

Suppose the employee has been given 1,000 shares under a stock appreciation right (SAR) agreement. This agreement says that, at the end of five years, the employee will be given a bonus equal to the increase in value of 1,000 shares of company stock. If the shares are selling at $100 a share when the agreement is first signed, and $150 a share five years later, then this SAR agreement would result in a bonus to the employee of $50,000. This is a bonus. The company deducts this amount as a payroll expense and the employee pays a tax on it just like any other wage income received during that year. SARs are particularly attractive for lower paid workers who might have trouble coming up with the money to buy the shares through a stock option plan. However, lower paid employees will have to pay Social Security taxes on this money, which is a problem because they will automatically lose 15.3 percent right off the top.

Because SARs are a promise to pay employees an amount at a future date, the financial statements of the company must show this "debt" each year based on what the current price of the stock is. For example, as stock prices increase, the SAR bonus liability of the company increases, and this must be shown on the company balance sheet. Of course, when the bonuses are finally paid, they are then no longer debt and show up as part of the personnel expenses for that year.

The fact that SARs have to be shown on the balance sheet and stock option plans do not is one incentive to use stock options instead of SARs. During the 1990s, more and more companies switched from SARs to stock options to avoid this effect on the company books. Because a stock option is simply a promise to sell something, if the employee wants to buy it, it is not shown on the books until the option is actually exercised. The net long-term effect of both on the company will be similar, and many accountants believe that accounting rules should be changed to reflect that fact.

In some cases, the company may grant stock options and stock appreciation rights at the same time. Then when it comes time for the employee to exercise the option, the bonus money from the stock appreciation right can be used to make the purchase.

Securities and Corporate Law Issues

In the United States and many countries, a distinction is made between "public" companies and "private" companies. A public company has hundreds of stockholders and is subject to strict government regulation of its relationship with those stockholders. This usually means providing the stockholders with an annual report and other information that is expensive to compile as well as complying with other regulations.

If a company is already a public company, then providing employees with stock options and selling them stock when those options are exercised will not be difficult. If a company is not yet a public company, then selling employees stock when they exercise their stock options can cause problems. If too many employees buy stock, the company may find that it must comply with the public company regulations before it is ready to do so. Some companies have dealt with this problem by putting in the stock option that it can only be exercised six months after the company has its initial public offering. This not only prevents the triggering of "public company" rules but also gives employees an incentive to help the company get ready for that all-important initial public offering that the founders and the venture capitalists are counting on to make themselves rich.

There is a tendency in the United States to think only of federal laws when thinking about securities and corporation laws. In the United States, a company must also comply with the securities laws of all 50 states, each of which is different. Corporations must also comply with the rules of the state in which they were incorporated. Some states limit the percentage of a company's stock that can be subject to stock options at any one time. Also, some states will not allow an initial public offering in their state if too much stock is subject to stock options when the offering takes place. These state laws may limit the amount of stock options granted to employees. Many states also require that corporations incorporated in their state get the approval of a majority of the stockholders (meaning the stockholders of more than 50 percent of the shares) before granting stock options to officers, directors, or employees. Many stock exchanges have similar rules, requiring stockholder approval of "special remuneration plans" for officers, directors, and employees.

If the employees resell their shares before the company has "gone public," this can cause problems. In the worst case, it can force the company to comply with stock registration rules before it is ready to do so. To avoid this, some companies require that anyone selling stock provide the company with a right of first refusal (the company has the right to buy shares at the price being offered) until the company has completed its initial public offering.

Many exceptions to U.S. securities laws allow companies to exempt themselves from regulation at the national level. For example, most small companies are exempt from federal securities laws if their stock is sold only to the residents of a single state. A small company that has all of its employees in one state and is incorporated in that state can usually simply comply with the corporation and securities laws of that state until it is ready to go public and expand into other states.

One set of federal securities regulations that usually apply even if a company does business in only one state are the rules designed to prevent corporate officers and directors from making money by using their special "inside" knowledge. These insider trading regulations are very complex and can result in criminal convictions if violated. One of the basic rules is that insiders, as a general rule, may not sell stock for at least six months after they purchase it (known as the Section 16 rules). In 1992, these rules were amended to allow the six months to begin to apply when a stock option is granted. This means that if an employee holding a stock option waits at least six months to exercise it, he or she does not have to wait another six months after the purchase date to sell it in order to avoid violating this rule.

One way for a small company that has not yet gone public to avoid all of these potential securities law problems is to give employees stock appreciation rights instead of stock options. The employees have an incentive to see the value of the shares go up without having to worry about state and federal securities laws.

Advantages and Disadvantages of Stock Options

Are stock options a good idea? From the point of view of the employee who has the money to exercise them when the time comes (usually higher paid employees), stock options are an excellent idea. The more higher-paid executives have experienced the advantages of stock options, the more stock option plans have flourished in the Western world. The employee makes money if the stock price goes up without having to suffer the risk that the stock price will go down.

Are they a good deal for the other stockholders? That depends. Yes, stock options encourage employees to work harder and smarter in the hope that the price of the stock will go up. At the same time, stock options are short-term incentives. Chapter 4 notes that investors buy stock options on the Chicago Board of Trade because they think the price of a particular stock is going to go up significantly over a short period time, a matter of months. While an employee stock option may be for several years, the orientation is still on the short term.

Suppose Sandra is the CEO of a major corporation, and she has a stock option to buy shares of her company at $100 a share. The shares are currently selling for $102 a share and her option has one more year to run. She is nearing retirement and would like to make a killing before she leaves the company. She will not make a killing at $102 a share. The chief financial officer comes to her with his belief that the French franc is going to significantly increase in value against the dollar in the next few months. Because this company does a lot of business in France, it usually has a significant balance of French currency on hand. The chief financial officer suggests that the company increase its level of borrowing, postpone investing in a new factory, and instead buy as many French francs as possible. Sandra goes along. The chief financial officer was wrong. Instead of increasing in value, the French franc takes a significant fall because of a general strike that paralyzes the country. When word leaks out that Sandra and her chief financial officer have gambled and lost, the price of the company's shares falls to $80 a share. Sandra retires and the chief financial officer is fired. The stockholders have lost billions of dollars. What did they expect, giving her a stock option like that!

The same short-term perspective, with less danger, applies to lower level employees. Their focus is on the period of the option, not the long term. While their ability to do what Sandra did is limited, middle managers in any large organization make thousands of decisions during any year that involve the short term (less than 5 years) as opposed to the long term (more than 10 years). The Japanese beat their competitors over the long term because they think in terms of the long term. Some Japanese corporations have business plans through the year 2500!

Also, even for the average employee, stock options have no downside liability. Risks, large and small, that might increase the value of the shares over the short term are more likely to be taken, with less concern that the shares will go down in value. If the purpose of spreading ownership to executives and employees is to force them to begin to think like stockholders, that is not exactly what happens with stock options. With stock options, employees begin to think like stockholders who cannot lose money on the downside but who can make money on the upside.

On the other hand, some people argue that one of the problems with large corporations is their unwillingness to take risks. It can be argued that stock options help to overcome this bureaucratic tendency and, therefore, are a good thing.

It was not uncommon during the 1980s to issue stock options to executives with a strike price well below the market price of the shares when the option was granted. For example, assume that a CEO is granted an option to buy 100,000 shares of stock at any time during the next five years at $50 a share and that on the day the option is granted the market price is $100 a share. If the company were selling such an option on the Chicago Board of Trade, it would command a value of $50 times 100,000, or $5 million. In other words, this executive has been given an additional $5 million in compensation this year. Why do it this way? To hide it. The shareholders see that the CEO is paid $1 million a year, a little steep, but not out of line with the pay of other CEOs running similar businesses. The shareholders also read that the CEO was given a stock option. It is only if they read the fine print that the stockholders will find out that the CEO's stock option has a strike price that is significantly *below* the current market price!

Despite the potential for abuse, stock options certainly have their place. A very good example is Lee Iacocca of Chrysler. When Chrysler was on the verge of going out of business, Iacocca hired on as the CEO for $1 a year. How does a dying corporation get an excellent executive to come to work for $1 a year? With stock options. These were options that only paid off if the price of the stock rose. It did rise, as everyone knows. During 1987, for example, Iacocca's stock options showed a gain of $9.6 million. Is a CEO worth that kind of money? In this case, while Iacocca made millions on his stock options, the stockholders made billions from the increased value of their stock, and the third largest automobile manufacturer in the United States was saved from bankruptcy. That sounds like a pretty good deal.

It is also possible to structure a stock option for CEOs and other executives that seems fair for the shareholders. Give them long-term options with a strike price that is significantly *higher* than the current market price. For example, let's assume that the current selling price is $100 a share. While hypothetical situations are seldom typical, it is reasonable to assume that if this company pursues a growth strategy, and there is growth potential in the business, the price of the shares should rise at least 6 percent on average over the course of 10 years. We would hope the price would rise significantly more than that. We can give the executives a generous stock option with a large number of shares, but they can purchase these shares only after our "reasonable target" is reached. In this case, a 6 percent compounded growth rate in stock price would result in a price of approximately $180 a share in 10 years.

If we are going to give top executives what Wall Street calls an "out-of-the-money" stock option, why stop there? Why not set a strike price even higher? The point of giving top executives an out-of-the-money stock option is to say that they should not be rewarded for below-average performance. At the same time, stock prices are affected by much more than just the performance of the company. Stock markets go up and down in relation to factors such as interest rates, inflation, world economic growth, and a hundred other factors over which corporate executives have no control. By putting the strike price within reach, and then increasing the number of shares that can be purchased over what would otherwise be given, the stockholders are truly saying to executives, "Come on in and get wet with us, the water's fine."

The ironic thing about stock options is that they make more sense for rank-and-file employees than for top executives, but most companies do not offer them to anyone other than the top executives. While top executives are in a position to gamble with the company and take large risks in the hope of making a killing with their stock options, the average employee is not in a position to do that. If a stock option makes that average employee begin to pay attention to the thing that matters most to the stockholders, the price of the shares, it may well be worth the cost.

Some would argue that employees should be rewarded not based on stock price, which is subject to so many other forces beyond the control of the employee, but on the basis of company performance as measured by such things as profitability. The response to that is that if the company is making a large profit but the share price is going down, then more money should be reinvested in the business as opposed to being given out as employee bonuses. While this sounds cruel to some employees, it would make sense to employees who also owned a significant number of shares. They can have a bonus now, which will shrink significantly after Social Security and income taxes are taken out, or they can have the value of their shares go up, and not pay taxes until they sell the shares.

9

Stock

While stock options may give employees the opportunity to think "sort of" like stockholders, many would agree that the only way to get anyone to think and act like an owner is to make sure they actually own stock in the company. That way if the stock goes up, they make money; if the stock goes down, they lose money. If the stock pays a dividend, they make money (without having to pay Social Security taxes on the money); if it does not, they do not make money. There are four main ways companies have tried to encourage their employees to own stock: require them to purchase stock, give them an incentive to purchase stock, give them stock, or give them restricted stock.

Required Stock Purchase Plans

Some would argue that the only way to make employees, from the rank and file to the chief executive officer, really act and think like stockholders is to require them to purchase stock in the company. In that way, they actually have some of their own money on the line, just like the other stockholders. They receive all the benefits, and suffer all the pitfalls, of risking real money by purchasing stock in their company.

Required stock purchase plans were popular during the 1920s in the United States. In some cases, a significant amount of the capital of the company was raised by selling stock to the employees, particularly to the future executives of the company. In many cases, employees borrowed money, using personal loans (or mortgaging their homes) to fulfill the stock ownership requirement. With low interest rates and rising stock prices, this looked like a better and better deal during much of the 1920s. Then, in 1929, the New York stock market crashed. Suddenly, thousands of workers not only found themselves without a job, but they were also in debt because of their stock purchase loans. Many of them were driven into bankruptcy when they could not pay off the loans.

Because of this, some states and countries passed laws making the required purchase of stock by employees illegal. Today, for example, both California and Canada have laws against required stock purchase. That does not mean that required stock purchase no longer exists. One of the best-known U.S. companies with a required stock purchase plan is America West Airlines based in Phoenix, Arizona. Under its plan, when employees come to work for the company, they must purchase stock equal in value to 20 percent of their first year's base salary. The company will sell the stock at 85 percent of the current market price and will even lend the employee the money to buy the shares at an attractive interest rate. This allows the employee to pay off the loan through payroll deductions over a five-year period. America West Airlines reports that most of its employees in California have taken advantage of the plan even though the company cannot require them to buy shares under California law.

At the same time, the America West plan demonstrates the problems with required stock purchase plans, particularly when the employees must go into debt to make the purchase. America West is in a battle with Southwest Airlines for the short-haul travel dollars in the southwestern part of the United States. As this book is being written, America West is technically in bankruptcy along with several other airline companies in the United States. Will America West employees end up like thousands of workers did in the 1920s, out of work and personally bankrupt? Of course, America West is not out yet. If it can survive the current shakeout in the American airline industry, it could still turn out to have been a good investment for the employees. Also, if America West does survive, it might be in part because the employees, as stockholders, were willing to make the short-term sacrifices necessary to get the company out of bankruptcy.

Optional Stock Purchase Plans

Any company can set up a plan to allow employees to buy stock, perhaps through a payroll deduction every payday. Of course, the securities laws may make this difficult unless the company is already a public company whose stock is already freely traded on a stock exchange. Assume that it is, and that the employees are paying the company the full market price of the stock at the time of purchase. Before the stock is purchased, the employees will pay Social Security and income taxes on their wages (which might take out anywhere from 30 to 60 percent, depending on the tax bracket of the employee and the country involved). The money from the sale of the stock is placed in the capital account, just as it would be if the company sold stock to anyone else. The employee has saved the cost of paying a stockbroker's commission and has enjoyed the ease of purchase that comes from having everything done automatically by payroll deduction, but the employee has not received any tax benefit. Even without special incentives, simple stock purchase plans were popular in the United States during the first three decades of the twentieth century. They became less popular after the stock market crash of 1929.

The Bureau of National Affairs (BNA) was begun in 1929 and has evolved into a publishing and electronic giant reporting on government activity and laws to professionals in many fields. BNA's founder, David Lawrence, began selling the company to the employees in 1947 through a simple stock purchase plan. Today about three-fourths of the company's 1,600 employees own stock. Employees buy stock either through payroll deductions or by making an offer to buy in an in-house stock market.

Science Applications International Corporation (SAIC), based in San Diego, California, has a slightly different approach. Workers and directors own 46 percent of the company's stock outright, while 41 percent is owned by the employee stock ownership plan and the 401(k) plan. In other words, employees own most of the stock either outright or through a trust. During the 1970s and 1980s, the value of SAIC stock rose at a 27 percent annual compound rate, although that pace slowed at the beginning of the 1990s. Once each quarter employees can buy and sell shares through Bull Inc., a broker-dealer subsidiary of SAIC. The value of the shares is determined by an outside appraiser and is tied to the financial performance of the company and the price/ earnings ratios of its major competitors. Almost 7,000 of the 13,500 employees own stock outside the trust plans. To encourage better performance, only employees recommended by their managers can buy SAIC stock on the quarterly trading days (anybody can sell). Founder and President J. Robert Byster (who owns 2.5 percent of the company stock) strongly believes that ownership provides the incentive to keep the company growing. In the mid-1980s, two-thirds of SAIC's business was defense related. By 1992, the company had diversified so that less than half of its business was with the Defense Department. The company moved into both health care and pollution prevention and cleanup.

In Sweden, one way that companies encourage their employees to buy stock is through the use of "convertibles." Employees buy convertibles that can then be converted to shares of the company. If an employee decides not to convert to shares, the convertible is paid off by the company just like any other debt instrument. This has become a popular form of stock participation in Sweden with over 200 companies and 200,000 employees participating in 1991.

Incentive Stock Purchase Plans

Because some governments believe it would be good for employees to own stock in the companies they work for, these governments allow companies to sell stock to employees at a discount. In the United States, this is controlled by Section 423 of the Internal Revenue Code. Essentially the law allows a company to sell stock at 85 percent of the market price to employees. The company must have a plan approved by the shareholders; employees who own 5 percent or more of the company's shares cannot participate. The plan must be available to all the employees (except part-time, new, and highly compensated employees), and every employee must be given the chance to purchase the same percentage-of-salary in stock. No employee may purchase more than $25,000 worth of stock in any one year. If all the requirements are met, the company may sell stock to employees at 85 percent of market price. The employees do not pay taxes on this windfall until the stock is sold. If the employee holds the stock for at least six months, any increase in value is treated as long-term capital gains. The employer places the money received for the stock in the capital account.

The incentive stock purchase plan at Amdahl, a computer company based in California's Silicon Valley, is typical. Employees have the option of setting aside 2, 4, or 6 percent of their compensation every payday. The money is placed in a special account; at the end of each quarter, company stock is purchased from the company at 85 percent of the lowest market price during the quarter. Employees can stop participating in the plan at any time and must stop once they no longer work for the company.

The Canadian provinces of Ontario and British Columbia passed statutes in 1988 and 1989, respectively, to encourage the creation of stock purchase plans. In both cases, only smaller companies that spend at least 25 percent of their total wages within the province are eligible. If a plan is adopted and approved, employees may purchase stock and receive a 15 percent cash grant (in Ontario) or a 20 percent tax credit (in British Columbia) up to a maximum amount each year. To receive the grant or tax credit, the stock may not be sold for a period of years after purchase (two years in Ontario and three years in British Columbia). While both provinces call these employee stock ownership plans (ESOPs), we would not because there is no trust and no provision for borrowing money to allow the employees to purchase a large block of stock. They are in reality subsidized employee stock purchase plans.

Australian law made any kind of stock purchase plan difficult and expensive until 1988, when the laws were changed. Today Australian companies may sell stock to employees at a 10 percent discount up to a maximum amount of stock each year without any tax problems. Companies are free to sell shares at an even greater discount and many do, but there are tax consequences for the employees. While both political parties and many labor leaders are in favor of more employee ownership through stock purchase plans, the amount of stock actually held by employees in Australia is still very low. There are some examples of significant employee ownership, however. Siddons Industries is about 20 percent employee owned, and about 60 percent of the employees own stock through the stock purchase plan. Siddons allows employees to buy stock at a significant discount and to pay for the shares over 10 years with an interest-free loan. The shares are held in trust until they are fully paid for, at which time they are given to the employee.

In Great Britain, companies may set up an "approved savings-related share option scheme." Under British law, such a stock purchase plan must be available to all full-time employees. Under the plan, employees agree to save a fixed amount each month for five years. The interest earned on this savings account is tax free and, after five years, the employee may take the money and buy shares under the stock option granted when the savings plan began. The option price cannot be less than 80 percent of the fair market price at the time the option was granted. If all of the rules are followed, the employee does not pay any income tax on money made because the shares increased in value until the shares are sold, at which time capital gains taxes are due. Under the British plan, the employee may decide to keep the cash after the five years are up and not exercise the option.

An optional stock purchase plan allows employees to buy stock at a discount (in the United States or Great Britain) or to receive a tax rebate (in some Canadian provinces) if the rules are followed, which is an extra incentive for employees to own stock. At the same time, the money used by the employees to purchase the stock is "after-tax" dollars. That means the employee has already lost a significant amount of money to the government before buying the stock. While the discounted price or tax rebate makes up for this somewhat, it remains a problem from the employee's point of view. Also, there is a problem for the employer. In the United States, the employer has given the employee something—stock worth more than the employee paid for it—but the employer does not get a tax deduction for that benefit. At the same time, this transaction does not show up as an expense for the corporation.

A Gift of Stock

A company can also give stock to its employees. The company takes a tax deduction for a personnel expense based on the value of the shares given to the employees, and the employees pay income taxes at the time the shares are given based on the value of the shares. The fact that employees have to pay income taxes on any outright stock gifts makes it difficult for average employees to do anything but turn around and sell the shares. The major exception to this is if the company is very new and the shares are worth very little. Then the employee can pay income tax on this not-worth-very-much gift and hold onto the shares, hoping they will be worth much more in the future.

Life USA, a Minneapolis-based life insurance company, pays all of its employees 10 percent of their salary in the form of company stock. The employees pay income tax on the value of the stock, and the company deducts that value as an employee compensation expense. The stock given to employees has full voting rights and is not restricted. Unlike many benefit plans, there is no vesting period. The founders of the company envision an employee-owned company, so the personnel department is called the "owner services department" and the entrance to the building has a sign calling it the "owner's entrance."

Between 1985 and 1987, Bank of America lost $1.8 billion. In 1988, bank performance improved and the management looked around for a way to reward employees. They decided to give 10 shares of stock to each of the 50,000 employees located in seven states and 44 foreign countries. The share gift was announced two days after the general corporate dividend was announced, and the shares were handed out a month later at special ceremonies held at each bank location. This "surprise" gift seems to have had the desired effect. Thousands of employees sent thank-you cards to the CEO. A company survey found that almost every manager and employee contacted felt that this was a significant boost to employee morale. The survey also showed that the employees were much more impressed by a gift of stock than a gift of money. The stock given away cost more than $10 million (500,000 shares times $20.75 a share). By the end of 1989, Bank of America's profits had soared to $1.1 billion, the most in its 85-year history and the largest of any U.S. bank in 1989.

Restricted Stock

What are the basic problems of giving stock to employees? First of all, the employees might turn around and sell it. If the idea is to make employees into owners, that does not happen if the stock is sold right away. Second, employees have to pay income taxes on the stock when it is given to them. Again, this forces many employees to turn around and sell the stock, defeating the whole idea of giving them stock in the first place. Both of these problems can potentially be minimized, if not eliminated, through the use of restricted stock.

Restricted stock is simply stock given (or sold) with restrictions on it. The main restriction we are concerned with is the restriction that the employee not sell the stock for a period of time. Commonly, restricted stock cannot be sold for 5 or 10 years after it is given to the employee. Some restricted stock also requires the employee to remain employed with the employer during the term of the restriction or forfeit the stock. This stay-with-me requirement might decrease over time. For example, for every year the employee stays with the company, he or she gets to keep 20 percent of the restricted stock.

Restricted shares have a number of advantages. The employees do not have to come up with any cash (or, if the shares are sold at a nominal price, not much cash). The employees do not pay any income tax on the shares when they are given (as a general rule in the United States). The shares pay dividends, and the employee gets to vote them just like any other shareholder.

The corporation deducts the current fair market value of the shares (in the United States) just as if it had given the employee unrestricted shares (like any other personnel expense). The value of the shares is placed in the capital account. Why is this good for the corporation? Assume that the corporation is paying 40 percent of income in income taxes. The corporation gives $10 million worth of restricted stock (what it would have made if it had sold the stock on the stock market without restrictions). The corporation then has the full $10 million to reinvest in the company. If the corporation had not given the restricted stock, it would have had to pay $4 million in income taxes and had only $6 million to reinvest in the company. If the corporation had paid out the $10 million in bonuses and wages, it would have had nothing left to reinvest in the company. The employees have received a kind of bonus, and the company still has the money to reinvest in the growth of the company.

How is all of this taxed to the employee? Differently in different countries. The United States provides an example of what other countries should not do. The employee has a choice. The employee can receive the restricted stock and not pay any income tax until the restrictions lapse (in our example, in five years). At that time, the employee has to pay income tax on the stock based on its value at that time (when the restrictions lapse). If the stock has gone up in value, the employee will have had the opportunity to think like an owner for a few years but will then probably have to sell the shares to pay the tax bill. Or the employee can elect (under Section 83 of the IRS Code) to pay a tax on the restricted stock when it is first received. In that case, the employee pays income tax on the full value of the stock just as if the shares had no restrictions. In other words, the employee has a large tax bill when given the stock and cannot even sell the shares (because they are restricted) to pay it.

In Great Britain (as this is written), the employee receiving restricted stock must pay income tax at the time the shares are received, but the tax is on the value of the stock taking into account the restrictions on the stock. Because this restricted stock is worth less than stock that can be sold immediately, this amounts to a kind of tax break for the employee receiving the restricted stock. At the same time, there are problems with this as well. How much is restricted stock worth? With transferable stock options, there is a market where such things are bought and sold. There is no open market for restricted stock.

Worker Stock

I would like to make a proposal to the United States, Great Britain, and every other country that might resolve the tax problem on restricted stock: Pass a law saying that restricted stock will be taxed as income to the employee when it is given to the employee based on its value at the time it is given, taking into account the restrictions that have been placed on the stock. Then pass a law saying that stock that cannot be sold for one year will be presumed to be worth 80 percent of stock not so restricted (and so on). In other words, five-year re-stricted stock would be worth nothing (for tax purposes) at the time the shares are given to the employee; the shares would not be taxed as income to the employee until they are sold (and then as long-term capital gains). The law should also specify that the corporation receives a deduction based on the current market price of unrestricted stock (the same deduction it would receive if it sold or gave to employees unrestricted stock). Also, dividends paid on all shares, regardless of who owns them, should be deductible to the corporation (but the corporation would otherwise pay an income tax of, let's say, 40 percent on any money left over after expenses and dividends were deducted).

What would be the net result of all of this? Companies would have a strong incentive to grant "worker stock" to the employees instead of giving them money. The corporation would then have more money to reinvest in the company, leading to growth for the company and economic growth for the country. Why would the employees go along with this? Because they are receiving something of value and not having to pay any income taxes on it until it is sold, at which time they get whatever break the law allows for long-term capital gains. Also, their shares would pay dividends and, in most countries, people pay lower income taxes on dividends than they do on wages (in the United States, dividends are not subject to Social Security taxes). In a few countries, such as the Netherlands, individuals do not pay any income tax on dividend income.

Why would the government want to forgo all of these taxes? Because in the long run, the government ends up with larger, more successful companies and a population of workers who are also owners, workers who own stock and earn dividends and are not forced onto welfare the minute they are laid off or given a forced vacation because of a slowdown in the economy.

Currently in Ireland or Great Britain, a similar result can be achieved using an employee stock ownership plan or a profit-sharing plan. The law allows companies to place shares of stock in trust for the employ-ees. The company receives a tax deduction, just as if it had sold the shares, but the employees pay no income taxes at the time the shares are placed in the trust. After the shares have remained in the trust for the required length of time, they are then given to the employees and, again, the employees pay no income taxes. When the shares are ultimately sold, the employees will then pay taxes on the money, but that income will be treated as long-term capital gains.

A country could even take this idea of worker stock a step further. In the United States every month billions of dollars are invested in the U.S. stock market by pension and benefit plan trustees. If a country did not want to go down that trust road, it could still encourage, even require, its workers to invest in the local stock market by having them buy worker stock from local corporations. The workers would not pay income taxes on the wages they invested in this way. They would be buying restricted stock in any one of thousands of local corporations. The workers would pay full market price but could not sell the stock for some length of time, let's say five years. During that time, they would receive dividends and the right to vote their stock just like any other investor. When they sold the stock, they would pay only long-term capital gains taxes rather than ordinary income taxes.

Why would a country want to give its workers this kind of tax break? For the same reason that the United States gives tax breaks to pension and benefit funds. The country would end up with a population that owned stock for retirement, or reinvestment. The country would also have available more money for investment by its corporations than would otherwise be the case.

It is also important to keep in mind that when a government gives individuals a tax incentive to invest in the society, it is only postponing the collection of taxes, not forgoing it altogether; and, if the investment pays off, the government will end up with more money in the tax coffers at the end of the road than it otherwise would.

Let's suppose we are advising the government of Ireland. Ireland essentially has an income tax of 50 percent on all income except for the first few thousand punts (the Irish currency is called a punt, and the income tax rate is 30 percent on the first £6,500 and either 48 or 53 percent after that). Let's assume that we talked the Irish government into taxing long-term capital gains made on the sale of stock in Irish companies (stock held for more than five years) at 25 percent instead of 50 percent (half the gain in any one year would be tax exempt).

The Irish government currently exempts from income tax money made gambling, which encourages Irish citizens to waste their money on lotteries and the sweepstakes instead of investing it in the long-term growth of Ireland. Let's also suppose that Ireland allowed workers to buy up to £6,000 a year of restricted stock with pretax pounds. Given the tax rate of 50 percent, this means that if a worker did that every year, the government would not collect £3,000 in each of those years.

But the story is not over. Let's suppose that a worker did that every year for five years and suppose that the stock went up in value at a reasonable rate every year during those five years. The government has not collected £15,000 in income taxes during those years. However, the government has collected income taxes on dividend income this worker would not otherwise have had. Also, a total of £30,000 has been invested during those years, creating jobs for other Irish citizens (in 1992, Ireland had an unemployment rate of between 16 and 18 percent, the highest in the European Community). Finally, even at a lower tax rate, the government begins collecting capital gains taxes as the stock is sold.

To illustrate. Assume that the first shares purchased for £6,000 are sold after five years for £9,000. Even with the tax break, the government collects 25 percent of this, or £2,250. Suppose the worker takes the rest, £6,750, and uses it as a down payment on a much nicer house (that has just been built by Irish workers, also bringing in more income taxes). The government collects a sales tax of 6 percent on the purchase of a house worth £70,000 (the current rate in Ireland is 6 percent for any house valued at more than £60,000). This brings in another £4,200 in sales taxes. We could go on estimating the complete tax implications. Suffice it to say that Ireland has given up £3,000 in taxes the first year and taken in three times that amount in taxes over the next five years because of the economic activity stimulated by that investment.

It is important in this scheme that the money be invested in Irish companies. I would define an Irish company as any company that spent more than 30 percent of its payroll in Ireland, regardless of where it is incorporated. This would make sure that the money is invested in creating jobs in Ireland, not in some other country. In fact, if the long-term capital gains tax break applied only if the shares were held at least five years, there would be no need to make it restricted stock. The tax incentive would encourage most workers to hold onto their stock for at least five years to receive the tax break (they might hold onto it even longer once they see the benefits of stock ownership).

Securities and Corporate Law Issues

As with stock options, if a company is already a "public" company, it would have few problems in selling or giving stock, or restricted stock, to its employees. If it is not already a public company, it would have many potential problems. If stock is "sold" to employees, then federal and state securities laws will apply (many of these laws do not apply if the stock is given to the employees and no money changes hands). Selling stock in a private company may require a stock registration, which will be very expensive. If the company fits into an exception to the federal securities laws—for example, all of the employees buying the stock live in only one state—it will still have to comply with the securities laws of that state.

To help companies provide employees with a chance to purchase stock as part of their compensation, the United States Securities and Exchange Commission has promulgated Rule 701. This rule exempts the sale of securities to employees from federal securities regulations if the sale is part of a compensation plan or a benefit plan. Rule 701 limits the amount of stock that can be sold, depending on the size of the company and the total amount of stock the company has already issued.

The company is also subject to the laws of the state in which it was incorporated. That state may require the consent of the shareholders if stock is given or sold to officers, directors, or employees for anything other than its full cash value. If the stock is bought with a promissory note, a host of corporate, tax, and securities law problems arise.

If the company sells or gives away stock to too many people, it may find that it has become a public company by virtue of the number of shareholders it has before the company is ready to begin an initial public offering. This problem can be minimized by giving the company a right of first refusal to buy back the shares before the company becomes a public company. However, some state corporation laws limit the ability of corporations to repurchase their own shares, which can be a problem.

Because each of the 50 states in the United States regulates the sale of stock in their state, anyone thinking of having an initial public offering has to realize that giving away too much stock to employees may cause problems. Some states will not allow an initial public offering if too much "cheap stock" is in circulation. It is not always clear exactly how much is "too much" and what is meant by "cheap stock."

While most state securities commissions are mainly concerned that purchasers receive complete and accurate information about the stock and the company, a few states will not allow stock to be sold in the state unless the commission feels the sale is "fair." These states are California, Florida, Illinois, Ohio, Pennsylvania, and Texas. Again, it is not always easy to predict what the securities commissioners in these large states will consider to be fair.

Because of these problems, it is usually easier for companies that are not yet public companies to share ownership with a large number of employees through a trust plan such as a profit-sharing plan or an employee stock ownership plan. These plans will be discussed in more detail in the next chapter.

Advantages and Disadvantages of Stock Ownership

The major advantage of any kind of stock purchase or stock gift scheme is to assure that the employees, be they top executives or rank-and-file workers, really do own stock. It is stock that can go up or down in value, depending on the performance of the company. Owning stock is not a short-term gamble with no downside risk like owning a stock option.

The major disadvantage is the tax consequences. In general, either employees buy stock with after-tax dollars (allowing them to buy less stock than would be the case if they could use pretax dollars), or they are forced to sell the stock quickly to pay taxes (defeating the whole idea of making them stockholders in the first place).

If the tax laws were changed to allow employees to receive restricted stock and not pay any taxes until the stock is sold (and then pay only long-term capital gains taxes), restricted stock could become a significant way for rank-and-file employees to be given an ownership stake in the companies they work for.

Without favorable tax laws, restricted stock is mainly something given only to the top executives in the company. Graef S. Crystal, in his book *In Search of Excess* (W. W. Norton & Co., 1991), provides a number of examples of how restricted stock has been used by CEOs in the United States to rip off the stockholders. Crystal points out that in the United States, in most cases, the executive receiving restricted stock is receiving something like a stock option with a strike price of $0. When the restriction runs out, the executive sells the stock because the tax man is at the door with a large income tax bill, so most restricted stock is sold as soon as the restrictions lapse. This means that it is not a vehicle to encourage long-term stock ownership.

For the executive, five-year restricted stock is better than a five-year stock option for several reasons. Suppose the executive has a choice of receiving either a five-year stock option to buy 100,000 shares, or 20,000 shares of restricted stock. The stock is currently selling for $100 a share and the option has a strike price of $100 a share. With the option, the executive makes money only if the stock price goes up. With the restricted stock, the executive receives dividends on the stock (just like any other shareholder); and no matter how low the stock goes in price, the restricted shares are going to be worth something when the five years are up. Suppose the stock is selling for $100 a share five years later. The executive with the stock option makes nothing. The executive with 20,000 restricted shares sells them and makes $2 million (in the United States, the tax man then takes a share of that, of course). For the executive with the stock option to make that kind of money, the share price would have to rise, in this case, to $120 a share. Then he could exercise his option, buy 100,000 shares at $100, and sell them at $120 for a net profit (before taxes) of $2 million.

Graef S. Crystal points out that, in many cases, restricted stock has been given to CEOs simply to hide an outrageous bonus. He chronicles how dozens of CEOs received tens of millions of dollars in restricted stock on top of already generous salaries, and concludes that restricted stock is just a sophisticated way for executives to rip off the shareholders. Under current tax law in most countries that is true. It does not have to be that way. If restricted stock were not subject to tax until sold (rather than when granted to the employee or when the restrictions lapse), it would provide a vehicle to encourage long-term stock ownership by rank-and-file employees. Also, if restricted shares were given *instead* of salary, it would be a boon to the shareholders. They would have more money to reinvest in the company than would otherwise be the case, and the employees receiving restricted stock would have a real incentive to begin to think like owners.

Without changes in the tax laws, restricted stock will continue to be simply another way to provide a special bonus to the highest paid executives in a company, a bonus that may or may not be reasonable from the stockholder's point of view, depending on the circumstances.

APPENDIX

Reading and Writing Employee Stock Purchase Plans

A typical Section 423 stock purchase plan requires any employee who wishes to participate to sign a STOCK PURCHASE AGREEMENT. This agreement will discuss many issues. A simple stock purchase agreement would cover the following:

1. *Purchase Rights.* This section will describe how much stock the employee is entitled to purchase during the year and point out that the law limits any one employee to the purchase of not more than $25,000 worth of common stock in a year (based on the current fair market value). It will explain how the money will be removed from the employee's paycheck. Many companies place the money in an account during three-month periods and sell stock to the employees at the end of the period at 85 percent of the lowest market price during that period. Most plans set an absolute limit on the total number of shares that can be purchased through the plan in any year or period.

2. *Payment and Exercise.* This section will describe how money will be withdrawn from employee paychecks and placed in a fund for the purpose of buying stock in the company.

3. *Termination of Purchase Rights.* This section will set out how and when the employee can withdraw from the plan. Most plans state that employees who terminate their employment cease immediately to participate in the plan. Any funds remaining in the employee's stock purchase account will be refunded.

4. *Rights as Stockholders.* This section will make clear that the employees have no rights as stockholders until stock is actually purchased for them through the plan.

5. *Assignability.* Generally, rights under a stock purchase plan cannot be assigned or transferred by the employee.

6. *Merger or Liquidation.* This section will spell out what will happen to the employees' right to purchase stock if the company merges or is sold to another company. Generally, most agreements give the corporation the right to cancel the plan if this happens.

7. *Proration of Purchase Rights.* Most plans set a limit on the number of shares that can be sold during any period. If more employees want to purchase shares than there are shares available, a provision usually allows the employee to buy a prorated percentage of the shares that are available for sale to employees.

8. *Termination or Amendment.* Most agreements spell out what will happen if the plan is terminated or amended.

9. *Notice of Disposition.* Because the corporation may be entitled to some kind of tax deducation when the employee ultimately sells the shares, most agreements require the employee to notify the corporation when the shares are ultimately sold.

10. *Continued Employment.* Most agreements explain that employees reserve the right to quit and the company reserves the right to fire them without regard to the existence of a stock purchase agreement with the employee.

11. *Interpretation.* Most agreements explain that the agreement is intended to qualify under Section 423 of the IRS Code and should be interpreted under that section and Sections 421 and 425 of the IRS Code.

10

Trusts

In the United States, the most popular way to encourage workers to own stock in both the company they work for and other companies is through the use of trusts. There are four basic ways that employees can own shares in the company they work for through trusts: a defined-benefit pension plan, a thrift plan such as a 401(k) plan, a profit-sharing plan, or an employee stock ownership plan (ESOP).

Pension Plans

Millions of employees own shares in the company they work for and do not even know it. That is because they own those shares through their pension plan. While rules restrict the amount of its assets that a pension plan may invest in any one company (as a general rule, not more than 10 percent), this can be a significant amount of stock when a large pension fund is involved. The problem with a company's pension fund owning stock in the company is that it is usually a small percentage of the assets of the fund, and the fund owns only a small percentage of the company's stock. In other words, the fact that the pension fund might own some shares of the company's stock does not really enter anyone's consciousness. There is no reason for employees to think or act like owners. They don't know how much stock they

121

own because they own stock only as part of a large group. There is no account with their name on it and a number showing how many shares they own. If the price of the stock goes up or down, it does not affect the financial picture of the pension fund much because only a small percentage of the fund's assets are invested in any one stock.

Thrift Plans

Employees can own stock in the company for which they work in two different ways through a thrift plan. In 401(k) plans—the most popular thrift plan in the United States—the normal procedure is for the employee to invest money every payday into the plan. The employee is generally investing money on which Social Security but not income tax has been paid. Employees have a number of investment options for their money, and one of these options can be a fund that buys shares in the company they work for. In most 401(k) plans, the employer matches the employee's contribution by some percentage, perhaps 50 or 100 percent. This match can be made by placing stock of the employer company into the plan. When employees buy stock, or have stock placed into their accounts through a 401(k) plan, they do have an account with their name on it that shows how many shares they own and what the value of those shares are. They can begin to think like owners. Those shares will be in that account for a long time—for most people, until retirement—so the employees have become long-term shareholders concerned with the long-term health of the company they work for. Also, because the employees actually own the shares (through a trust), they suffer if the price of the stock goes down, and benefit if it goes up. If the stock pays dividends, these are usually reinvested to provide the employee with even more shares (without the dividends being taxed).

In Japan, more than 90 percent of all companies listed on the Japanese stock exchange have a *mochikabukai* trust with more than 40 percent of their employees participating. While these trusts generally do not own more than 1 or 2 percent of any company's stock, the average employee was estimated to own over $16,000 worth of the employer's stock in 1989. This figure undoubtedly rose and fell during the 1989–1992 years, when Japanese stocks went up to high levels and came back down. The Japanese *mochikabukai* trust functions much like a thrift plan in the United States except that the employees invest only in the stock of their employer. The company sells stock at a small discount, and the employees use after-tax income to purchase the shares. The stock is held in trust, but employees have the right to withdraw their shares when more than 1,000 shares have been purchased. A trustee called a "general director" votes the shares held by the *mochikabukai* trust without consulting the employees who actually own the shares. In theory, the participants in the trust elect the "general director"; in practice, the personnel director of the company usually acts as the "general director."

In France, employees can invest in something similar to an American thrift plan with pretax francs up to a yearly maximum, and employers can make matching contributions to these plans. In most cases, the funds are invested in mutual funds owning a large number of different stocks, but they can be invested in the stock of the employer. If a company issues new shares to be placed in these plans, they may be sold at 20 percent below current market prices. These funds may also borrow up to 10 percent of their assets to purchase a large block of stock. As of 1992, only a small percentage of these funds were invested in the stock of the company the employees work for.

Profit-Sharing Plans

Until the 1980s, the most popular way to provide a large group of employees with stock in the company they worked for was through a profit-sharing plan. The term *profit-sharing plan* can refer to anything from plans that provide employees with a cash bonus to plans that use part of the employer's profits to buy stock for employees and place that stock in trust for their retirement. French law requires companies with more than 100 employees to have a profit-sharing plan, but it can be either a cash bonus plan or a trust plan. The purpose of the French law is to encourage employees to think about the bottom line, not to make them owners of company shares.

In the United States, profit-sharing plans have a very long history.

Procter and Gamble had a cash bonus profit-sharing plan in 1887, Eastman Kodak created its plan in 1912, and Sears created its plan in 1916. In the United States today, most profit-sharing plans place money into a trust for the employees. The trustees use the money to buy stock for the employees, with the employees receiving money from the plan when they retire. Under U.S. law, a profit-sharing plan can be written to allow up to 100 percent of the assets to be invested in the stock of the company for which the employees work. Also, recent changes in the law allow a company to place money in the profit-sharing plan whether the company makes a profit in that particular year or not. Remember, a profit-sharing plan trust is a defined-contribution benefit plan. Each employee has an individual account showing the number of shares that employee owns in the company he or she works for, and other companies in which the trustee has invested.

In the 1990s, many U.S. companies have profit-sharing plans that own significant amounts of the company's stock. For example, the Hallmark company is about one-third employee owned through a profit-sharing plan, while Southwest Airlines has approximately 9 percent of its stock owned by its profit-sharing plan.

Under Canadian law, "deferred profit-sharing plans" can do most of the things that American profit-sharing plans can do, including buying stock for employees and placing that stock into the employees' profit-sharing accounts using pretax dollars. As long as the shares remain in the profit-sharing plan, the employee does not pay any income tax on the increase in value or the dividends received. However, as in the United States, a company is limited in the amount of money it can place into its employees' retirement plans, including profit-sharing plans.

In Great Britain, shares of the company for which the employees work may be placed in the individual accounts of the employees using a profit-sharing plan (an Inland Revenue Approved Profit-Sharing Scheme). When the shares have been in the account for five years, they can be distributed to the employees and the employees do not pay income tax on the shares until they are sold, at which time they pay a capital gains tax. The company receives a tax deduction based on the value of the shares when they are placed in the profit-sharing plan.

Employee Stock Ownership Plans

The fourth major way employees own stock in the companies for which they work is through employee stock ownership plans (ESOPs). An ESOP works much like a profit-sharing plan. There is a trust, and shares of company stock are placed in the trust. While profit-sharing plans have the option of investing a majority of the money in shares of the company for which the employees work, ESOPs are designed (and are generally required) to do just that.

ESOPs have a major advantage over profit-sharing plans because they can borrow money (with the loan guaranteed by the company) to buy a large block of shares in the company. As the loan is paid off, the shares are placed in the accounts of the individual employees. ESOPs can use leverage the same way average people use leverage to buy a house. When families buy a house, they often end up paying about the same amount they would have paid in rent each month, only now they are making mortgage payments. By using a mortgage loan to buy a house, buyers get to have their cake and eat it too (that is, live in the house before it is entirely paid for).

The same can happen with an ESOP. The company would like employees to own a significant number of shares, and the employees would like to own those shares. The company could require the employees to take out a personal loan and buy some shares (as discussed in the last chapter). This may be a financial hardship for some employees. Also, the employees will be buying their shares with after-tax dollars. Taking Social Security and income taxes into account, this means the employees will be able to buy significantly fewer shares than would otherwise be the case. With an ESOP, the dollars being used to buy the shares (or to pay off the loan taken out to buy the shares) are pretax dollars. This means that more shares can be purchased with the same amount of money. The money used for this purpose is a deduction for the company (just like any other personnel expense).

With an ESOP, employees can begin to think like owners from the first day of work (after the system is explained to them). As they work and as the company makes contributions to the ESOP to pay off the loan, shares are placed in the individual employee's account. Dividends on these shares can be used to pay off the loan even faster, putting even more shares into their account. If other employees leave the ESOP without vesting, their shares are also divided up among the remaining employees. Finally, while under U.S. law a company cannot spend more than 15 percent of its payroll on these kinds of funds, a company can use up to 25 percent of payroll to pay off the principal on an ESOP loan (and deduct the full cost of the interest on the loan as well). This allows the company to buy a significantly greater number of shares for employees than would otherwise be the case.

Joseph Blasi and Douglas Kruse, in their book *The New Owners* (Harper Business, 1991), estimated that by the end of 1990 more private-sector employees owned stock in the companies they worked for than belonged to trade unions. The authors compiled a list of the 1,000 largest companies whose the stock was publicly traded and whose employees owned a significant block of stock (mainly through the various trusts we have just discussed). This list includes a third of the Fortune Industrial 500 companies and a fifth of the Fortune Service 500 Companies. Companies with a significant level of employee own-ership accounted for almost a third of the market value of all public companies and for about a fifth of all the employees working for companies with publicly traded stock. Blasi and Kruse found that the average company on this list had more than 12 percent of its stock owned by employees and that the employees, as a group, were the largest single shareholder in almost half of these 1,000 companies. They estimated that by the year 2000, more than a quarter of all the public companies in the United States will be at least 15 percent owned by their employees and that a quarter of all private-sector employees will work for those companies. A 15 percent stake will make the employees the largest single shareholder in most cases.

Securities and Corporate Law Issues

We saw in the last two chapters that securities and corporate laws can make it difficult for a company that is not yet a public company to sell shares to its employees. Most of these problems do not apply if the shares are purchased and held by a trust fund such as a profit-sharing plan or an employee stock ownership plan. Most states and the United States government exempt purchases of stock by sophisticated investors or accredited investors from the general securities law requirements. The employee benefit plan trustee is usually going to qualify as a "sophisticated investor" or an "accredited investor." Many states specifically exempt the sale of securities to a qualified employee benefit plan. Also, when the shares are held in trust, they are technically owned by only the trustee, meaning there is only one shareholder for securities law purposes even though those shares are being held for the benefit of hundreds of employees. This keeps the company from becoming a public company because its shares are owned by too many stockholders.

The same will not be the case if employees use their own money to buy stock "voluntarily" through a thrift plan such as a 401(k) plan. In that case, the law considers a sale of securities to have taken place. For this reason, most companies will not allow employees to invest in the company through a thrift plan until the company has become a public company. However, if the company uses company stock as a matching contribution to such a plan, most securities law problems can be avoided. That is because the employee is not making a voluntary purchase of securities with his or her own money. Also, Rule 701 of the Securities and Exchange Commission may allow some purchase of stock through a thrift plan if the requirements of the rule are met.

While people often overlook state securities and corporation laws, such laws can have a significant impact on the use of employee benefit plans that own stock. In 1981, Continental Airlines tried to sell a large block of stock to a new employee stock ownership plan. The company was trying to place the stock in the friendly hands of its employees to prevent Texas International Airlines from taking over Continental Airlines. The California commissioner of corporations issued a stop order to prevent the sale of the securities to protect, he said, both the employees and the current stockholders. Continental Airlines was taken over by Texas International, which ultimately resulted in unemployment for many of the employees and a trip to bankruptcy court for the stockholders. We will never know what would have happened if the employee stock ownership plan had been allowed to come into existence.

Advantages and Disadvantages of Trusts

From the point of view of the company that wants its employees to own a significant amount of its stock, the main advantage of trusts is the assurance that the company's contributions of stock or cash are fully deductible from its taxes. It can also be sure that the employees covered by a trust are going to be long-term owners. In most cases, the employees will not be getting their stock until they retire (or several years after they leave the company). Also, everyone is in the same trust. There is a trust fund, and not only do the employees know that they own shares in the company but they also know that the other employees are in the same boat. At every level in the company, long-term stockholders are at work every day with a very real chance to make the long-term prospects of the company much brighter than they otherwise would have been.

From the point of view of the employees, the main advantage of trusts is the tax benefits they enjoy. The money placed in these trusts usually has not been taxed, except for 401(k) plans, where the Social Security tax has been paid. Taking into account both Social Security and income taxes, this could mean a significant increase in the amount of stock the employees can purchase. Also, with a leveraged ESOP, 25 percent of payroll can be used to pay off the principal on the debt, allowing for a significantly larger contribution than would otherwise be the case. This is why studies by the General Accounting Office have found that the average ESOP participant has an account growing at a significantly faster rate than that of other pension and benefit plan participants.

Another potential advantage of trusts for both employers and employees is the trustee. Employees, even executives, do not feel that they have time to worry about their investments. That is why mutual funds have become so popular in the United States. With a trustee, who is bound by law to look out for the beneficiary's best interests, the employees have some assurance that a sophisticated individual is watching the financial statements. At the same time, the employer has one person, the trustee, to deal with, not thousands of employee-owners. Although unfounded in most cases, some corporate executives fear having to deal with thousands of employees who take an active part in being owners. These executives seem to think that some kind of "mob psychology" might take over and result in the destruction of the company. The trustee, however, is going to be a sophisticated business person with experience in corporate finance.

The main disadvantage of a trust for both employers and employees is that, by law, the trustee must act when he or she feels that the best interests of the employees would be served. This could mean selling shares to a corporate raider. While such an action could be in the short-term financial interest of the employee beneficiaries, it could also cause some of them to lose their jobs. Also, while lawyers and accountants can explain over and over that the employees own their shares, some people never feel like real owners until they actually hold the shares in their hands. ESOPs in Ireland and Great Britain deal with this by placing the shares in the hands of the employees after a period of years have passed. This, too, has its disadvantages.

If the purpose of an ESOP is to make long-term owners out of employees, and those employees receive their shares after a few years, this purpose could be circumvented. Many of these employees might sell their shares upon distribution, take their capital gains tax break, and reduce their ownership. They will still own some shares, of course. But if the purpose of an ESOP is to build up a significant level of employee ownership so that most employees really feel like they have a financial stake in the company, this may never happen following the Irish and British models. The current U.S. ESOP model, where employees do not receive their shares until many years after leaving the company, or upon retirement, guarantees that employees will have a higher stake in the company they work for.

Simulating Trusts

Many countries do not have the legal concept of a trust. A trust is, after all, a special kind of person who owns property but is bound to use that property for someone else's benefit. Fortunately, in most countries, a nonprofit corporation or association can be set up to do what pension and benefit trusts do in the countries that inherited their legal system from the British. For example, in Egypt, the Alexandria

Tire Company (Egypt's first ESOP) has shares owned by an employee shareholder association. The association owns the shares for the employees just as a trust would in Great Britain or the United States.

In several Latin American countries, employee associations called *solidarista asociaciós* can be set up to perform many of the functions that a profit-sharing or ESOP trust would perform. These associations can even borrow money to buy a block of stock, and the employer-corporations can make contributions to the associations with tax-deductible dollars. The stock held by the solidarista asociaciós is placed in individual accounts and is given to the employees when they leave the company. These associations are particularly popular in Central America, with more than 2,000 companies currently participating in these associations. The most famous solidarista asociación may be La Perla, which is a large agricultural corporation in Guatemala. A majority of the stock is owned by the Arenas family, but a significant minority position (approximately 40 percent) is owned by the employees through their association. When guerrillas attacked the plantations in 1985, the worker-owners beat back the attack.

Land reform is a major political goal in many developing countries. At the same time these countries are faced with the reality that only large plantations can efficiently produce the cash crops that these countries depend on. Giving workers shares in a corporation, or placing those shares in a trust or employee association, is one way to share ownership without breaking up the plantations into uneconomical units. President Aquino's family farm has done just that in the Philippines. The Hacienda Luisita is owned partly by the Aquino family and partly by the employees through the use of stock.

Trusts or ownership associations can also be used as part of a government privatization plan. The newly freed countries of Eastern Europe (and the former Soviet Union) are currently struggling with how to privatize the former state industries in a way that gives them a real chance to succeed as independent enterprises. These countries also do not wish to see these enterprises controlled by investors from outside the country.

Some strategists have suggested giving current employees shares in these companies as part of the privatization process. Others have pointed out that this will not "encourage" those employees to work harder in the future. Another approach would be to put a large block of stock into a trust (or association) to be distributed to the employees over the next 10 or 20 years. This would have the advantage of both rewarding past and current employees by making sure that they get a share of the company and encouraging them to stay with the company and make it a success in the future as well. As with all trusts, the employees will know that they are all in the same boat and that they all will either have an investment nest egg worth real money, or have nothing, depending on how hard they work in the crucial years to come. It also allows new, outside investors to deal with a trustee (or equivalent) instead of a large group of shareholder-workers who may need a significant amount of time to "get the hang" of capitalism.

Putting It All in a Trust

So far we have been discussing putting some of the shares of a company into a trust. In a few cases, all the shares of a company have been placed in trust. This has been done to make sure that only current employees enjoy the benefits of ownership. This can best be explained with a hypothetical situation.

Suppose Mr. Jones has built the Jones Corporation into a large company with thousands of employees. He wants to sell the company to the employees, but he also wants it to be run like a worker cooperative. At the same time he wants more experienced employees to have more say in the company rather than all employees having an equal voice (most cooperatives are required by law to operate on the one-worker, one-vote principle). He also wants long-term employees to receive more of the benefits of ownership, with higher dividend payments (most cooperatives are required to base payments on work done not on time spent with the company). Mr. Jones does not want the employees to take any ownership with them when they leave the company or retire. Their retirement has been taken care of through a pension plan. When they leave the company as active employees, he does not want them to continue to have any say in how the company is run or to receive any financial benefit from the profits of the company.

To accomplish these goals, Mr. Jones sets up the Jones Company

Trust and works with an attorney to spell out his desires in the trust documents. The trustee will poll the employees when it comes time to elect the board of directors, giving each employee one vote for each year of service with the company. That board of directors will provide bonuses to the employees based on the profits of the company and the number of years each employee has been with the company. The trust will also buy Mr. Jones's shares over a period of years, using company profits (or the company will buy the shares back from Mr. Jones if that has more tax advantages for either Mr. Jones or the company). Mr. Jones will pay income tax each year on the money he receives as payment for his shares, something he might have avoided if he had sold his shares to a true cooperative or an ESOP. However, Mr. Jones doesn't care about the tax payments because he is getting old and figures he would have to pay the taxes at some point anyway.

A trust can be structured to accomplish almost any purpose of the retiring owner. The largest candy company in the United States, the Hershey Company, maker of everything from Hershey Kisses to Reese's Peanut Butter Cups to Mounds candy bars, is owned by a trust set up by Mr. Hershey to perform a number of charitable functions. His concern was helping underprivileged children rather than making his employees owners, but the principle is the same.

This kind of trust can be set up to simulate a cooperative, an ESOP, a profit-sharing plan, or whatever the outgoing owner wishes, but minimizing whatever feature of these options the owner does not like. The owner could set up the trust to benefit the employees along with a charity or members of his family. The options are almost endless, limited only by the owner's imagination and the requirements of the tax code.

The Problem with Trusts

While trusts can accomplish a lot of worthwhile purposes, a trust has a fundamental limitation. A trustee is not a real owner. A trustee is bound by law to act in a prudent way, which means to avoid risk. But a vibrant economy needs investors who are willing to take risks. While some of these risks will fail, others will succeed and whole new companies or industries will be born as a result. The history of the United States is a story of people who took risks, in some cases failing several times before finally making good. Mr. Hershey had failed in several other businesses before making a success of his chocolate company. Mr. DuPont had tried and failed to set up a farm cooperative when he convinced people to lend him the money to begin a gunpowder factory on the Brandywine River in Delaware. People laughed at Thomas Edison, Henry Ford, and a thousand others. In each case, these people found other people willing to provide "risk capital" to make their dream a reality. Trustees can do a lot of things but, in general, they cannot provide risk capital.

The American economy is well down the road to trustee-capitalism (or trustee-socialism, take your pick). Pension and benefit fund trustees will own a majority of common stock in American companies by the early years of the twenty-first century. The political system has to recognize this and realize that these trusts have a role to play in helping to finance the continued growth of the American economy, but they will not be able to provide "risk capital." They will be able to buy out venture capitalists once an enterprise has proven itself and "gone public." They will be able to finance the takeover of obsolete companies in need of significant restructuring (but only if the law does not insulate these companies from the takeover that will mean short-term hardship and long-term prosperity for the company involved). They can even be an instrument of foreign policy, investing in the emerging companies of the developing world.

Trusts will not provide capital for new companies. During the 1980s and 1990s, the United States debated what tax incentive to give those willing to take that particular risk. The debate has seemed almost silly to outside observers. President Bush asked for a significant long-term capital gains tax break. The Democrats responded by saying they were unwilling to encourage the purchase of such things as gold and antiques by the very rich. The answer is to structure a long-term capital gains tax break so as to reward only those who invest over the long term in U.S. corporations and not those who buy paintings by van Gogh. By increasing the "normal" income tax rate that the rich must pay, while simultaneously giving a tax break on money made by in-vesting in the stock of U.S. companies, both the goals of higher tax revenue and higher levels of investment could be achieved. Rules could also allow "average" people to receive a similar tax break if they also invest in U.S. companies through mutual funds. Through the creative use of trusts, pension funds, and tax laws, America could once again return to the path of significant economic growth.

APPENDIX

The Philosophy of Profit Sharing

The conflict between employer and employee has come to be regarded as the unchangeable norm in industrial relations. This does not have to be the case. Throughout the twentieth century, management theory has come more and more to recognize the importance of the contribution employees make to any enterprise. From Elton Mayo's experiments at Western Electric's Hawthorne plant to Douglas McGregor's famous Theory X and Theory Y, the role of employee relations has gained an important place in every large corporation. More recent authors credit the chief executive, the corporate structure, and other factors that also contribute to the success or failure of a corporation.

I believe the best approach to understanding and managing the corporation begins by recognizing that the corporation has been granted the privileges of limited liability and perpetual life in exchange for the responsibility of contributing to the long-term economic welfare of the community. There are six parties, each with rights and obligations, that make up the world of the corporation. The six are the State, the local community, suppliers, customers, employees, and the owners. Each is essential to the continued successful operation of any corporation. The State provides services and is entitled to receive taxes in return. The local community provides a working environment for the corporation and is entitled to expect that the corporation will help preserve that environment in return. Suppliers provide goods and services and expect payment, while customers expect quality goods

---

This special contribution is by Dr. J.I. Fitzpatrick, director of the Planned Sharing Research Association in Dublin, Ireland.

and services in exchange for their money. Employees expect compensation for their labor, and owners expect a return on their investment.

The basic measure of success for modern free enterprise is profit. The key question is: Who should be entitled to receive a share of that profit? I believe the employees, as the literal heart and soul of the organization, deserve to share in that profit as much as the investors. An organization is basically the combination of labor and capital, and both should have a claim on the profit of the corporation. The nineteenth century witnessed the stormy growth of the trade union movement and a concept of labor-management relations that focused on conflict. I believe the better approach would be to view labor and capital as partners in a joint enterprise. If this idea of partnership is accepted, I believe it will have great benefit for the corporation and for the various parties that have a relationship with the corporation.

Profit is to the corporate body as food is to the human body, essential for survival. It is, therefore, a "good thing." That is not to say that more is better. A surfeit of it can damage either body. In both cases, survival implies growth. A corporation's needs for that are determinable, and constitute the prior charge on its profits. Once that level of reserves has been reached, whatever is surplus should be disbursed in the best interests of the corporation and its component parties.

The purpose of a corporation is to produce wealth. The more effectively and the longer it does that, the greater its virtue. To discontinue, for any reason, temporarily or permanently, is to harm the community; suppliers lose customers, customers lose a supplier, employment is jeopardized, and investment endangered. It follows that corporate survival should be the principal goal of management. That long-term survival, and even growth, depends on the ability of management to provide each of the six players with what they want from the corporation: taxes, protection, payment, products, salaries, and dividends. Profit is not just an end for the corporation but the means to achieve these other goals. To accomplish this, enough of the profits must be retained to ensure the long-term survival and growth of the enterprise. The long-term dedication and interest of each employee may be the single most important factor in helping to guarantee the long-term survival and prosperity of the corporation.

The shareholders are entitled to a fair return on their investment, based on the going interest rate at the time. By investing in the corporation, they should receive a return commensurate with the risk they take. Employees are entitled to a fair wage for fair labor. If employees contribute beyond the basic, and above-average corporate performance is achieved, who should participate in that above-average corporate profit? Should not the employees (who made it possible) participate along with the State (that will receive higher taxes) and the shareholders (who will receive higher dividends or share values)? Would this not provide a real incentive for employees to continue to provide above-average performance to the corporation of the kind that customers desire and deserve? Would this not help to ensure the long-term health and profitability of the corporation so that it can fulfill its obligations to all six of the parties interested in its growth and survival?

In any industry, most corporations cluster around a midpoint, setting the norm in costs and profits, and providing the standard for judging excellence of performance. Those corporations that move ahead of the pack provide an example of what can be done. These successful corporations will be the ones able to move beyond the labor-management confrontation of the past decades. A realistic approach would be for management to:

1. Assess the additional profit that might be earned with the full cooperation of every employee.
2. Discuss with the employees how this additional profit could be shared between owners and employees.
3. Write up a document to cover this principle, with feedback from employees, that will take time and patience.
4. Create a practical format to continue this management-employee dialogue to ensure the further success of the corporation.
5. Establish plans to achieve excellence, goals to assess financial progress, and a scheme to share the increased profits that should come from better management-employee cooperation.

Thomas J. Peters and Robert H. Waterman, in their now classic book *In Search of Excellence* (Harper & Row, 1982), found that successful corporations were concerned more with the quality and reliability of customer service than with simply making a profit; that they decentralized decision making, encouraged direct communication within the corporation, and respected their employees. I believe all of these goals, and the broader goal of corporate survival and corporate profit making, will best be served if employees are given a fair share of the corporation's profit.

11

Cooperatives

Cooperatives (co-ops) go back at least to the Middle Ages in Europe. In Russia, rural cooperatives formed the basis of agriculture in many regions. In medieval cities, guilds—associations of skilled craftsmen—pooled their resources to provide a number of joint services for their members. Today there are thousands of cooperatives around the world. Legally, a cooperative in most countries is a strange cross between a corporation and a partnership.

In a partnership, the income of the enterprise is divided among the partners, and the business enterprise itself does not pay income taxes. A major advantage of a partnership is this "single taxation" feature. On the other hand, every partner is personally liable for the debts of the partnership. That means that if the partnership injures someone, each partner could find himself virtually bankrupt after paying for the losses. Lloyds of London, the famous insurance firm, is in reality a group of partnerships. Members of each partnership (partners are called "names") pledge their personal wealth if a loss requires it. In 1992, these partners had to come up with almost a billion dollars to make up for the difference between what Lloyds took in as premium income and what it had to pay out as losses. The partners in Lloyds learned the danger of joining a partnership with potentially limitless losses.

With a corporation, an artificial person is formed, chartered by the government, to carry on a business. The government expects to make

Exhibit 11.1   Comparing Corporations, Partnerships, and Cooperatives

	Corporations	Partnerships	Cooperatives
Liability	Limited	Unlimited	Limited
Taxation	Double	Single	Single
Control	Based on capital	Based on agreement	Equal
Receipt of earnings	Proportional to investment	Based on agreement	Based on work done
Transfer of interest	Easy	Difficult	Controlled
Effect of death	No effect	Terminates partnership	No effect

money on this deal and imposes corporate income taxes. This means that the income of the corporation is taxed first at the level of the corporation and then again when dividends are paid out to the shareholders. This "double taxation" feature is the major disadvantage of corporations. On the other hand, the shareholders of a corporation are not personally liable for the debts of the corporation. If Lloyds of London were a regular corporation, it might have gone bankrupt in 1992, but it could not have passed through its losses to the shareholders. This "limited liability" feature is considered one of the major advantages of corporations.

As Exhibit 11.1 illustrates, a cooperative has, at least in theory, the best of both worlds. On the one hand, it is an artificial person, chartered by the government, and the individual members are not liable for the debts of the cooperative business enterprise (just like shareholders in a corporation). On the other hand, the income of a cooperative is taxed only once, at the level of the members (just like partners in a partnership).

However, cooperatives also differ from both corporations and partnerships. While the shareholders of a corporation can own very different amounts of stock, have very different claims to control, and receive different amounts of income from the corporation, members of a cooperative must be treated equally. Members of the cooperative can be paid in proportion to the amount of work they do, but this usually means that every member is paid about the same as every other member. Each member has just one vote, without concern for how long the individual has been a member or how much effort the individual has put into the organization.

In a cooperative, membership is limited to those allowed in by the other members. While a shareholder can simply sell shares, a cooperative member may not. Cooperative membership cannot be "sold" except according to the rules of the cooperative and, in most cases, with the approval of the cooperative board of directors. In a corporation, ownership is essentially divided up based on the amount of capital each person puts into the corporation. If someone puts up $1 million and someone else puts up $1, the first person would own a million times more shares in the corporation than the person putting up only $1. In a cooperative, control and access to the profits are not based on the amount of money put into the cooperative by the members.

With partnerships, the death, bankruptcy, or withdrawal of a partner requires a termination of the partnership and perhaps the creation of a new partnership with new partners. That is not the case with a cooperative. If one member dies or withdraws, the cooperative goes on, just as a corporation would if a shareholder died or withdrew.

In the United States, most cooperatives, like most corporations, are chartered by the states, not the federal government. At the same time, it is the Internal Revenue Service that decides how the income of the business enterprise is to be taxed. You can end up with an enterprise that the state thinks is not a cooperative but that the IRS thinks is, or vice versa. For the IRS, a cooperative must have three major characteristics: its control is not based on the amount of capital invested in the enterprise; the members control the enterprise on a democratic basis; and the members share the earnings in proportion to their dealings with the enterprise.

The single tax treatment means (under Subchapter T of the IRS Code) that the cooperative is allowed to deduct the "patronage dividends" (meaning the dividends paid to members) from its income for income tax purposes. This dividend must be paid based on the amount of work done by the members. Also, the same rules must apply to all members equally. For example, in a partnership, the partners are free to agree that one partner will receive twice as much profit while another partner will have more of the liability for the partnership's debts.

Cooperatives cannot operate this way. Equality is the key with cooperatives.

If a corporation wants to use some of its earnings to invest in the enterprise to create growth, it simply pays its corporate income taxes and reinvests the money instead of paying it out as dividends. A cooperative can do the same thing. It gives members "written notices of allocation," meaning the members get a statement telling them that the cooperative earned money in their name but that they are not going to receive it. This money is "retained" by the cooperative for investment in the enterprise (this money is called a "retain"). Of course, the workers have the unpleasant experience of paying taxes on money they have not actually received. It is a task of the cooperative to explain that because the individual workers are in a lower tax bracket than the cooperative would be if it were taxed as a regular corporation, it is better to handle reinvestment this way.

As with all businesses, the biggest problem for a new cooperative is money—how to acquire the capital needed to begin the business. Some of this capital may come from membership fees charged to the members of the cooperative. Cooperatives can, of course, borrow money and can also use any of the methods a regular corporation might use to raise funds. It can even issue "preferred stock" in the cooperative. This stock does not entitle the holder to vote for the board of directors or share in the increased value of the company over time. It does allow the holder to receive dividends and to redeem the stock for the amount paid for it. In other words, it operates the way a bond might operate if the cooperative had a good enough financial picture to be able to issue bonds.

Many people imagine that a cooperative is some kind of grand experiment in democracy, with every decision of any importance being decided by a meeting of the members. While a few small cooperatives operate that way, most do not. The members elect a board of directors that controls the operation of the business enterprise and selects the president of the cooperative just like any other corporate board of directors. The members meet once a year to elect the board of directors. At the same time, cooperatives are different from corporations; the members often meet more often and make decisions that might be left to the board of directors in most corporations.

Capital Retains in a Cooperative

One of the principal responsibilities of membership in a cooperative is to provide investment funds for capital purposes (i.e., to finance the acquisition of assets). These funds are provided under the members' agreement to provide such funds. Members can agree to provide investment funds either by out-of-pocket investments (through the purchase of membership or stock certificates), by investing a portion of their patronage refunds arising from the operations of the cooperative, or by contributing capital based on the dollar value or physical volume of business to be done with or through their cooperative. This last form of investment, known as a "per unit retain," is based on a preexisting obligation to contribute investment capital to the cooperative prior to performance of the cooperative's obligation to the contributing member. A per unit retain (contribution based on a unit or value of business to be done with the cooperative) is distinguishable from capital contributed as a result of a patronage dividend. Patronage dividend capital contributions are contributed after the cooperative has performed its marketing, service, or processing obligation for the member and after all operating expenses have been deducted from the net earnings of the cooperative. Conversely, per unit retains reflect an amount determined without reference to the net earnings of the cooperative. Per unit retains are contributed to the cooperative in the form of a deduction from the members' price of product or services sold or marketed through a cocperative as opposed to patronage dividend contributions, which are deducted from net earnings. The member agrees to "invest" capital "up front" through per unit retains. Under the patronage dividend method, the member authorizes deductions for operating purposes from the proceeds of members' business done with the cooperative, with a portion of the net income remaining to be invested in the cooperative. Because per unit retains are up-front investments, they can be used as a "quick fix" for cooperatives in need of capital.

A. Fred Holm, Esq.
Cooperative Auditing Service
Princeton, Minnesota

Northcountry Cooperative Development Fund

Northcountry Cooperative Development Fund (NCDF) was founded in 1979 as a member-controlled, self-help organization by several cooperative businesses in Minnesota interested in establishing a permanent financing and development resource for cooperatives in the upper Midwest. Since that time, more than $1.8 million has been loaned to worker co-ops, consumer co-ops, producer co-ops, and housing co-ops in rural and urban areas all over the Midwest for a variety of needs, including expansions, new equipment, building improvements, and working capital. In all that time, the fund has experienced total accumulated principal losses of less than $5,000—a remarkable record by any standard. Northcountry Cooperative Development Fund is a cooperative itself, with membership open to any cooperatively run business in the upper Midwest. Assets of the fund are currently at approximately $750,000 and growing every year. Funds for lending come from three sources: 45 percent from the savings of cooperative members, 45 percent from socially responsible institutional investors, and 10 percent from loans made to the fund by individual investors interested in making their money work for a cooperative economy. Individuals and organizations making socially responsible investments in the fund receive a competitive rate of interest.

Margaret Lund, Managing Director
Northcountry Cooperative Development Fund
St. Paul, Minnesota

The Mondragon Model

In the late 1950s, Father Arizmendiarrieta, a parish priest in the Mondragon region of Spain (in Basque country), decided that the key to controlling the economic future of the region was money. He formed a new bank, the *Caja Laboral Popular* (Bank of the People's Labor), to change the way capital was invested. The bank, with the savings of the people of the region, financed a group of worker cooperatives called the Mondragon cooperatives. The goal was to have people employ capital rather than to have capitalists employ people. The Empresarial Division of the bank helped new cooperatives begin a business much as a venture capital firm might do in other countries. This division was eventually spun off into a separate cooperative. The Mondragon cooperatives succeeded beyond anyone's wildest dreams. Every cooperative has been a business success. The combination of capital, business start-up expertise, and committed worker-owners brought relative prosperity to the Basque region in a very short period of time.

The Mondragon cooperatives developed a set of governing institutions in each cooperative that looked more like a political system than a business enterprise. Members meet as a general assembly (*Asamblea General*) to make major decisions just as a legislature might in a country. They elect a board of directors, called a *Junta Rectora*, to oversee the running of the business. However, the Mondragon cooperatives do not stop there, as most cooperatives would. They also elect a watchdog council called the *Consejo de Vigilencia* to watch the finances of the cooperative and act much like an audit committee acts in many large corporations. The workers also elect a social council, *Consejo Social*, to perform many of the functions that a union might perform in a normal corporation.

To some extent, the Mondragon experiment shows what an underdeveloped region can do when money generated by the region is reinvested in that region instead of sent to absentee owners for investment somewhere else. These cooperatives also demonstrate that a properly organized and executed cooperative can be a safe investment.

Italian Cooperatives

Italy has approximately 20,000 worker cooperatives with some 300,000 members. While the northwest region of Italy has many large enterprises with traditional labor unions and traditional labor-management relations, the northeast region has had an economy based on small enterprises that manufacture such products as clothing, shoes, leather goods, and machinery. This emphasis on small enterprises has helped worker cooperatives to flourish in northeastern Italy. Worker cooperatives have also flourished because during the economic crisis of 1981–1984, both government and trade unions agreed to encourage the formation of cooperatives to employ the unemployed.

Italian law on cooperatives has evolved over the years. The original Reform Act of 1947 allowed cooperatives to avoid paying corporate income taxes. At the same time, the law limited the ability of a cooperative member to sell his or her individual share for a significant profit upon leaving the firm. Return on employee investments was limited and, if a cooperative went out of business, its assets and reserve funds were distributed to charities, not to the members. In other words, under Italian law, worker cooperatives were treated more like nonprofit corporations designed to perform a public service (employ the unemployed) than like real businesses. In 1985, the Marcora law set up a financial company to help employees buy out troubled firms and turn them into worker cooperatives. During its first year, the company financed 40 buyouts, setting up cooperatives that employed more than 1,600 workers.

In 1988, the De Vito law established a support system to aid in the formation of cooperatives in southern Italy, where many young workers were unemployed. Business innovation centers and job creation companies were set up to aid new cooperatives. Each new cooperative is given a "tutor," which might be a major corporation such as Fiat or Olivetti. Public funds are used to provide start-up capital for these new cooperatives.

Until the end of the 1980s, the idea was to put the unemployed to work, not to make capitalists out of workers. Three large trade unions control the Italian labor movement, and they were not very interested in turning workers into capitalists. Also, the Italian stock exchange has never functioned effectively. This has been true in part because there are no private employee pension and benefit funds such as those in countries like Great Britain and the United States with capital to invest in Italian stocks.

In 1992, the Italian Parliament passed a new law effective in 1993 to allow members of worker cooperatives to participate in the financial gains generated by their enterprise. A member's share can now reach a value of $100,000. Also, cooperatives may sell stock to members or outside investors to raise capital. Shares sold to outside "venture capital partners" may not control more than one-third of the votes in the company. Members can receive the cash value of their shares when they leave and pay only capital gains taxes on that cash. Members can also make interest-bearing loans to their cooperatives. It is expected that these changes will allow cooperative members to begin to think and feel more like real owners of a real enterprise with a real profit motive.

Irish Cooperatives

In countries such as the United States, it is an advantage that the income of the cooperative is taxed at the rate of the individual workers. If a corporation must pay an income tax rate of 40 percent and workers a rate of 20 percent, then paying the workers' rate provides much more money to reinvest in the enterprise. The opposite is true in Ireland. Corporate income in Ireland is taxed at 40 percent while most workers' pay is taxed at approximately 50 percent. This being the case, a group of workers who wanted to form a true cooperative in Ireland would form a standard corporation instead. To the extent that they wanted to pay themselves money, they would simply pay out wages and deduct that money from the corporation's income for tax purposes. If they wanted to retain money and reinvest it, then they would pay the 40 percent corporate income tax rate and use the rest to invest in new plant and equipment. They would not pay corporate income taxes and then declare a dividend to be taxed again at the individual level.

Advantages and Disadvantages of Cooperatives

The advantages of cooperatives as a way to turn employees into owners come from a cooperative's structure and tax-favored status. A cooperative is a corporation that enjoys limited liability for its worker-members and avoids the double taxation of profits under which most corporations suffer. Every cooperative member has an equal vote, which avoids some of the resentment that comes when some people are "more equal" than others.

The major problems with cooperatives revolve around money. First, where will the money come from to begin the cooperative? In Mondragon, this problem was solved with the development of a new kind of bank.

The other major problem with cooperatives has to do with how much money a member may take out when the member leaves the organization. Using the normal business valuation techniques discussed in Chapter 5, the cooperative could place a value on each member's interest in the cooperative. For discussion purposes, let's say that each member's interest is worth $100,000. The problem is, no new worker-member can afford to buy that share. How, then, do you bring in new worker-members to be equal with the old worker-members when the old members feel that their share is worth so much money?

The Mondragon cooperatives deal with the problem of how much money an exiting member can take out by keeping an account for each member based on the amount of "retains" credited to that member. The account draws a small amount of interest each year and, when the member leaves, he or she takes that money and nothing else. In the United States, a number of states have passed special employee cooperative acts to go into the statute books alongside the "usual" cooperative law. These laws allow worker cooperatives to be set up on the Mondragon model, with much of the value of the cooperative unallocated to any individual member.

Other cooperatives make no pretense of "paying" an exiting worker-owner the value of his or her ownership when the worker leaves the business. The member paid a fee upon joining and gets back that fee upon leaving. If the value of the business has increased during the period of ownership, that's great for the next member who joins, but of no use to the departing member. This is a problem only if the members think it is. Many members do feel that way. They see fellow workers who purchased shares in the corporations they work for either through share purchase plans or ESOPs leaving with tens of thousands of dollars worth of stock. They know that their share of the cooperative would come to a similar amount if it were a corporation, and they resent it.

Another problem with cooperatives is the fact that individual workers must pay income taxes on the money "retained" in their name by the cooperative for reinvestment in the business. While this retention can be explained, that explanation often comes when the worker-owner has to come up with tax money he does not have. Many cooperatives that could have been successful businesses have been unable to expand because of the unwillingness of the members to pay taxes on money they do not actually receive. The Mondragon cooperatives avoid this in part by borrowing money from the bank and paying interest on that loan. The interest is tax deductible to the individual cooperative, and the bank pays higher interest rates to its depositors instead of taxes on income. The depositors are rewarded for taking the risk of lending to a cooperative (not much of a risk, in this case), and the individual cooperative does not have to use its own profits to grow and expand.

Thinking Creatively about Cooperatives

In law schools and business schools in the United States and most other countries, the students learn all about corporations and partnerships. They do not learn about cooperatives. That is a shame because the cooperative form could provide the answer in many situations. There are basically three types of cooperatives: worker, producer, and consumer. We have been discussing worker cooperatives. A producer cooperative operates on the same principle. Suppose a group of farmers who grow cranberries decide to skip the middlemen and market their product directly to the consumers. They would use a producer cooperative. The cooperative would buy their cranberries, turn them into cranberry juice, and sell the juice to grocery stores. The profit made on the juice operation would be passed back to the growers on a proportional basis, depending on how many pounds of cranberries they grew. In a sense, by using a producer cooperative, the farmers have enabled themselves to get a higher price for their products. That is exactly what OceanSpray is, a producer cooperative. In fact, many

Americans would be surprised to learn that many of the brands they are familiar with, such as Sunkist, are really producer cooperatives.

A consumer cooperative—for example, a food cooperative—works on similar principles. The members are consumers, not workers. They pay a small membership fee and try to buy as much as possible from the cooperative. At the end of the year, if the business made a profit, it is returned to the consumer members in the form of a "patronage refund." The more money the members spend at the cooperative, the more money they get back at the end of the year. Many people in the United States belong to a credit union, which works on the same principle except that members get higher interest rates rather than a patronage refund. Many people also belong to a public television station, which does not provide a patronage refund at the end of the year but uses any leftover funds to provide more and better television programs for the members.

While it might take a new statute, no laws of nature prevent combining these three forms. For example, what about a grocery store that is owned by the farmers who grow the food, the workers who work at the store, and the consumers who buy the food? The farmer would be paid market prices; the workers would be paid going wages; and the consumers would be charged market prices. At the end of the year, any money left over would be divided three ways—a third to the producers, a third to the workers, and a third to the consumers. Or imagine any combination of the three: a worker-consumer cooperative, or a producer-worker cooperative. Imagine a producer-worker art gallery, with the profits being divided between the artists who make the art and the workers who sell the art. That would be fairly easy to create under existing law in many parts of the world.

Simulating a Co-op with an ESOP

If the major problems of a co-op are the inability to borrow money for growth and the difficulty of allowing members to receive the true value of their share when they leave, we can overcome both of these problems by setting up an employee stock ownership plan (ESOP) inside a regular corporation instead of using a cooperative. Imagine that we have 20 original members, each able and willing to invest $2,000; another $60,000 is needed to begin operation. A regular corporation is set up with an ESOP, which then borrows the entire $100,000 ($40,000 from the members, $60,000 from a bank). The bank receives a mortgage on the machinery and building that the new company will own. The members agree to "subordinate" the money they are owed to the bank, meaning the bank gets paid off first if there is a problem. The bank is willing to make this loan because all of the company's stock is owned by the ESOP and the ESOP is controlled by a trustee, in this case another banker. The lending bank trusts this trustee and knows this trustee will do everything possible to repay the loan. Also, the lending bank is allowed to elect one member of the board of directors as long as any money is owed to it. This is something banks often demand and that cooperatives generally cannot allow (it would violate the law in most cases to allow a nonmember to sit on the board of directors or to vote for a member of the board of directors).

The ESOP trust is structured so that votes on all issues, including the members of the board of directors (other than the member appointed by the lending bank), are passed through to the employees on the basis of one vote for each worker. ESOPs are allowed to do this, even if different workers have different amounts of stock. At the same time, the trustee has the power to override any vote to protect the interests of the lender (this would be written into the bylaws and the trust agreements to give comfort to the bank lending money to the company).

Through the ESOP we have created a new company with 20 shareholders and 20 employees. Imagine that the loans are for 10 years. Each year as a tenth of the loan is paid off, 10 percent of the stock is placed in the individual accounts of the workers. During the course of the first 10 years, our new company grows. As new workers are hired, they are added to the ESOP trust and they, too, receive stock at the end of each year. The initial 20 members get the money they lent to the ESOP back with interest and receive stock in their individual accounts, along with the other workers. Because they worked at the company from the beginning, the 20 initial members have more stock in their accounts to compensate them for the sacrifices they made in those early, lean years.

Imagine that after 10 years the company employs 50 workers and wants to expand further. Again the ESOP borrows money to buy newly issued shares (the money is borrowed at a reduced interest rate for reasons that will be explained in the next chapter), and again shares are placed in the accounts of individual workers as the loan is paid off.

It is now 20 years since the company was formed, and the original founding members would like to leave. They have the most stock in their ESOP accounts for the simple reason that they have been with the company the longest. The ESOP borrows money so it can buy the retiring members' shares at the current fair market value. Again, as that loan is paid off, those shares are divided up among the current active workers. The outgoing workers are happy because they received a substantial sum of money for their 20 years of hard work, and the remaining workers are allowed to "buy them out" as a group in a fairly painless way over many years. Instead of the workers having to borrow the money on their own, the ESOP borrows the money and pays off the loan as money is paid to the ESOP each year by the company.

During the early years of our ESOP company that is acting like a co-op, wages are low as the company struggles to find a market and meet the competition. The worker-owners are willing to receive low wages because they see the value of their individual ESOP accounts go up each year as the company becomes profitable and the ESOP loan is paid off. Eventually, the workers are receiving reasonable wages, and there is still money left over. An ESOP is allowed to pass through to the workers any dividends paid on the stock held in the ESOP, and the company is allowed to deduct the cost of those dividend payments because they are made to an ESOP. The workers decide to declare a dividend and receive money on their shares. They realize that workers with more shares will receive more money, but they think this is a fair way to recognize the past sacrifices and added experience those older workers bring to the job. By avoiding the payment of Social Security taxes (over 15 percent of wages), these employees receive more money than would otherwise be the case.

This company is in a position to use borrowed funds to finance

growth, just like any other corporation. At the same time, the ownership is held by the worker-owners, not outside investors. Each worker
has one vote on all issues, including electing the board of directors.
But they can use that vote to place people who are not workers on the
board so that the company can benefit from their advice. When workers leave the company, the ESOP buys back their shares based on an
objective evaluation of the shares' worth. The workers have made
money in the same way that they would have if they had formed a
"regular" corporation instead of this ESOP corporation. Because this
was explained in detail to each new employee, only people who feel
that this is the way things should be handled have signed on with this
new kind of company.

We will come back to this question of simulating a co-op with an
ESOP in Chapter 15, after we have described in more detail what an
ESOP is and how it works.

The Future of Cooperatives

Cooperatives have gotten a bad name in some parts of the world
because that word *cooperative* has been misused. In the former countries
of Yugoslavia and the Soviet Union, organizations that were in reality
owned by the state were often called cooperatives. That is not what
we mean by the word *cooperative*. In other countries, cooperatives
are not allowed to function in the same way that other corporations
function, or they are denied access to capital because bankers do not
believe they have a future. This "belief" becomes a self-fulfilling proph-
esy. The Mondragon region of Spain has demonstrated what cooperatives can do when they do have access to capital.

Many people believe that cooperatives work fine if there are fewer
than 20 members but are impossible if the membership is larger. The
Mondragon experience should put that idea to rest. Do cooperatives
have a future? Yes, limited only by the willingness of people to band
together for their own mutual economic self-interest. It is always
going to be "harder" to start a cooperative than to "get a job" or "go
shopping," but the rewards can be tremendous.

APPENDIX

The Mondragon Cooperative Complex

Among those interested in various forms of employee ownership, the Mondragon cooperative complex, in the Basque country of Spain, has come to be recognized as the most impressive development of worker cooperatives currently in existence. Furthermore, it has no close parallels in the previous history of worker cooperatives.

The success of Mondragon challenges some widely held beliefs that worker cooperatives will survive only precariously in economic niches of little interest to private firms, that they will be limited to highly labor-intensive operations, that workers will be unwilling to forgo current income in order to invest in growth, and that a financially successful cooperative will eventually revert to private ownership.

The complex began with the founding of the first firm by 23 workers in 1956. By 1992, the complex had grown to 99 industrial or agro-industrial cooperatives, with total employment of over 23,000.

Mondragon is the leading manufacturer of machines for kitchens and laundries in the Spanish market. Mondragon cooperatives are heavily involved in a wide range of other businesses, from machine tools to construction, from furniture making to financial and computer services. Some of the cooperatives export more than 50 percent of their production.

The founder and guiding spirit of cooperative development in Mondragon until his death in 1976 was Father Jose Maria Arizmendiarrieta. When he began his ministry in 1941, Mondragon was a small industrial town of about 8,000 population. In the aftermath of the Spanish Civil War, in which the Basques had lost out to the Franco forces, the youth of Mondragon had no opportunity to get an educa-

This special contribution is by William Foote Whyte, research director, Programs for Employment and Workplace Systems, New York State School of Industrial and Labor Relations, Cornell University. He is also coauthor with Kathleen King Whyte of *Making Mondragon: The Growth and Development of the Worker Cooperative Complex*, 2d ed. (ILR Press, 1992).

tion beyond high school or even to learn industrial skills in school. Don Jose Maria began working with the young men of blue-collar families in a variety of youth and community-development projects. He also met with groups for discussion of social and economic issues. In 1943, he got together with the blue-collar youth and their parents to establish an educational program in industrial skills for boys from 14 to 16 years of age. Over the years, that educational program has been extended into college years, with the emphasis now on industrial engineering.

Through arrangements made with the University of Zaragosa, five of the first graduates of the industrial skills program were able to study industrial engineering in absentia to gain university degrees. They then left their blue-collar jobs in the leading private firm to found the first worker cooperative. Capital came from their personal savings and from contributions from fellow citizens in a campaign in which they worked with Don Jose Maria.

How do we explain Mondragon's success? Some critics attribute it to the Basque culture. Some Basques speak of "our associative tendencies," and there are indeed many more worker cooperatives in the Basque region outside of the Mondragon complex. These outside cooperatives, however, are all small and isolated from each other.

Others attribute success to the extraordinary leadership of Don Jose Maria, which, they argue, cannot be reproduced elsewhere. If we want to build on Mondragon's experience, we need to focus on the social inventions and social structures that he and his associates created.

Mondragon is an integrated system. The cooperative bank supplies investment capital and loans. The entrepreneurial division of the bank (now an independent cooperative) provides support services for groups planning to begin a cooperative and intervention services to revive and reorganize a failing cooperative. The two research and development cooperatives keep the cooperatives up to date on technological developments and work with individual firms on the development of new products and processes. The cooperative that provides social security protection to the members also offers assistance on industrial medicine, and sells individual insurance policies.

When ownership and control is based upon a share of stock purchased when the firm is founded, a cooperative can cease to exist either if it goes bankrupt or becomes highly successful. In the latter case, when the original owners reach retirement age, the value of their stock has risen so high as to be out of reach for those hired in later. The original owners then sell out to private interests.

In Mondragon, control is based on labor, not capital. The founding members make their contribution in the form of a *loan* to the cooperative. This establishes a *capital account* in the name of each member. That capital account draws interest from the cooperative and increases through the distribution of profits. When the cooperative loses money, that loss can be covered through deductions from the members' capital accounts. Nonmembers are limited to 10 percent of total employment. Each member has one vote, and a financially viable cooperative can only be converted to private ownership if a majority of members vote to sell out.

The Mondragon complex grew rapidly in the 1950s and 1960s in an economy that was then sheltered by high tariffs. The 1970s were marked by sharply reduced profits and slower growth as Spain adjusted to the shocks of soaring oil prices. The early 1980s was a period of recession in which the creation of new cooperatives practically ceased, and Mondragon concentrated on rescuing failing cooperatives (with extraordinary success).

From the early 1980s onward, Mondragon leaders have concentrated on reorganizing to confront problems arising from the elimination in 1993 of all tariff protection by countries of the European Community. What began as a system linked together only through relations with the cooperative bank has recently evolved into the Mondragon Cooperative Corporation, with an overall chief executive and vice-presidents of eight industrial divisions. This sweeping change came about in stages, with each change ratified by the cooperative Congress, representing each cooperative, first established in 1987.

Can the Mondragon model—or parts of it—be applied to other countries? In the United States, the most active not-for-profit agency working to develop worker cooperatives and employee-owned firms, the Industrial Cooperative Association, uses aspects of that model with worker cooperatives and seeks to develop democratically managed

ESOP firms along Mondragon lines. There is growing interest in Latin America and Asia. In Eastern Europe and the former Soviet Union, the drive toward privatization is spurring interest in various forms of employee ownership—but so far (1992) adaptations of the ESOP model have proven more popular with those seeking alternatives to government ownership.

PART
THREE

EMPLOYEE STOCK OWNERSHIP PLANS

12

Creating an ESOP

An employee stock ownership plan (ESOP) in the United States is a special type of employee benefit trust. Unlike a normal pension or profit-sharing plan, an ESOP is required to have most of its assets invested in the company its beneficiaries (the workers) work for. In this chapter, we will look at why ESOPs were invented and why anyone would want to set one up in the company they own, manage, or work for.

Louis Kelso and the Invention of ESOPs

The story of ESOPs begins with Louis Kelso. As a boy growing up in Colorado during the Great Depression, Louis Kelso watched as the passenger trains passed by empty followed by freight trains loaded with people. He wondered how an economic system could have gotten so messed up that this bizarre situation could be the result. He continued to think about this strange phenomenon during World War II. Kelso decided the problem lay in a capitalist system in which most people did not own capital (in the form of stock) and in which most people did not have access to capital (in the form of credit). Having decided that the problem was one of access to capital and credit, he wrote down his ideas, ultimately creating a manuscript of more than

1,200 pages. He reasoned that people make money from both their labor and their capital, and that the more evenly capital is distributed, the less likely the economy would find itself with more products to sell than it had buyers to buy. As money flowed to capital, as a return on investment, it would flow to millions of people, who could spend it, instead of to a few thousand very rich people would could not. Also, if everyone owned capital investments, they would have a second income that could grow over time and provide them with financial security. People would not need welfare payments if they were receiving dividends on their shares, even if they were temporarily unemployed. In a very real sense, Louis Kelso had a vision for America. It was a vision that had much in common with the vision millions of immigrants had when they came to America. They came from societies where only a few could ever be "owners" and they came in search of ownership.

The problem was the Industrial Revolution, which made only the largest economic enterprises successful at the expense of the small shops those immigrants had dreamed of. As a good lawyer, Louis Kelso knew that just because modern economics required large enterprises was no reason to keep the average person from sharing in ownership. He knew that with corporations everyone could own a "share" of the company, even the people who worked for the company. Capitalism was, at least in theory, a game everyone could play.

He found upon his return to the United States at the end of World War II that the leaders of the country were not interested in his ideas. The Full Employment Act of 1946 stated that the major goal of the federal government was finding a job for everyone, not turning everyone into stockholders. Louis Kelso put away his manuscript and became first a professor at the University of Colorado and then an attorney in San Francisco, California. He would eventually meet Mortimer J. Adler, who would look at the old manuscript and agree to help coauthor a shorter version for the general public. The result of their collaboration was published in 1958 as *The Capitalist Manifesto* (Random House). Over the next three decades, Louis Kelso continued to write and work to realize his dream of a capitalist system in which everyone could be a capitalist.

H. Ross Perot, during his presidential campaign in 1992, talked a great deal about the need to provide "capital and credit" to revitalize the inner cities of America. This was a message Kelso had begun to preach decades before. But how do you provide capital and credit to the average worker? They have to spend most of their wages on basic living expenses. They cannot borrow large sums of money because they do not have mansions or jewelry to put up as collateral.

Louis Kelso, as an attorney, knew that most rich people do not use their mansions or their jewelry as collateral when they purchase a business. They use the assets of the business itself as the collateral. In other words, they use the assets of the business being purchased to secure the loan needed to purchase that business. As a simple example, suppose a taxi driver buys a taxi. Instead of saving up the money needed to pay the entire purchase price of the taxi, he pays a small down payment and borrows the rest of the money, intending to pay off the loan with the profits generated by the taxi business. Louis Kelso knew the same thing could be done on a large scale with almost any business.

The key was getting a bank to lend money to a group of workers who might want to buy a business for themselves. He believed this could be done through the use of a defined-contribution employee benefit plan. The plan could borrow the money, buy stock in the business, and pay off the loan as the company made contributions every year to the benefit plan. In 1956, the owners of a 72 percent interest in the Peninsula Newspapers came to him with a desire to sell their stock to their employees. The employees obviously did not have enough money to buy the stock outright. As individuals, they would also not be able to find loans enabling them to buy the stock. Kelso amended seven company profit-sharing plans to allow the plans to buy the stock, financing the purchase by giving notes to the sellers themselves. The company then made tax-deductible payments to the plans each payday, which in turn made payments on the notes. The 20-year notes were paid off in 8 years, and the first ESOP was a success. By using the assets of the company to secure the loan, the employees had done what rich people do all the time. By using the profit-sharing plans, the company was able to deduct both the principal and the interest as the loans were paid off.

ESOPs did not spread like wildfire across the United States in part because many attorneys were not sure this maneuver was legal. Could profit-sharing plans borrow money like this? Was it really légal for them to invest most of their funds in the stock of one company, the company the employee-beneficiaries worked for? In 1973, Louis Kelso met Senator Russell Long of Louisiana. Senator Long believed, like his father, the legendary Huey Long, that the wealth of America should be more evenly divided. At the same time, he did not think taking money from the rich and giving it to the poor was the solution. Senator Long saw in ESOPs the potential for turning workers into owners in a way that would make them realize the value of what they owned because they would have earned it for themselves.

In 1974, Senator Long was a key author of the Employee Retirement Income Security Act (ERISA). He made sure the law provided clear legal authorization for the creation of ESOPs, with the authority to borrow money from anyone who would lend it, and gave employing companies the authority to make or guarantee such loans. The first major advantage of an ESOP for a company was now written into law: the company could borrow money through an ESOP and deduct not only the interest (as it could regardless) but also the principal used to pay back the loan. As a general rule, when a corporation borrows money and repays it, this repayment of principal is not deductible. With an ESOP it is because the principal payment is considered a contribution to a defined-contribution employee benefit plan.

Over the following years two major provisions were passed and then repealed. The first provided a tax credit for companies setting up ESOPs. The second provided a tax break on estate taxes in some situations for retiring owners who sold to an ESOP.

In 1980, the United States Congress passed legislation allowing the Small Business Administration to guarantee loans for companies with ESOPs and requiring Chrysler to set up an ESOP as part of the Chrysler bailout. The Chrysler employees eventually sold their stock and shut down the ESOP after a significant increase in the value of the stock.

In 1981, federal law was amended to allow a corporation to make tax-deductible contributions to a leveraged ESOP of up to 25 percent of payroll. This made it clear that when an ESOP borrowed money to buy stock, the company could deduct whatever the interest payment came to plus up to 25 percent of payroll to repay the principal on the loan. The general rule was, and still is, that companies may not contribute more than 15 percent of payroll to these types of benefit funds. If the ESOP is not leveraged, the 15 percent limit generally applies. This new law meant, in cases where companies were for sale, that an ESOP could now make a reasonable bid against the corporate raiders bent on buying and dismantling the company.

Also in 1981, the "put option" was changed. Federal law allowed employees, when it came time for them to receive their stock, to "put it to the company," meaning force the company to buy it at a fair market price if the stock of the company was not freely traded on a stock exchange. The employee had the option of taking the stock or demanding cash. The 1981 changes allowed a company to force the employee to sell the stock back to the company and take cash if the corporate charter or bylaws restricted ownership in the company to employees and employee trusts. This would make it easier for an ESOP to be used to simulate a cooperative.

There was one problem. Many owners of small- to medium-sized businesses found that selling out to a large corporation had a major tax advantage. If they traded their stock in the small business for stock of a large corporation, the Internal Revenue Service did not view this as a "tax event." This meant that they did not pay any income tax on the deal until they subsequently sold the stock of the large corporation, which they could do over a period of years as they needed retirement income. Obviously, the same thing could not happen if they sold their stock to an ESOP.

To remedy this disparity, Congress, in 1984, created what has come to be called the *1042 rollover* (covered in Section 1042 of the IRS Code). This new law allowed someone selling stock to an ESOP to roll over the proceeds by purchasing stocks and bonds and not pay any income taxes until those new securities were sold. The law required the new securities to be issued by U.S. corporations. Also the provision was not available unless the ESOP owned at least 30 percent of the company's stock after the sale. The law also allowed people selling stock to a cooperative to receive the same benefit, providing the same limitations were met. If the deductibility of principal payments was the first major advantage of ESOPs, and the ability to deduct up to 25 percent of payroll the second, this rollover provision was the third.

The 1984 law also allowed a corporation to deduct dividends paid on stock held by an ESOP if the money was passed through to the employees. This became the fourth major advantage for ESOPs, the ability to deduct dividend payments. Also, the 1984 law allowed banks, insurance companies, and other commercial lenders to exclude 50 percent of the interest income they made on ESOP loans if the money was used by the ESOP to buy company stock. This is called the *133 interest income exclusion* (covered in Section 133 of the IRS Code). Much of the benefit from this tax break is passed on to the ESOP, providing the fifth major advantage for ESOPs, that they can borrow money at a lower interest rate (provided the requirements of Section 133 are met).

In 1986, the law was amended again to allow for the deduction of dividends paid on stock held by an ESOP if the dividends were used to pay off the ESOP loan. Later amendments made it clear that only dividends paid on the stock purchased with the loan proceeds could be used in this way. Also, in that year, Congress added "mutual funds" to the list of entities that could lend money to ESOPs and receive the 50 percent interest income exclusion. The 1986 law also imposed a 10 percent penalty tax on money taken out of pension or benefit funds before retirement (unless they are rolled over into an Individual Retirement Account) but exempted dividend payments made on ESOP stock and passed through to the employees or used to pay off the ESOP loan.

The 1986 law also required ESOPs to offer employees the option of diversifying some of the value of their ESOP account when they reach age 55 (and have been in the ESOP for 10 years). At that point, the employee can ask that 25 percent of the value of his or her ESOP account be used to purchase a diversified portfolio of stocks and other securities. At age 60 (after 15 years of participation in the ESOP), the employee can ask that the account be invested 50 percent in diversified securities. This diversification requirement applies only to shares purchased by the ESOP after 1986. The 1986 law also required that stock of companies not publicly traded be evaluated once a year by an independent appraiser.

In 1989, Congress limited the Section 133 interest income exclusion to situations in which the ESOP owned more than 50 percent of the

company's common stock. Also, to receive the exclusion, the employees would have to be allowed to vote the stock purchased with the
loan proceeds, just like any other stockholder, and the loan could not
be for more than 15 years. This change came about because Congress
felt that too many large, public companies were taking advantage of
this interest rate break to place an insignificant amount of stock into
an ESOP. Also, in 1989, Congress decreed that people selling stock
to an ESOP and enjoying the rollover benefit had to have owned their
stock for at least 3 years prior to selling it to the ESOP. In 1989,
Congress also limited total contributions made in the name of any one
employee to ESOPs and other benefit plans to $30,000 a year. Previ-
ous law had allowed ESOPs to contribute more than this limit. This
mainly decreased the attractiveness of ESOPs for highly paid employees who would have been eligible to receive more than $30,000 a year
in stock under the previous law.

As of 1992, the five major advantages of ESOPs over other employee benefit plans or other methods of sharing ownership with
employees are: (1) the company may borrow money using an ESOP
and deduct the principal payments on the loan along with the interest
payments; (2) the company can contribute up to 25 percent of payroll
to a leveraged ESOP, or a combination of a leveraged ESOP and other
benefit plans (such as a profit-sharing plan), subject to limits such as
the current $30,000-per-employee limit imposed by the law; (3) peo-
ple who sell their shares to an ESOP and roll over the proceeds into
other securities do not pay any income taxes until those "rollover
securities" are sold, provided a number of restrictions are met and the
ESOP (or co-op) ends up owning at least 30 percent of the company's
stock after the sale; (4) dividends passed through to employee stockholders or used to pay off an ESOP loan are deductible to the corporation; and (5) interest charged on an ESOP loan is lower providing the
lender is qualified to receive the interest income exclusion, the employee stockholders have full voting rights concerning those shares,
and the ESOP ends up owning at least 50 percent of the company's
stock once the loan is made and the stock is purchased with that loan
(with a loan term of not more than 15 years). Lenders qualified to
receive this benefit include banks, insurance companies, mutual funds,
finance companies, and other corporations that usually engage in the

business of lending money. ESOPs can issue bonds that qualify for this interest exclusion as long as they are owned by the proper type of company. The fact that the bonds might have been owned at one time by someone who was not qualified to receive the interest income exclusion does not keep the exclusion from applying once the bonds are owned by the proper party.

The Major Uses of ESOPs

While we will discuss the many uses of ESOPs in detail in the next two chapters, it is important to realize early on the major things ESOPs have been used for in the United States during the 1980s and 1990s. The major use is to buy out owners of small- to medium-sized businesses who wish to retire. These owners often find it difficult to find a buyer willing to pay what they believe is a fair price. If these owners sell out to an ESOP (or a co-op), they receive the rollover benefit, meaning they can use the money to buy stocks and bonds and delay paying income tax until those replacement securities are sold. If the ESOP ends up owning at least 50 percent of the company's stock, the interest payment on the loan is less. The company can also deduct both principal and interest payments, making it easier to pay off the loan and making a bank more willing to make the loan in the first place. Once the ESOP owns 30 percent of the stock of a private company, stockholders who might have had a hard time finding a buyer for their stock can sell to the ESOP and receive the rollover benefit.

Of course, an ESOP can simply be an additional employee benefit, one that gives the employees a greater stake in the success of the company they work for. It may also provide a partial defense against unfriendly takeovers by placing stock in the usually friendly hands of the employees. ESOPs can also be used as part of a leveraged buyout, providing a lower interest rate on the loan, a greater incentive to the employees to make the new company a success, and a higher probability that the loan will be repaid (given the lower interest rate and the deductibility of principal payments). Similarly, a large corporation can spin off a division and finance the sale by using an ESOP. The new company has debt, but this should be easier to repay because of the ESOP advantages. In some cases, an ESOP has been used to save a failing company, with employees trading current wages for stock in an ESOP that will be worth a significant amount of money if the company can be saved.

Louis Kelso believed ESOPs would be used primarily to finance new corporate growth. This is almost never the only reason an ESOP is created. When companies wish to expand, their two basic choices are to issue more shares or take on more debt. If the company issues more shares, this dilutes the ownership interest of the current stockholders, something they are not happy about. If the company takes on more debt, more money has to be spent on interest payments, which leaves less for dividends or other uses. Again, the stockholders are not happy. If a leveraged ESOP is used to borrow money for expansion, both of these things happen—more shares are issued (to the employees through the ESOP), further diluting the current stockholders ownership interest; and additional debt is taken on, requiring more money for interest payments. For most companies, this is simply the worst of both worlds.

Once a company already has an ESOP, perhaps created to buy out the shares of a major shareholder who wished to retire from the business, using additional ESOP loans can be a very attractive way to finance corporate growth. Suppose the ESOP owns 60 percent of the company's stock. Suppose a million dollars is needed to finance growth, and this requires issuing new stock worth 10 percent of the current value of the company's stock. The majority stockholders, the employees, are not going to object to this dilution of stockholder interest because they will ultimately receive those shares. The company can borrow money at a lower interest rate, and deduct both principal and interest (as well as using deductible dividends to help repay the loan), making the debt much easier to pay back than would otherwise be the case. In other words, using additional ESOP loans to expand the corporation is a temptation that most companies with an existing ESOP will not, and should not, resist.

In 1989, George Updike, the majority owner of the trucking company Speedy Inc., wanted to sell most of his stock to his employees and also raise money for expansion. An ESOP loan was used to buy majority control of the company from Mr. Updike ($650,000), to refinance $385,000 of existing debt, to obtain a $915,000 mortgage, and to finance a $1.25 million expansion of facilities. By doing all of this at once through an ESOP loan, the company received a lower interest rate and all of the other advantages of an ESOP loan. They also made their loyal employees, who had stayed with the company through thick and thin, owners with an even greater incentive to help the company grow in the years ahead.

The biggest advantage of ESOPs, when compared with other forms of employee ownership, is their ability to place a large block of stock in the hands of employees quickly. This has already happened in many American companies. As of 1992, employees in the United States, through ESOPs, owned a majority of the stock in two of the largest hospital management companies, two of the largest shipbuilding companies, two of the largest construction companies, and three of the largest steel companies. It is doubtful that any other mechanism would have allowed employees to increase their ownership stake in large companies so quickly.

Leveraged Buyouts and Corporate Restructuring with ESOPs

To make it easier to see why someone would want to use an ESOP as part of a leveraged buyout (LBO), let's imagine a world in which both banks and corporations pay an income tax rate of 50 percent. Let's suppose a group wants to buy a large block of stock, $7 million worth of which will be paid for with a loan. Let's also assume for illustration that the bank wants to end up with 6 percent interest income after taxes on the loan are paid. If the bank must pay 50 percent in taxes, then the interest rate to the company without an ESOP will be 12 percent. If the company has an ESOP, half of the interest income is tax deductible, therefore the interest rate charged by the bank is 8 percent (4 percent plus half of 4 percent equals a 6 percent return).

Let's assume a seven-year loan. Exhibit 12.1 shows what this loan will look like over the seven-year life of the loan assuming an equal payment of principal each year. The total interest payment is

Exhibit 12.1 Repayment of $7 Million Loan by Company without ESOP

Year	Principal	Interest	Taxes	Pretax Earnings Needed
1	$1,000	$ 840	$1,000	$ 2,840
2	1,000	720	1,000	2,720
3	1,000	600	1,000	2,600
4	1,000	480	1,000	2,480
5	1,000	360	1,000	2,360
6	1,000	240	1,000	2,240
7	1,000	120	1,000	2,120
Totals	$7,000	$3,360	$7,000	$17,360

Note: Assume a corporate and bank income tax rate of 50 percent, an interest rate of 12 percent, and a loan term of seven years. (All figures are in thousands of dollars.)

Exhibit 12.2 Repayment of $7 Million Loan by Company with ESOP

Year	Principal	Interest	Taxes	Pretax Earnings Needed
1	$1,000	$ 560	$0	$1,560
2	1,000	480	0	1,480
3	1,000	400	0	1,400
4	1,000	320	0	1,320
5	1,000	240	0	1,240
6	1,000	160	0	1,160
7	1,000	80	0	1,080
Totals	$7,000	$2,240	$0	$9,240

Note: Assume that both principal and interest are tax deductible, the interest rate is 8 percent, and the loan term is seven years. (All figures are in thousands of dollars.)

$3,360,000. Because the money used to pay off the principal is not tax deductible (assuming a 50 percent tax rate), the corporation has to earn two dollars for every dollar used to pay off the principal of the loan. Over the course of the seven years, the pretax earnings needed to pay principal, interest, and income taxes comes to $17,360,000.

Let's suppose an ESOP that can both deduct principal and qualify for a lower interest rate is used to borrow the money, as illustrated in Exhibit 12.2. Because both principal and interest are tax deductible, and the interest rate is lower, the company has to earn only $9,240,000

Exhibit 12.3   Repayment of $7 Million Loan by Company with ESOP and Deductible Dividends

Year	Principal	Dividend	Interest	Taxes	Pretax Earnings Needed
1	$1,000	$ 700	$ 560	$0	$2,260
2	1,000	700	424	0	2,124
3	1,000	700	288	0	1,988
4	1,000	700	152	0	1,852
5	200	0	16	0	216
6	0	0	0	0	0
7	0	0	0	0	0
Totals	$4,200	$2,800	$1,440	$0	$8,440

Note: Assume that both principal and interest are tax deductible; the interest rate is 8 percent; a 10 percent dividend is paid every year on stock, further reducing interest payments; and the loan term is seven years. (All figures are in thousands of dollars.)

in pretax income over the life of the loan in order to make the payments. Because of the lower interest rate, only $2,240,000 is paid out in interest, saving $1,120,000 in interest costs. If a 10 percent dividend is paid every year on the stock and that money is used to help pay off the loan, the loan can be paid off faster with an even lower total interest expense. Exhibit 12.3 illustrates this possibility. Only $8,440,000 in pretax earnings are needed to pay off this $7 million loan. Only $1,440,000 is paid in interest, for an interest saving of $1,920,000. In other words, by using an ESOP the company has saved almost $2 million in interest and has been able to service the loan with much lower pretax earnings.

Having explored the general principle, let's examine a possible real-world LBO. Exhibit 12.4 shows what the numbers might look like if a group of outside investors were considering buying a company with leverage. The company has 10 million shares outstanding. We are assuming that if these shares were freely traded they would sell for $40 a share. A minority interest would sell for 50 percent less than that, or $20 a share, while a controlling interest would sell for 50 percent more, or $60 a share—not an unreasonable assumption.

If the ESOP buys 60 percent of the shares and pays the control premium price of $60 a share, the ESOP's shares will cost $360 million ($60 times 6 million shares). The outside investors pay the minority

Exhibit 12.4 ESOP versus Non-ESOP Leveraged Buyout

Assumptions:
10 million total shares.
$440 million price tag.
10-year loan at 8% (ESOP loan) or 12% (non-ESOP loan).

With ESOP and ESOP Loan

ESOP Buys	**Investors Buy**
60% of stock for $360 million	40% of stock for $80 million

First Year of Loan

Principal	**Interest**	**Taxes**	**Pretax Earnings Needed**
$36 million	$28.8 million	0	$64.8 million

Without ESOP and ESOP Loan

Investors Buy	**Bank Lends**
100% of stock for $200 million	$240 million

First Year of Loan

Principal	**Interest**	**Taxes**	**Pretax Earnings Needed**
$24 million	$28.8 million	$16 million	$68.8 million

interest price of $20 a share, or $80 million for 40 percent of the shares ($20 times 4 million shares). We are also assuming the total price of the company is $440 million and that it has current profits (pretax earnings) of $60 million (seven times pretax earnings is a fair price for many companies).

If we assume a 10-year loan and an 8 percent interest rate on the ESOP loan, the first year's principal payment would be $36 million, the first year's interest payment would be $28.8 million, and the total pretax earnings necessary to service the loan would be $64.8 million. Because the company can deduct both principal and interest, there are no income taxes this first year. The company has to come up with $4.8 million more in pretax earnings, which it accomplishes by firing 240 employees (assuming an average employee made $20,000 per year). However, with the ESOP, after the loan was paid off, the remaining employees would own 60 percent of the company and would have stock worth in excess of $360 million.

What if they had done this LBO without an ESOP? As Exhibit 12.4 illustrates, the investors would have had to come up with a lot more cash. Because the principal payments would not be tax deductible, the bank would lend only $240 million (not $360 million). The investors had to come up with $200 million cash instead of $80 million. The higher interest rate (assume 12 percent instead of 8 percent) means the interest cost is the same, $28.8 million, the first year of the loan. Assuming the corporation is in the 40 percent income tax bracket, it had to earn $40 million in pretax profit to make a principal payment of $24 million, with $16 million of that going for income taxes. The company had to increase earnings the first year to $68.8 million, which meant laying off another 200 employees.

Both the investors and the employees are much worse off than they would have been had an ESOP been participating in this LBO. With the ESOP, the investors have to put up only $80 million instead of $200 million (note that the investors end up paying the same $20 a share whether they use an ESOP or not). Most investors would prefer to spread their money around; in other words, investors would rather spend $80 million for 40 percent of a company than $200 million for 100 percent. The employees are much worse off. First, another 200 have lost their jobs. Second, the remaining employees end up with nothing at the end of the 10 years although they have had to work just as hard to keep this company out of bankruptcy as they would have with the ESOP loan.

Some people argue that it is not fair for the ESOP to pay $60 a share while the investors pay only $20 a share. The only answer to that is this example. Which is fairer to the employees? The employees have put up no cash, only their ability to provide a larger loan with a lower interest rate. The investors have put up cash. In the real world, cash is always difficult to come by and always commands a high price.

One of the factors that enabled some investors to realize high returns during the 1980s was the fact that corporate raiders were willing to pay a control premium for the shares they purchased. If there is no corporate raider, a company can manufacture such a raider by using an ESOP. That is exactly what the Parsons Corporation did. The ESOP had been instituted to help buy the stock of founder, Ralph Parsons. The company also went public. Eventually the ESOP was able to make a $32-a-share tender offer (much higher than the current market price) and purchase stock to make the ESOP the owner of some 93 percent of the company stock. A total of $557 million had to be financed to complete the deal. The selling stockholders received significantly more for their shares than they would have realized on the open market, and the 7,000 employees became owners of the company. Because the special requirements of Section 133 were met, the ESOP paid a lower interest rate than would otherwise have been the case and, because the company "went private," it no longer had the expense of fulfilling the reporting obligations a public company must fulfill.

In the early 1980s, National Intergroup of Pittsburgh decided it could no longer make a profit with its Weirton steel plant and that it made no sense economically to invest the large sums needed to modernize the facility. In 1983, the employees used an ESOP to buy the company from National. National avoided substantial shutdown costs, and the employees agreed to reduce their pay by 20 percent. The company began making a profit and was the only American steel company to consistently post quarterly earnings during the mid-1980s. It also paid significant cash profit-sharing bonuses to the employees. In 1989, the 8,000 employees decided to begin a $740 million capital improvement program and to have the shares listed on the New York Stock Exchange.

The 1042 Rollover

Because the most significant use of ESOPs is to buy shares from retiring owners, the rollover provision has encouraged a substantial number of U.S. companies to establish ESOPs. Section 1042 of the Internal Revenue Code spells out the rules that must be followed.

First of all, the stock being sold to the ESOP must be in a private company, not stock in a company whose shares are readily traded on a stock exchange. The seller must have owned the shares for at least three years before the sale to the ESOP, and the ESOP must own at least 30 percent of the company's shares after the sale is complete. The seller must purchase the replacement securities during a period that begins three months before the sale to the ESOP and ends 12 months after the sale to the ESOP. The ESOP must own the stock for at least three years or pay a penalty tax if the stock is sold. An officer of the corporation must sign a statement that the corporation is aware of this three-year holding period, and this "statement of consent" must be filed by the selling shareholder with his or her income tax return.

The selling shareholder must also file with the IRS a statement of intention to elect rollover treatment and another statement listing which securities have been purchased with the money received from the ESOP. The selling shareholder must not have received the stock being sold to the ESOP as compensation or as a distribution from another qualified benefit plan.

To receive the rollover tax treatment, the seller may only purchase "qualified replacement securities." These must be securities (stocks, bonds, rights, debentures, notes) of U.S. domestic (incorporated in the United States and not controlled by a foreign company) operating corporations. An "operating corporation" uses more than 50 percent of its assets in the active conduct of a trade or business, and receives not more than 25 percent of its gross receipts from passive investments. Mutual funds and Real Estate Investment Trusts (REITs) do not qualify. An exception is made to the "passive investments" rule to allow sellers to invest in financial institutions such as banks. While some companies obviously do not qualify, the vast majority of U.S. corporations do. Also, the seller may use the money to buy an interest in a privately held American corporation. This means part of the proceeds of the sale can be used to invest in another small company with growth potential (or to put more capital into a spouse's struggling small business).

Once the rollover is completed, the basis (for tax purposes) of the rollover securities is the amount of money originally invested to purchase the original stock. In other words, if someone took $10,000 to start a company and 20 years later sold the company to an ESOP for $1 million, and rolled over the proceeds into replacement securities, the basis of those replacement securities is $10,000. Any money made from selling those replacement securities is considered a capital gain.

Also, once the replacement securities are purchased, there is no limit on how they may be used. They may be put up as collateral for a loan, sold, given away, or left to the heirs in a will. If left to the heirs, estate taxes will be due, but the securities will receive a step-up in basis to their value at the time they are inherited. The heirs will pay capital gains taxes only on the increase in value they enjoy after they inherit the securities.

This 1042 rollover provision puts the selling shareholder of a private company in a much better position than would be the case if the shareholder were selling to a large corporation and doing a stock trade. With a stock trade, the selling shareholder has all his eggs in one basket. While the basket is bigger and less likely to go under, that is still a possibility. With the 1042 rollover, the selling shareholder can buy stocks and bonds from dozens of different companies. If the selling shareholder takes advantage of the 1042 rollover, the shareholder's family members (and those owning a large amount of the company's stock) will probably not be able to participate in the ESOP. An exception is made for lineal descendants, but as a group they may not receive more than 5 percent of the stock that the retiring owner sells to the ESOP. This provision keeps sellers from setting up an ESOP for their employees, all of whom happen to be their children, in order to receive the tax break. As a general rule, this cannot happen. However, a family of people unrelated to the seller can, of course, work for the company and participate in the ESOP. It has been suggested that the "family farm" of the future will be a corporation with an ESOP in which the employee-family members participate.

The rollover money cannot be used to buy government securities or municipal bonds. It can be used to buy bonds with floating interest rates that some financial corporations have created to provide selling shareholders who take advantage of the 1042 rollover with a long-term security that will pay the going interest rate over a long period of time.

These rollover advantages also apply if the shareholder sells to a cooperative. Because of the availability of the 1042 rollover, anyone selling a business should consider selling to an ESOP or a co-op.

Another possibility is to use an ESOP in conjunction with a charitable remainder trust. Let's suppose the retiring owner would like to give controlling interest of his $2 million business to his son and sell the rest of his interest for cash to have money to retire on. In the real world, no one would buy this minority interest in this small business because no one wants to be a silent partner for the son. However, an ESOP would be willing to be just that.

Now suppose the retiring owner feels that much of his success was due to the education he received at AAA University. He can give the son 60 percent of the shares ($1,200,000 worth should be exempt from gift taxes if the retiring owner and his wife both make the gift). He sells 40 percent to the ESOP, and rolls over the proceeds into stocks and bonds worth $800,000 (because of the requirement that the company must repurchase shares from its employees, the ESOP is willing to pay a fair price for the shares without the minority discount, whereas an outside investor would have been unwilling to pay this price because of the anticipated difficulty in selling the shares). The retiring owner then puts those stocks and bonds in what is called a charitable remainder trust. This trust pays the owner an income as long as he lives. When he dies, the stocks and bonds are given to AAA University without any inheritance taxes because they are a gift to a charity. The retiring owner used some of the income from the trust to pay life insurance premiums so that, upon his death, the son received $1 million in life insurance tax free. The son ends up with controlling interest in the family business plus $1 million cash from the life insurance; the employees end up with a benefit plan where there had been none before; AAA University ends up with stocks and bonds worth $800,000; and the retiring owner ends up with a retirement income from the trust that is much larger than would have been the case if he had been forced to pay capital gains taxes when he sold his stock.

The Repurchase Requirement

When it comes time for employees enrolled in an ESOP to receive their stock, they have the option of demanding cash instead, unless the stock is readily traded on a stock exchange. If there is no ready market for the stock, most employees should take advantage of this "put option" and take the cash. Under the law, employees receiving stock in a private company may put the stock to the company within

60 days after receiving the stock, and again during a similar 60-day period one year later. Some people call this a "repurchase liability," but this is a misnomer. As we discussed in Part One, repurchasing stock is often an excellent strategy, particularly if many of the shareholders plan to hold their stock until retirement. They receive the benefit of ever-increasing stock values and do not pay any income taxes on that increasing wealth until they retire and sell the shares.

To see how this works, suppose a company has one million shares currently valued at $10 a share. Also suppose that more than 50 percent of this stock is owned by the ESOP. During one year a large number of employees retire and the company buys back $1 million worth of stock. Is this a good deal for the other shareholders? Their stock, formerly worth $10 a share, is now worth over $11 a share. The shareholders' net worth has gone up without paying taxes, and they will receive that much more for their shares when they sell or (if they are employees in the ESOP) when they retire or leave the company. In many situations, this is the best use that could be made of company profits or, if necessary, of borrowed money.

Basic ESOP Rules

Once an ESOP is set up, it operates like any other employee benefit plan. It is subject to the regulations of the Internal Revenue Service and the U.S. Department of Labor. There are also special rules that only apply to ESOPs.

Contributions

Generally, only 15 percent of payroll may be contributed to employee benefit plans such as ESOPs. If the company has a leveraged ESOP (or in a few other limited situations), this limit is raised to 25 percent. Also, no one employee can have more than $30,000 placed in these kinds of plans in any one year. If the contribution is based on pay, only the first approximately $220,000 of pay may be taken into account. This salary limit increases each year with inflation.

A company with a leveraged ESOP can contribute even more than

25 percent of payroll when dividends are taken into account. This means that an ESOP account can potentially grow faster than any other type of employee benefit fund, assuming the stock is stable or going up in value. While in most cases contributions to individual employee accounts are a percentage of salary, it does not have to work that way. The company could contribute the same amount for each employee or base the contribution on some other criterion, such as number of hours worked in the year or number of years with the company.

Disclosure

The Employee Retirement Income Security Act (ERISA) requires companies to provide their employees with information about the company's employee benefit plans and the effect of such plans on the employee's financial status. Employees (or anyone receiving benefits from an ESOP) must be given a summary of the plan and a summary of the annual report (which is filed with the federal government). Employees must also be given an annual statement showing their personal account balances. Employees also most be given access to the full plan, and any other documents, contracts, or agreements that relate to the plan.

Participation

As a general rule, employers must allow employees to participate in the ESOP when they are over the age of 21, have been with the company full-time for more than one year, and continue to work at least 1,000 hours a year for the company. There are, of course, exceptions. For instance, employees covered by a collective bargaining agreement may be excluded because these employees are probably already covered by some kind of pension or benefit plan. Of course, the company and the union are free to renegotiate the contract to include these workers in the ESOP. Many managers have gotten into trouble for saying that anyone belonging to a union cannot be part of the ESOP. This is not true, and to discriminate against union members would be a violation of federal labor laws.

Vesting

Employees vest in an ESOP the same way they vest in any other defined-contribution benefit plan. Federal law allows a company to begin vesting in the third year, in which case employees would vest 20 percent a year and be fully vested in the seventh year. Alternatively, the company can cliff vest, meaning employees are not vested at all until the end of the fifth year, when they become 100 percent vested. Companies may vest faster than this. For example, many companies vest 20 percent a year, beginning in the first year, which leads to full vesting after five years.

Voting

When employees own stock through most pension and benefit plans, they cannot vote the shares in their account. Voting is done for them by the plan trustee. In the case of an ESOP, employees must be allowed to vote the shares in their account on major decisions, such as whether to merge with another company or whether to sell most of the corporate assets. If the shares of the company are publicly traded, then the employees vote their shares just like any other shareholder on all shareholder issues, such as deciding who will sit on the board of directors.

If the company is a private company, the employees do not have to be given the right to vote for the members of the board of directors (except for shares purchased with a low-interest Section 133 loan). Generally, the trustee votes the shares that have not yet been allocated to individual accounts, but the ESOP can require that the trustee vote those shares in proportion to the way the employees vote the shares in their individual accounts. In this way, employees can be given the power to vote a large block of stock even though the loan has not yet been paid off.

Distribution

In most employee benefit plans, employees receive their money when they retire, die, or become disabled. Currently, ESOPs are also required to provide the employees with the stock in their account no later than the close of the sixth calendar year following the year they leave the company (this special rule applies only to stock acquired by the ESOP after 1986). Companies have the option of paying the money out over five years, with interest.

Retirees can choose to delay their distribution, but generally they must begin receiving benefits when they reach age 70½. Under current law, employees receiving their stock or cash prior to the age of 59½ must either pay a penalty tax on the money or roll it over into an Individual Retirement Account. Employees can usually take their stock. If the stock is not generally traded on a stock exchange, the employee has the option of forcing the company to buy back the stock.

If the company charter or bylaws require that substantially all of the company stock be owned by employees or employee benefit plans, then the company can force the employee to take cash, not stock. In most cases, the ESOP can delay paying out shares until any loan on those shares has been paid off. If the employee takes stock and chooses to pay income tax rather than roll it over, he or she pays income tax only on the original cost of the stock. When the stock is subsequently sold, the employee pays capital gains taxes on any increase in value that has been realized since the stock was originally purchased by the ESOP.

Diversification

Participants who attain the age of 55 and who have participated in the ESOP for at least 10 years may require that 25 percent of their ESOP account be diversified into other investments instead of the stock of their employer. This chance to diversify must be offered to them in each of the succeeding five years. At the end of the fifth year, such participants (now 60 years old) must be allowed to diversify up to 50 percent of their account into investments other than the stock of the employer. This requirement does not apply to ESOPs that only own stock purchased prior to 1987.

Dividend Deduction

When a dividend is paid on shares held by an ESOP, that dividend payment can be deducted from current income by the corporation to the extent that the dividend payment is passed through to the employees or is used to pay off the loan currently owing on those particular shares. The deductible dividend may not be used to pay off a loan owing on other shares owned by the ESOP. Also, the dividend payment must be reasonable in the eyes of the Internal Revenue Service. These dividend payments passed through to employees are not subject to Social Security taxes.

Creating an ESOP

To see how these decisions are made, let's look at one company that set up an ESOP. This company began in 1958 as a nonprofit drug treatment program called Synanon. During the early years, Synanon was financed by contributions. By the mid-1960s, it had grown to a community in southern California of more than 500 people. To raise money, Synanon began AdGap (Advertising Gifts and Premiums Department). AdGap sold advertising specialties such as pencils with a company's name, address, and phone number printed on them. By the mid-1980s, AdGap employed over 100 people, had sales revenue of over $25 million, and had offices in five states. At that point, there was a dispute with the Internal Revenue Service over whether AdGap was part of a charity or was a business subject to normal taxes.

In 1988, it was decided to turn AdGap into a profit-making company. This was done by taking out a loan, making the necessary payments to the state attorney general, and paying Synanon the value of the AdGap division. In the United States, when most nonprofit corporations are turned into profit-making companies, a small group of executives end up owning the company when the "privatization" is complete. The executives of the new AdGap Group were determined to share ownership with all the employees through an ESOP.

A committee of employees was set up to make the many decisions necessary when an ESOP is established. This committee held meetings with the employees to solicit their opinions and, on December 7, 1990, the committee's recommendations were adopted by the board of directors without amendment. What did the employees decide?

Participation

The employees decided that employees should begin to participate in the ESOP after completion of their 90-day probationary period. The older employees wanted new employees to begin to think like owners as quickly as possible.

Allocation

Should the past service of AdGap employees be recognized? Some employees believed that this was a new company and everyone should begin on an equal basis. Other employees felt that the years they spent building up the company, years when they were paid very little for their efforts, should be recognized. It was decided that the first allocation of stock should be based half on years of past service, and half on pay. This would bring long-time low-paid and recent high-paid employees closer to the mean. Future allocations would be based 90 percent on pay and 10 percent on length of service.

Vesting

Some felt that employees should vest quickly while others believed a slow vesting schedule would encourage employees to stay with the company. They decided on a common compromise: employees would vest 20 percent at the end of the first year, and 20 percent each year thereafter. People would only begin to vest in 1990, when the new company was formed; service prior to that would not count for vesting purposes.

Voting Rights

It was assumed that all shareholder issues, such as who would sit on the board of directors, would be passed through for a vote of the employees. The only question was how to weigh that vote. Some argued that the ESOP should operate on the one-person, one-vote principle allowed by law. This would make every employee feel like an equal partner in the company. Others felt that people with more stock should have more of a vote, just like in a real corporation. The employees decided on the one-person, one-vote formula.

Contributions

The employees had to decide how quickly the shares of the company should be placed in individual employee accounts. This is usually controlled by the ESOP loan. As the loan is paid off, a proportional number of shares are distributed to the employees. In the AdGap case, the loan used to buy the company from Synanon was not tied to the ESOP so the employees were free to set up their own schedule. The committee decided that 21 percent of the company stock should be contributed at the beginning of 1991, and 10 percent a year thereafter. This would allow employees to gain ownership over time based on their performance in the decade of the 1990s.

This AdGap example is particularly instructive to the thousands of companies in Eastern Europe that are considering using an ESOP as part of their privatization procedure. The employees in those companies will have to make the same decisions the AdGap employees made under similar circumstances.

The Annual Valuation

Federal law requires a company that has an ESOP and does not have stock freely traded on a stock exchange to have an annual valuation of the stock. This is an annual cost that must be considered when a private company sets up an ESOP. However, this requirement can also be an advantage. Executives in many smaller, privately held companies often have difficulty telling exactly how their company is doing from year to year. A large, public company has an annual report to the shareholders that the competition can read. There is also a published share price, which is the ultimate mark of performance. Smaller private companies do not have these guides to performance. With a proper valuation, everyone can know if share value has gone up. Also, a correctly done valuation offers guidance about what must be done to improve share value in the future. An analysis of the competition, which is part of a valuation report, provides another benchmark of performance.

One fear that executives of smaller, private companies have when considering an ESOP is that the employees would have access to the company financial records and could leak information to the competition. Because of the structure of an ESOP, only the ESOP trustee is a true shareholder and only the trustee has any claim to examine the books. With an objective, outside valuation each year, even the trustee will usually not need to examine the books. "But," people ask, "won't the employees feel cheated if they can't examine the books?" No, not in most cases. When someone owns shares in any company, they may have a right to examine the books but almost never exercise that right. Employees don't care about the specifics any more than do average shareholders in any company. Employees want to know what every shareholder wants to know: What are my shares worth? The annual share valuation answers that question.

A properly done valuation will discuss the price paid for similar companies, if any have been sold recently; the value of the company's hard assets; and the projected value of the company's shares based on the earnings times an appropriate price/earnings ratio (see Chapter 5). The valuation will consider the fact that a minority interest in a private company is not valued as highly by the marketplace as the shares of a public company that can be sold easily. Also, the valuation will take into account the value of a controlling interest in the company, which applies whether a company is public or private. If the ESOP owns more than 50 percent of the shares (or is buying more than 50 percent of the shares), the share value will be based on that control premium.

There is also the question of company debt. Because the company has guaranteed the payment of the ESOP loan, that loan must be carried as debt on the company books, thereby reducing the value of the shares. This is not so hard to understand. When someone buys a house for $100,000 and borrows $90,000 to make the purchase, their equity in the house after the purchase is $10,000, not $100,000. The same thing happens when an ESOP borrows money to buy stock. The

Why Shares in Closely Held Companies Are Valued Less Than Shares in Comparable Public Companies

Valuation experts believe that shares of companies for which no public market exists are worth less than shares of comparable public companies. Why should this difference exist? Publicly-traded stock can be quickly sold through a broker and cash received in five business days. Selling shares that are not traded on a recognized market, such as the New York and American Stock Exchanges or on NASDAQ, can be a lengthy and expensive process. For this reason, investors are not willing to pay as much for these shares. Studies using actual transactions in restricted stock and other studies that compare the price of stock before and after an initial public offering have measured this discount. The average discount has been in the range of 35 to 50 percent.

A number of factors affect the level of the discount and may lead to a discount much higher or lower than this average range. One in particular has great importance to employee-owned companies: a put option that allows the employee-stockholder to sell shares to the company. Put options are required for ESOP plans if the stock is not publicly traded and are usually part of other plans. The discount for these shares is much less, usually in the range of 5 to 20 percent, and in some cases a discount of zero can be justified, depending on the company's financial strength, its funding plan, and its track record of redeeming shares.

Should the valuation expert make any other special consideration in the appraisal of privately-held companies, such as applying a P/E ratio that is lower than those of the comparable public companies? No, but the appraiser must take into consideration the company's size, diversification, management depth, and access to capital, all of which may lower the value of the privately-held company.

In conclusion, a discount to the value of stock of privately-held companies is a real phenomenon, and its level has been measured in numerous empirical studies. The appraiser must consider the individual circumstances in each case to determine the appropriate discount.

George Moosburner
Howard, Lawson & Co.
Philadelphia, Pennsylvania

price paid for the stock is based on a company that is without this debt. After the ESOP purchase, the shares are "worth" only what the company is worth given the new debt.

Just as equity in a house grows as the loan is paid off, the value of the ESOP's shares increases over time as the ESOP debt is paid down. This ability to use leverage is a major advantage of ESOPs and this has to be kept in mind by everyone involved. After all, in most cases, the employees did not even put up what in the house-buying situation would be called a "down payment." They have paid nothing for the stock; and if the shares are worth anything after the transaction, it is usually a good deal for the employees.

The ESOP Trustee

Some people think that because the trustee actually "owns" the shares, the employees covered by an ESOP don't really feel like owners. But, it can be pointed out, in many situations the employees vote the shares in their account just like any other shareholder. That being the case, it could be argued that they have the best of two worlds.

Most owners of stock in large corporations receive a proxy statement and an annual report once a year. They either vote for the slate of candidates recommended by management for the board of directors or they don't vote. Generally they do not attend the annual meeting nor do they have a representative in attendance. Because of this, many people have decided to place their money in mutual funds and let the mutual fund trustees vote their shares and even buy and sell shares as they see fit.

Employees with stock in an ESOP have the right to vote on major issues and, in some cases, even for the board of directors. This is more voting rights than they have when they own stock through any other pension or benefit plan or through a mutual fund. In a normal pension or benefit plan, the trustees buy and sell stock and vote the shares without ever consulting the employees who are the beneficial owners of those shares. With an ESOP, the employees also have the benefit of a trustee who is bound to provide them with unbiased information, information that may be at odds with the information provided by the company's managers. The employees also have a representative at the annual meeting who is bound by law to look out only for their best financial interests.

Of course, the proper role of the ESOP trustee must be explained to the employees, along with the employees' role in voting their shares and receiving information from the trustee. If this process is properly explained, everyone should feel confident that their interests are being looked out for and that they are better off than they would be without the ESOP trustee.

While it was feared that ESOPs would be difficult to establish in countries without any kind of trust law, that has proved not to be the case. In Egypt, for example, a nonprofit corporation called an Employee Stockholder Association can be established to own the shares and perform the functions performed in the United States by the ESOP trustee. The association is formed for the benefit of the employees, and the employees vote the shares in their individual accounts just as is done in the United States. Similar nonprofit corporations are being formed in the countries of the former Soviet Union and in Eastern Europe to perform the same function.

Accounting for ESOPs

As we saw in Part One, accountants are concerned with three major documents: the balance sheet, the income statement, and the cash flow statement. The balance sheet shows the assets of the company balanced against the liabilities of the company. Whether the ESOP borrows money guaranteed by the company or the company borrows money and then lends it to the ESOP, the ESOP debt must be shown on the company balance sheet as a liability. That is the whole point of an ESOP loan, that the assets and credit worthiness of the company are being used by the ESOP to borrow money to buy stock in the company. While that debt may be a special kind of debt, the ESOP debt is still company debt. This is true even if the company does not guarantee the ESOP debt. The lender expects the company to make the necessary contributions to the ESOP to pay off the ESOP debt, regardless of the actual "on-paper" arrangements. Because other rules applied before June 1989, ESOP loans made before that date may not show up on the balance sheets of some companies.

The entry of the ESOP debt in the liability section of the balance sheet means that the equity section shows less equity for the shareholders than would otherwise be the case. The equity section will contain an "unearned compensation" entry (sometimes called an ESOP loan contra account). This negative entry in the equity account will shrink as the loan is paid off. In other words, as the ESOP loan is paid off, the debt section of the balance sheet will shrink, and the equity section will increase.

When payments are made to the ESOP to pay off part of the debt, how should this show up on the income statement? Remember that the company makes one payment to pay off interest and another payment to pay down principal. The income statement shows an expense item for the payment of interest and another expense item, listed under compensation, for the payment of principal. This is a fairly simple process if an equal amount is paid on principal each year. If the loan amortizes like a home mortgage, with small principal payments in the early years and large principal payments in the later years, the compensation expense can be evened out over the life of the loan by following Labor Department regulations.

The cash flow statement simply shows that cash is going out to repay the ESOP loan, thereby providing a special benefit to the employees.

An accountant dealing with an ESOP in a financial report will be expected to explain in the footnotes how the ESOP affects both the debt of the company and the benefit payments to employees. The structure of the loan and the plan should also be discussed. While the obligation to repurchase shares is not a liability in the true accounting sense, the amount of money required to repurchase shares by the company over the last two years should be stated.

Remembering the ESOP's Purpose

In the next two chapters, we shall discuss in detail all the things a company can "do" with an ESOP. It is important to remember that the most important thing an ESOP does is provide employees with productive wealth they would not otherwise own. This productive wealth is different from the stocks, bonds, and real estate holdings that their pension or benefit plan owns in their name because, with an ESOP, employees have a real chance to increase the value of the stock in the company they work for. Congress, in creating and encouraging the use of ESOPs, believes that the dream of millions of immigrants to America can be realized. People can have a significant ownership stake in the company they work for, even if it is a giant corporation. Congress also believes that this ownership stake will make a difference in the way American workers think and act, and the American economy will benefit as a result. In the competition to provide quality goods and services to the world market, every country is trying to provide itself with an edge. America has placed the ESOP in the basket of tools American companies may use to meet that competition.

APPENDIX

Major Criticisms of American ESOPs

Despite the fact that employee stock ownership plans, or ESOPs, are the most common form and the most successful form of employee-ownership in the United States, only a small percentage of U.S. companies are employee-owned through an ESOP. As the president of the U.S. ESOP Association, and the former general counsel for over six years, I have firsthand knowledge of why the U.S. government has not done more to promote ESOPs and employee-ownership.

The decision makers in the U.S. government, either in the legislative branch or executive branch, who are effectively preventing the expansion of laws to promote ESOPs, rely on three basic arguments to counter the proponents of ESOPs.

These three anti-ESOP arguments are:

1. An ESOP is a bad retirement policy because ESOPs concentrate assets to be used for retirement income when a diversified set of assets is better.

This special contribution is by J. Michael Keeling, president of the ESOP Association, Washington, D.C.

2. ESOPs are a waste of taxpayers' money.

3. ESOPs are not real ownership by employees of corporations.

Taking each argument alone, the ESOP community and its many voices can counter each argument. For example, the centuries-old theory of diversifying investments is actually linked to an old English common law tradition that related to large amounts of wealth, not the usually small amount of assets found in a retirement plan of any type in the United States. Furthermore, ESOP advocates have clearly pointed to the large number of ESOPs providing more wealth at retirement to an employee than does a traditional diversified plan. (Please note that under U.S. law, an ESOP participant may diversify up to 50 percent of his or her account balance as the date of their retirement approaches.)

As to the idea of ESOPs being a waste of taxpayers' money, this criticism relates to a concept that may be unique to the United States. In the United States, each provision of tax law that is designed to encourage an activity is known as a "tax expenditure." In essence, the tax expenditure theory is that, except for the tax break, or incentive, encouraging the activity, the U.S. Treasury would have as revenue the foregone revenue saved by the taxpayer; or, another way of explaining the theory is to calculate the direct cost of the federal government's writing a check to the taxpayer to do the same thing. Therefore, ESOPs are a tax expenditure under U.S. tax policy analysis. The ESOP tax expenditure results in lower federal revenues of $1 to $2 billion per year. Since at best only 10 million Americans benefit from ESOPs, while there are approximately 150 to 170 million taxpayers in any one tax year, the critics charge, "Why should the 140 million taxpayers subsidize the 10 million? This is a waste of money!" (ESOP advocates counter that surely in a $5 trillion economy with a nearly $1.5 trillion federal budget, the U.S. government can afford to spend less than 0.1 percent to encourage employee-ownership.)

Of course, the final argument is very controversial, and goes to the heart of whether employee-ownership through ESOPs creates better and more productive corporations. Nearly everyone agrees that owners take better care of their assets and property than do nonowners. Nearly everyone agrees that owners will work harder than nonowners, all other factors being equal. Critics charge that ESOPs do not create real owners—employees cannot buy and sell the stock, as real owners do. They charge that owners control their property, whereas employee-owners do not exercise control over all decisions in an ESOP company. So the critics say that the argument is not about ownership, but about ESOPs and their failure to create "real" employee-ownership. ESOP advocates bristle at this charge, and claim that the definition of ownership is not a fixed definition. ESOP advocates point to the many ESOP companies where there is tangible evidence that the employees think like owners and act like owners.

Having committed my professional life to seeing the number of ESOPs expand in the United States because of a strongly held belief that they are good for America and American employees, I am very aware of the critic's view.

So, anyone, anywhere in the world, who wishes to create employee-ownership utilizing an ESOP-like device must be aware of the failure of the U.S. ESOP community to silence critics of ESOPs. Understanding the criticism of ESOPs will help those working to establish ESOPs meet the criticism that will arise and, in turn, provide their country with a solid base to move forward to establishing a fair, just, and productive free market economy.

13

Using an ESOP to Grow
a Company

The five major financial advantages of an employee stock ownership
plan (ESOP) are:

1. An ESOP company can deduct both the principal and the interest paid on the ESOP loan.

2. A company with a leveraged ESOP can place up to 25 percent
of payroll into the ESOP accounts of its employees.

3. Anyone who owns shares in a private company for at least three
years and who sells those shares to an ESOP, thereby increasing the
ESOP's ownership to at least 30 percent of the company's stock (unless
the ESOP already owns 30 percent), can roll over the proceeds of the
sale into the stocks and bonds of U.S.-operating companies and not
pay any income taxes until those replacement securities are sold (Section 1042 IRS Code). Someone selling to a cooperative can receive
the same benefit.

4. Dividends paid on ESOP shares that are used to pay down
the ESOP debt or are passed through to the ESOP participants are
deductible to the company, unlike other dividend payments, which
are not deductible.

5. A bank or financial institution lending money for the purpose of buying stock for an ESOP can exclude from income 50 percent of the interest earned on the loan if the ESOP ends up owning more than 50 percent of the common stock and the employees are allowed full voting rights for those shares (Section 133 IRS Code). The loan may not be for more than 15 years. This means that the ESOP can borrow money at a lower interest rate than would otherwise be the case.

In this chapter, we shall follow a hypothetical company, the WILDE Company, through various stages of growth and watch that company make good use of these five major advantages to help the company grow.

Selling the Small Business

William Wilde (known in the business as Wild Willy Wilde) was a famous musician in the medium-sized midwestern city that he grew up in. As he got older, he wanted to have something to leave to his son Bob, who had no musical talent, so he began a small music store selling sheet music and guitars. When Bob finished college, he took over the family business. Bob built up the business as the city grew, moving to a larger location and to a building that he owned instead of rented. By the time Bob reached retirement age, the company (legally a corporation for many years) had 20 employees, annual sales of $2 million, and hard assets (land, building, paid-for instruments) worth $300,000.

Bob's two sons did not have any interest in taking over the family business. They had both worked at the store during summer vacations and were sick of it. One wanted to be a famous singer; the other got a good job with a giant corporation that paid him much more than the music store ever could. Bob Wilde put the business on the market, but there were no takers. The music business was in a state of flux at the time, the sale of band instruments was down, and another music store had just opened in the city.

Bob Wilde was playing golf one day and complaining that he wanted to retire but could not find anyone willing to pay what he felt his business was worth. One of his golfing friends was an attorney who had just attended a one-day seminar on ESOPs. They began talking, and Bob liked the rollover feature of an ESOP (no giant corporation was interested in buying him out so he had expected to pay a large income tax at the time of the sale). The attorney explained that setting up an ESOP in such a small company could be difficult and expensive; however, a worker cooperative could be set up for much less.

The next day Bob talked it over with his employees and explained the options. They thought it was a good idea, so the attorney created a worker cooperative for them. This new corporation agreed to buy the business by buying Bob's shares (20,000 total shares in the original WILDE Corporation).

The difficult part of the process was agreeing on a price. Bob, like all owners of small businesses, thought his business was worth at least $1 million. A business valuation expert hired by the employees felt that $600,000 was a fair price. The store had earned, after taxes, between $60,000 and $90,000 a year. Generally, a small business is not valued with a price/earnings ratio of more than six or seven. Using earnings of $80,000 and a ratio of seven, the valuation expert came up with a figure of $560,000. The fact that interest rates were low, hard assets could be mortgaged for $300,000, and similar music stores had sold in the $600,000 range allowed the expert to value the business at $600,000.

Bob agreed to this price in part because he could roll over the money he received into stocks and bonds and delay paying income tax until these securities were sold. Besides, he knew that the $1 million figure had always been pie in the sky. The bank was willing to lend $200,000 in return for a mortgage on the land and building, which allowed the new worker cooperative to buy one-third of the outstanding shares of Bob's corporation. This met the over-30-percent ownership requirement that allowed him to roll over the proceeds.

The assets of the new worker cooperative consisted of the shares purchased from Bob. Payments on the mortgage would require $40,000 a year, and the worker cooperative agreed to buy $50,000 worth of shares from Bob each year over the next eight years. This meant that all of the projected $90,000 of annual earnings would be going to pay down debt and buy Bob's shares.

The bank would have been willing to loan more money, but it would have required Bob to place his replacement securities in the bank as added security for the loan. Because Bob did not plan to sell these securities anytime soon, this would not have been so bad. However, Bob decided to structure the deal so that this was not necessary.

The first year was rough, with a slowdown in the local economy, and each of the worker-owners had to agree to take a six-week vacation without pay that summer to get through it. The next year things picked up. Several of the employees began giving music lessons, and the storeroom in the back was turned into several small studios. These studios were also rented out to other music teachers who needed the space. The worker cooperative managed to pay off the debt and buy the remainder of Bob's shares in only seven years. The employees realized that if they failed to continue to make the mortgage payments or to buy the required number of shares from Bob, the business was still the WILDE Corporation and Bob had a contract with the cooperative that entitled him to sell his remaining shares to someone else if the cooperative could not complete the sale.

During those initial seven years, the company had expanded to a second location and hired 10 new employees. The new employees were not made members of the cooperative because the initial 20 members felt that these new employees had not sacrificed enough to justify their inclusion. To allow a gradual buyout of Bob, the cooperative technically owned shares in WILDE Corporation and had a contract to manage the assets of WILDE Corporation rather than to own the assets themselves.

When three years had passed after the last purchase of shares from Bob, the 20 cooperative owners decided to end their cooperative. The WILDE Corporation purchased the cooperative by trading shares in the WILDE Corporation for member interests in the cooperative. Each of the 20 employees now had 1,000 shares of WILDE Corporation stock, and the cooperative was dissolved. Because this was a stock-for-stock trade, the cooperative members paid no income tax.

The Venture Capitalists

A couple of years later, WILDE opened another store in another city. It was a success, and the 20 stockholder-employees felt that they were ready to expand into other cities. However, they would need $4 million. The only realistic way to get that kind of money was from a group of venture capitalists. The company now had earnings of $400,000 a year and unmortgaged assets of over $1 million. The venture capitalists were willing to invest $4 million in return for 50 percent of the shares. WILDE Corporation sold them 20,000 shares and used the money to expand into several nearby cities.

The venture capitalists demanded that the bylaws be changed to require the corporation to set up an ESOP if shareholders owning more than 30 percent of the shares requested it. The bylaws were also changed to require the company to go public when shareholders owning more than 20 percent of the shares requested it and the company had earnings of more than $2 million a year.

Expansion was successful, and earnings rose to $1.6 million a year in three short years. At that point, the venture capitalists wanted to get some of their money out of WILDE. It turned out that 10 of the original 20 shareholder-employees were interested in retiring. It was decided that an ESOP would be set up to buy just over 50 percent of the shares, which would allow the bank to offer a lower interest rate on the loan. The company was now big enough and had a history of earnings growth so that a bank was willing to make a large loan. The company was valued at $16 million ($1.6 million times a price/earnings ratio of 10).

Eight million dollars was borrowed so that the ESOP could buy 50 percent plus one share. The 10 retiring shareholder-employees received $4 million for their shares ($400,000 each), and they rolled the money over into stocks and bonds of large U.S. corporations. The venture capitalists took their $4 million and rolled it over into the shares of another small U.S. corporation with a lot of growth potential. The ESOP allowed them to get back $4 million and reinvest it in another venture without paying any income taxes. Without the rollover feature, half of this $4 million would have been considered capital gains and subject to tax ($2 million was original investment and $2 million was profit).

The company continued to do well. All the employees, including those left from the original 20, were part of the ESOP so they all had a real incentive to work harder and smarter to make the company a success. Earnings rose to $2 million in three more years, and the venture capitalists demanded that the company go public. They wanted out, and their remaining 25 percent interest would be worth more if the company went public.

An investment banker was found who believed the shares could be valued at 14 times earnings. This gave the company a value of $28 million. All of the remaining 10 shareholder-employees sold out along with the venture capitalists, so just under 50 percent of the company was sold on the public market for just under $14 million. The venture capitalists took their money to invest in other companies ($2 million was the original investment, so $5 million was gain; taxes took $1.5 million, leaving a profit on these shares of $3.5 million). Each of the 10 original shareholder-employees received $700,000 minus taxes of $200,000 for a profit of $500,000. They did not want to sell their shares to the ESOP and take the rollover benefit because they wanted to remain with the company and continue to participate in the ESOP. Generally, a person cannot sell shares to an ESOP, roll over the proceeds, and then receive some of those original shares back as an ESOP participant.

By going public, the company was no longer required to purchase the shares of departing ESOP participants. Because this ESOP took advantage of the low-interest-rate loan, the employees participating in the ESOP had full voting rights on the shares in their account, just like the outside shareholders. The trustee voted the unallocated shares, which made the outside shareholders more comfortable with this "employee voting" concept.

Expanding with an ESOP

Over the next few years, the WILDE Corporation used the ability to borrow money at a lower interest rate and deduct both interest and principal to sell additional shares to the ESOP and expand the company. As a growth company, dividend payments were small; however, those paid to the ESOP were used to pay off the ESOP debt even faster. Employees saw their account balances grow significantly as the company grew and the ESOP debt was paid down. The company also set up a profit-sharing plan and placed a significant amount in that plan for investment in the stock of other growth companies. The profit-sharing plan also purchased stock in small companies that the executives at WILDE believed might be possible takeover targets for the WILDE Corporation.

The WILDE Corporation did buy several small companies during the next few years. One manufactured guitars and had run into hard times. The stock was selling for a very low price and WILDE felt that it made a good purchase. WILDE also bought a small drum manufacturer and a printer of sheet music. Company management reorganized these new divisions and explained to the employees that 25 percent of payroll was being placed in an ESOP and a profit-sharing plan to provide them with as much tax-free wealth as legally possible. Employees were also told that their ESOP shares would increase in value as the company grew, giving them a new incentive to produce quality products.

That added incentive, together with the participatory management style that had always flourished at WILDE, worked wonders in most of the new divisions. In the case of the sheet music division, however, nothing worked and the operation's assets were eventually sold. Because it owned a large tract of land in California, WILDE Corporation still made money on the deal.

WILDE could purchase these private companies by making the sellers a very good offer. The sellers would receive half the purchase price in WILDE company stock. Because stock was exchanged, the sellers would pay no income tax until that stock was sold. The sellers sold the rest of their stock to WILDE's ESOP. The sellers took this cash and rolled it over into the stocks and bonds of large U.S. corporations. The WILDE Corporation had been able to use its ESOP to make the sellers an offer they could not refuse (half WILDE stock, half stocks and bonds of major corporations, no income taxes) and used low-interest ESOP loans to make the acquisitions possible.

After many years of regional growth, WILDE was on the threshold of going national. At that point, it attracted the attention of a large entertainment conglomerate, BIG MOUNTAIN, with a lot of cash in its bank account. BIG MOUNTAIN made an offer that no one in their right mind would refuse. The ESOP and profit-sharing plans were terminated, and the employees took all that money and rolled it over into Individual Retirement Accounts (IRAs). The three divisions of WILDE became three divisions of BIG MOUNTAIN.

The management style at BIG MOUNTAIN was very different from what it had been at WILDE. Many of the older employees decided to retire, something they could afford to do given the large balances in their IRA accounts. The next year, the major money-maker at BIG MOUNTAIN, the motion picture production division, produced a string of flops and the company lost money for the first time in its history. The divisions that had once been WILDE were also not doing well under new management. It was decided after several years to break up BIG MOUNTAIN into eight new companies.

The Big Breakup

BIG MOUNTAIN was losing money only because of its motion picture operation; the other divisions could be viewed as profitable, stable companies if they stood alone. This meant that the value of BIG MOUNTAIN broken up was 50 percent greater than its value as a giant conglomerate. Each of the eight new companies would institute an ESOP owning 51 percent of its shares. The old BIG MOUNTAIN shareholders would receive the cash from the ESOP loans as partial payment for their BIG MOUNTAIN shares.

Because BIG MOUNTAIN was more valuable broken up, this meant that the average shareholder received 75 percent of the current market value of his or her BIG MOUNTAIN shares in cash plus shares in each of the new companies. Each of the new companies had significant debt, but because the ESOP owned more than 51 percent of the shares, the loans were at a low interest rate and were being repaid with tax-deductible principal payments. This gave the new companies a very good chance of survival.

One of the smaller new companies went bankrupt, but the other seven thrived. As their ESOP debt was paid down, these companies issued new shares to the ESOP with new loans and used the money to expand. Three of the seven bought out most of their outside shareholders and went private. This meant that they were no longer listed on a stock exchange. By using the ESOP to purchase these shares, the value of each employee's stake in the company increased. It also meant that after a year the remaining shareholders could sell their stock to the ESOP and get the tax-free rollover benefit (the seller must have owned the shares for at least three years, and at least one year must have passed since the shares were publicly traded before a tax-free rollover is possible).

The Leveraged Buyout

The retail music store division, with 100 stores around the country, became WILDE Corporation again. The company experienced reduced demand for band instruments as school districts across the country dropped their school bands to save money. Earnings fell and employees were laid off. For several years, low earnings meant low stock prices. A Japanese billionaire came along and offered to buy the company for cash. Everyone, including the ESOP trustee, felt that this was the best offer the shareholders were going to get. WILDE Corporation became YAYA Corporation, and the ESOP employees rolled over the money they received from the sale and the termination of the ESOP into IRAs.

The new Japanese mangers of YAYA did not get along with the old employees. The company began to lose money; and, with each new cost-cutting initiative, morale sank lower and losses increased. Finally, the Japanese billionaire wanted out. He offered to sell the company to the highest bidder. An employee group formed to make a bid using an ESOP, but they knew the ESOP could not borrow enough money to pay the entire purchase price. Because the company had negative earnings for two years in a row, the ESOP could only borrow money based on the value of the hard assets (the land, buildings, and inventory). This was enough to raise 70 percent of a realistic price ($100 million). The employee group needed an outside investor to make up the difference.

The outside investor, Mr. Fatcat, was willing to put up $30 million cash, but he wanted to own at least 49 percent of the company. He reasoned that if he bought the company himself, using a loan on its assets, he could put up $30 million and own 100 percent of the company. The ESOP could supply a lower interest rate and provide deductible principal payments. He also knew that the new company would need some kind of employee benefit plan and that an ESOP would provide such a plan and also give employees an incentive to bring this company back from the edge of bankruptcy. Mr. Fatcat also liked the fact that as long as the new company was a private company, he could sell some of his shares to the ESOP and roll over the proceeds into investments in other companies.

All of these benefits were worth something to him. At the same time, he was putting up the cash, not the employees. If the company went under, the employees would lose their jobs, but they could get other jobs. The fact that the employees' ESOP stock would be worthless would be sad; but because they didn't pay any of their own money for it in the first place, it would not be the same, as far as Mr. Fatcat was concerned, as losing real money. An outside evaluator figured that because the ESOP was buying a controlling interest, it was not unreasonable for it to pay more for its 51 percent share of the company. The deal went through. WILDE Corporation was reborn with a 51 percent ESOP and 100 million shares valued at an average price of $1 a share (the ESOP paid more than $1 a share; Mr. Fatcat less).

Because this company had no debt and no earnings before the buyout, money had to be found to service the new debt. Even though the loan payments were lower because of the ESOP, the money had to come from somewhere. If this had been a non-ESOP buyout, Mr. Fatcat would have laid off a third of the employees to come up with this money. The WILDE Corporation employees agreed to a 20 percent pay cut and no layoffs. The employees reasoned that, without the buyout, they were all going to lose their jobs as the company slipped into bankruptcy. With an outside buyout, a third of them would lose their jobs. With an ESOP and a 20 percent pay cut, no jobs would be lost. If the company was able to turn around and pay off the ESOP debt, the employees would be paid back with a significant number of shares in their ESOP accounts worth a lot of money. Given the other two alternatives, a pay cut and an ESOP seemed like the best choice.

Of course, immediately after the buyout, the shares were valued at 30 cents a share, reflecting the massive debt of the company. This meant that Mr. Fatcat's 49 million shares were worth less than $15 million after the buyout even though he had paid $30 million for them. If he had not brought the ESOP into the deal, he would have owned 100 million shares with a value of $30 million. He had second thoughts, but it was too late.

The pay cut and the ESOP made it possible to pay off the loan in 7 years instead of the 12 years he had planned. This meant that after 3 years, the company was only $40 million in debt and Mr. Fatcat's 49 percent interest was worth almost $35 million. Because this was a loan that paid off $10 million of principal a year, the interest payments were very high the first year but went down quickly as the principal was paid off. After 7 years, the company was out of debt and expanding. Earnings were up, even after a pay raise that gave back most of the pay cut to the employees.

With earnings of $15 million a year (assuming a price/earnings ratio of 10), the company was now worth $150 million. Each share was worth $1.50. The pay cut that saved the employees' jobs had turned into a nice nest egg for each employee, thanks to the use of the ESOP. With 2,000 employees on the company payroll, the average employee now owned $37,500 worth of stock. Mr. Fatcat sold some of his shares to the ESOP to take advantage of the rollover; soon after that WILDE went public. With the higher price/earnings ratio that publicly-traded shares enjoy and the added shares purchased from Mr. Fatcat in their accounts, the average employee now had an account worth over $60,000.

Doing It in the Real World

Everything discussed above happened many times during the 1980s and 1990s. In 1931, Earle Wyatt opened a small cafeteria inside a Piggly Wiggly grocery store that he had purchased in Dallas, Texas. This grew into a successful chain of Wyatt cafeterias. In 1988, the shareholders, mainly descendants of Earle Wyatt, wanted to sell their shares in this large private company. Their major competitor, Furr's, offered a high price, but the shareholders did not want to sell to the competition. They decided to sell to an ESOP and take the tax-free rollover. When the smoked cleared, 6,500 employees had paid $173 million for the company.

During the 1980s, the employees of Avis found themselves being passed from one conglomerate to another. By 1987, Avis had changed hands five times in 10 years. The 12,500 employees used an ESOP to buy the company for themselves. The company introduced participatory management techniques and the value of the stock tripled in 2 years.

In 1977, the employees of BCM Engineers no longer wished to be part of Betz Laboratories. They used an ESOP to buy 75 percent of a new company that purchased BCM from Betz. The ESOP used a $3.8 million loan with an interest rate of 8.8 percent and a loan period of seven years. The value of the stock fell from $10 a share to $2.40 a share, reflecting the effect of debt on the new company's value. The employees were not worried. By 1989, the stock was valued at $38.50 a share. In 1990, a dividend was declared and passed through to the employees without paying Social Security taxes.

In the early 1980s, an aluminum plant in Goldendale, Washington, closed because its Australian owners could not make a profit. Three thousand employees were thrown out of work. In 1987, a local investor used an ESOP to buy and reopen the plant. Fewer employees were hired back and these were paid lower wages than had been the case before the closing. In return, these employees would own a large share of the company through an ESOP. The company made an amazing recovery. Shares that could have been purchased for 50 cents a share in 1987 were worth $150 a share by the end of 1989.

Is It Feasible?

We have explored how an ESOP can be used over the life of a company to buy out a retiring owner, buy out cooperative members, provide a tax-advantaged exit for venture capitalists, allow a large corporation to spin off divisions into new companies, and help ensure the financial success of a large leveraged buyout. While an ESOP can accomplish all of this and more, it is not magic. Before an ESOP is implemented, the shareholders, managers, and employees must take a hard look at whether or not an ESOP is really feasible.

The principal of an ESOP is paid off by contributions to a defined-contribution benefit plan. If the ESOP is leveraged, up to 25 percent of payroll can be placed in the ESOP, but this may not be enough to make the principal payments. This percentage can be increased by dividend payments on the stock, but it may not be possible to declare a dividend if the company is deeply in debt.

An ESOP is required by law to pay only a "fair" price for the shares it purchases. In some industries, such as the entertainment industry, companies sell for much more than their balance sheets and income statements suggest they are really worth. That is because some rich people get a kick out of owning these kinds of companies. That's fine, but an ESOP is not going to be able to play that game. Rich people are allowed to make stupid investments, ESOPs are not.

Why is the business for sale in the first place? If it is for sale because the owner wants to retire, buying it through an ESOP might be a good idea for everyone. If it is for sale because it is losing money and there is no hope of saving it, then it would be foolish for the employees or anyone else to buy it. While ESOPs, combined with fewer employees making lower wages, have saved dying companies and even turned some of them into very successful businesses, that does not always happen.

Once employees own a large percentage of a company, they have a right to expect that they will be treated differently. While they are not going to be consulted on daily management issues or allowed to come and go as they please, they should be shown some deference. Research during the 1980s by the National Center for Employee Ownership and others demonstrated that an ESOP can increase the growth and efficiency of a company, but only if it is combined with participatory management. This does not mean holding meetings every week to poll the workers about every decision. It does mean allowing each worker to have more say about how his or her particular job is done.

In one case, a company with a new ESOP asked the workers if they had any ideas about improving efficiency. The employees asked if they could move the machines around to save steps, and management agreed. The machines were moved and productivity increased 50 percent. When the managers asked why the employees had not done that before, the workers responded that they didn't think anyone would let them!

Finally, there is the financial issue. If the ESOP is going to be financed by a loan, whether the purpose is to buy out the owner, or to expand the company, or for any other reason, the company has to be able to make the loan payments. No bank is going to make a loan it does not think the company can repay. Some of the leveraged (non-ESOP) buyouts done in the second half of the 1980s ended up in bankruptcy court in a matter of months. Because these buyouts were financed with junk bonds, the company was saddled with high interest payments and not enough profits after operating expenses to make the payments. Although an ESOP loan has the advantages we have discussed, it cannot create cash where there is no cash. That is why investors in the 1980s gained a new appreciation for the importance of looking at a company's cash flow statement along with the balance sheet and income statement. Low cash flow plus high debt equals bankruptcy.

APPENDIX

Ownership Transfer Corporations

The basic idea of an Ownership Transfer Corporation (OTC) is that investors would give up their rights of ownership after the time period required by them to recover the cost of their investment, with enough profit to provide them with the incentive to invest. After this time period (the "investment time horizon"), the employees, customers,

---

This special contribution is by Shann Turnbull, Australian business executive and author of *Democratising the Wealth of Nations* (The Company Directors Association, 1975) and "Re-inventing Corporations," *Human Systems Management*, 10, no. 3 (1991):169–186

suppliers, and others (the stakeholders) would become the owners of the corporation. Since most venture capitalists invest with the idea of selling out in a very few years, setting up an OTC would simply provide a system for doing just that over time. Because the stakeholders know that they will eventually gain ownership of the corporation, they would have more of an incentive to help the investors attain their financial goals as quickly as possible.

An OTC creates a more efficient and equitable corporate structure because it avoids paying income to investors for a longer time period than the investors require to receive the desired return on investment. The investment time horizon for equity investments is typically less than 10 years (most venture capitalists expect to get their money back plus a handsome return within a 10-year period or less) even though the income stream may continue for much longer. The income obtained after the time horizon of the initial investors provides excess incentive to invest, or "surplus profits." Surplus profits are those profits that are not required to bring forth the initial investment.

OTCs could be used to transfer ownership, and thereby distribute surplus profits, to those individuals (other than the investors) who contribute to the increased value of the firm but do not contribute start-up capital. This increased value is contributed by employees, customers, suppliers, and the host community, which provides infrastructure and social services to the firm. By distributing surplus profits to these stakeholders through the eventual transfer of ownership from the investors to these stakeholders, control is also ultimately shared with those people whose lives are affected most by the operation of the corporation. This creates multiple cybernetic (information and control) circuits to allow corporations to become socially accountable, self-governing, and caring of the environment.

To convert existing corporations to OTCs, stockholders would change the corporate bylaws to create two categories of stock. One category would be described as investment stock; the other, as stakeholder stock. All economic and governance rights (the right to control the corporation) would initially belong to the owners of investment stock but would automatically transfer at a specified rate of, say, 5 percent per year to stakeholder stock. However, this 20-year flow of ownership rights would not begin until after the investment time horizon of the investors.

This arrangement would not create a disincentive for venture capitalists to establish new corporations because the dilution of their stockholder interest occurs only after their investment time horizon. The dilution of stockholders' interest, which is introduced into conventional existing corporations through the granting of shares or stock options to employees, could be eliminated because employees would automatically obtain a substantial interest through the ownership transfer process.

OTCs could be used to provide a more tax-efficient way to introduce employee ownership than ESOPs because OTCs would provide a way for the government to increase the amount of taxes collected. The tax base would transfer from firms toward individuals. Because of this, governments could afford to provide a tax incentive to those setting up OTCs. If government reduced corporate taxes from 40 percent to 30 percent on pretax profits of $50 million per year, this would increase after-tax profits from $30 million to $35 million per year. This 16.6 percent increase in after-tax profits would make the investment stock more valuable even if ownership rights fade out at a rate of 5 percent per year.

There are two reasons for this. One reason is that investors discount the value of future income on a compounding basis. The other reason is that, as their equity is fading out, investors would require OTCs to distribute all their profits each year. In most firms, this would more than double the level of dividend payments. Government taxes on dividends would more than offset the cost of the tax incentive. A win-win outcome is obtained for investors, government, employees, and other stakeholders.

Business expansion and new employment opportunities would be provided by OTCs establishing "offspring" corporations. These would be financed by stockholder rights to reinvest their dividends in activities initiated by the "parent" OTC in which they originally invested. Parent corporations would not necessarily hold sufficient stock in offspring enterprises to make them subsidiaries.

At the end of the ownership transfer period, the corporate bylaws would require that all residual assets and liabilities be transferred to a successor corporation. This would be financed either by the stakeholders reinvesting the proceeds they obtained from dissolving the original corporation or by new investors. Both stakeholders and investors would then acquire investment stock in the successor enterprise with a new 25-year corporate life cycle. The next transfer process would take 25 years. The extra 5 years would allow the new corporation 5 years for operations to become established.

An OTC provides a means for management and employees to act as "agents" for investors, to become principals in adding value to firms and the economy. Beside improving economic efficiency in this manner, OTCs would also improve the efficiency of the economy because reinvestment decisions would be transferred from firms to their owners. This process would expose the reinvestment of corporate cash flows to market forces. The most important way OTCs increase economic efficiency is through the minimization of surplus profits.

It is inconsistent with the moral and rational justification for a market system for people to be paid excess income. It is not good business or economic sense for any community, region, state, or country to pay alien investors more of a return than they actually require in order to make the initial investment. Existing corporations often result in resource-rich communities, regions, and countries becoming cash poor through the exporting of surplus profits. This also allows the greater concentration of ownership and control of the means of production. This wealth concentration forces democratic governments to transfer income through the use of taxes and welfare payments.

OTCs create a mechanism to distribute the wealth of nations without taxes or welfare and would thus allow for an eventual reduction in the size and influence of government. ESOPs are complementary in this regard, but they do not redistribute surplus profits. They can only switch them from investors to employees and then only in proportion to the ownership interest of the ESOP in the firm. OTCs would always switch 100 percent of the ownership and would allow stakeholders other than employees to share in the wealth of their nation. OTCs would provide a powerful technique for transforming Socialist countries to a private property economy. For all types of economic systems, OTCs would provide a more efficient way to attract foreign investment. They would also make foreign investment more politically attractive, as stakeholder ownership would increase local ownership and control.

Unlike OTCs, ESOPs do not create new firms to increase the total number of enterprises in the economy and so competition between them. However, ESOPs that issue newly created stock do provide a mechanism for making industrial development of any community self-financing with appropriate banking arrangements. ESOPs and OTCs are complementary. They are both mechanisms that allow for a greater spreading of ownership in free enterprise economies.

14

Other Uses for ESOPs

In the last chapter, we saw how an employee stock ownership plan (ESOP) could be used to buy out a retiring owner, provide capital for corporate expansion, allow a division to be spun off from a large conglomerate, or help with a leveraged buyout. There are other uses to which an ESOP can be put. In this chapter, we shall discuss how an ESOP can be used to help provide a cost-effective employee benefit, provide a defense against unfriendly takeover, save or resurrect a failing company, improve corporate performance, or provide a way to privatize a government-owned company.

Provide an Employee Benefit

According to a 1986 report from the General Accounting Office, the most often stated reason for setting up an ESOP is to provide a benefit for the employees. This emphasizes that an ESOP is, above all, an employee benefit plan. While a company must get stockholder approval before setting up some kinds of stock option and stock purchase plans, an ESOP does not require special approval from the stockholders.

In many cases, particularly with smaller companies, the management does not feel that it can afford to spend much money on employee benefit plans. Let's suppose the company is willing to spend $100 a month per employee for a normal defined-contribution plan, one that invests in a large variety of companies. At the end of the year, each employee has $1,200 worth of stock in a diverse group of companies. This does not provide them with an incentive to work harder for their own company, and $1,200 is not much money. Also, that $1,200 per employee has gone out of the company. Many companies feel that they can afford to place twice as much money in an ESOP because the money is coming back to the company in the form of capital paid in exchange for new shares issued by the company. The employees see $200 a month going into their accounts. They also know that they are now owners of stock in the company they work for.

Once an ESOP is in place, it is available to accomplish all the other goals that we have been discussing. In some cases, those other uses will be easier to accomplish if the company already has an ESOP in place. Expanding an existing ESOP is more prudent than waiting to put one in place when the time comes to borrow money or defend against takeover.

If the main motivation for setting up an ESOP is to provide an employee benefit, convertible preferred stock should be considered. Many of the large public companies that have established ESOPs, such as J.C. Penney, Procter & Gamble, Texaco, and Ralston Purina, have done just that. Convertible preferred stock receives a higher dividend rate and may be converted into common stock at a later date. Because dividends paid through ESOPs are tax deductible to the company, unlike normal dividends, this allows the company to pay a larger dividend on the ESOP shares, with the same after-tax effect as paying a lower dividend on regular common stock. Because the dividends received by the employees are not wages, no Social Security taxes (currently 15.3 percent) need be paid.

Convertible preferred stock has other advantages. It can have a floor price guaranteeing that the stock's value will never fall below a fixed amount unless the company goes bankrupt. Preferred stock is also safer because it is paid off before common stock, if the company does go bankrupt. If a loan has been taken out to buy these convertible preferred shares, the company can pay off the loan faster by making higher, tax-deductible dividend payments along with the usual contributions to the ESOP. By buying a large block of common stock and replacing it with a large block of convertible preferred stock sold to the ESOP, the company can avoid diluting the ownership interest of the remaining stockholders. It will also have prefunded an employee benefit plan.

Assuming equal principal payments over 10 years, and declining interest payments as the principal is paid down, the company ends up placing convertible preferred stock worth a great deal of money in the employees' individual accounts while the cost of doing this is declining each year as the loan is paid off. If the value of the common stock (which the convertible preferred stock can be converted into) is rising over the years, the value of the preferred stock will also be going up, which will add to the value of this employee benefit.

By using convertible preferred stock with a floor price, the company has maximized the benefits of an ESOP while minimizing the risk to the employees. While the employees' eggs are in one basket, that basket has a floor price and is paid off before common stock if the company goes bankrupt. Once the ESOP loan is paid off, the company can pass through the higher dividends to the employees, providing them with a special kind of bonus, one that is larger than would otherwise be the case because this bonus is not subject to Social Security taxes, as are other bonuses, or to corporate income taxes, as are other dividend payments. The employees have an incentive to make sure the company is profitable so that they continue to receive their dividends through the ESOP.

A company can certainly combine the desire to provide an employee benefit with other goals. In 1988, J.C. Penney used a leveraged ESOP to place 24 percent of its stock into the friendly hands of its employees (takeover defense), to replace existing profit-sharing and savings plans (benefits restructuring), and to replace common stock with convertible preferred (restructuring corporate finance).

Also in 1988, Champion Parts Rebuilders used an ESOP to buy 400,000 newly issued shares and used the money to replace debt costing 13.25 percent with an ESOP loan costing 8.5 percent. Of course, the employees received a new benefit that management hoped would make them more concerned with the company's bottom line.

There was also a desire to place stock in friendly hands because General Refractories was making an unsolicited bid to buy the company at the time.

An ESOP can be used to replace an open-ended retirement commitment with a definite-cost program. In the 1960s and 1970s, many American corporations promised their employees that when they retired, the company would continue to pay for their health insurance. During the 1980s, this promise became more and more expensive as the price of health insurance for people over the age of 50 continued to climb. In the late 1980s, the accounting community decided that the potential cost of this promise was so great that companies would have to begin showing it on their balance sheets by the 1990s as a type of debt (the promise to pay money in the future).

In 1989, a number of companies, ranging from Sara Lee to Boise Cascade, decided to replace this open-ended commitment with a definite commitment, an ESOP. These companies now place stock in their employees' ESOP accounts each year, and that stock will be available to pay medical or any other expenses after retirement. As a consequence of this changeover, the company balance sheet no longer shows a large liability in the form of potential retiree medical expenses, and the income statement simply shows the annual cost of the ESOP as another employee benefit expense. At the same time, the company can enjoy all of the potential benefits of an ESOP, including the greater identification of the employees with the long-term financial success of the company.

An ESOP can be combined with a 401(k) plan (frequently called a KSOP). The ESOP is used to buy a large block of stock with leveraged funds. This company stock is then used instead of cash to match employee contributions to the 401(k) plan. This allows the company to make a larger contribution than was previously the case. Tandycrafts uses its KSOP to provide a 200 percent matching contribution, meaning that for every dollar an employee contributes to the plan, the company matches that with two dollars worth of stock. When Syncor International Corporation decided to buy back 10 percent of its stock from a French company, it used a leveraged ESOP and established a KSOP to match employee contributions with Syncor stock.

Takeover Defense: A Tale of Two Companies

Throughout the 1980s, more and more companies felt they needed a defense against unfriendly takeover. A variety of defenses were developed. To understand these defenses we must first look at how a takeover works.

With a friendly takeover, a wealthy investor or another company tells the target company's board of directors that it wishes to buy the company. If the two sides can agree on a price, the board of directors of the target company accepts the offer. If the buyer is an outside investor, the stockholders of the target company usually get cash and notes or bonds in exchange for their shares. If the buyer is a company, the target company's shareholders may get stock of the buying company, bonds, cash, or a combination of all three in exchange for their shares.

If the board of directors of the target company refuses to go along, then the outside buyer has two main ways to proceed. The buyer can appeal to the stockholders to sell enough shares to allow the buyer to control the company. At the next shareholder's meeting, the buyer votes in a new board of directors that agrees to accept an offer on behalf of the remaining shareholders (including those who refused to sell) to merge the company into another company and take stock, cash, or both in exchange for their shares in the target company. Or, the buyer can simply appeal to the current shareholders to vote for a slate of directors at the next shareholder's meeting that will accept the offer and bring about the merger.

To limit takeovers, the state of Delaware (where most of America's large corporations are incorporated) passed a statute that requires a buyer who does not have the agreement of the target company's board of directors to either buy more than 85 percent of the target company's stock at one time or wait three years to complete the takeover (by exercising a merger with an existing or newly created company). Because most individuals and companies that might be interested in a takeover are not willing to wait three years to complete the deal, this prevents a hostile takeover unless the buyer can acquire more than 85 percent of the stock. This means that a company incorporated in

Delaware can prevent a takeover through outright stock purchase if it can place over 15 percent of the company's stock in friendly hands.

Employees, through an ESOP, offer the friendliest hands because they have the most to fear from a hostile takeover that could result in large layoffs. Stock held by employee benefit plans does not count unless the employees have the right "confidentially" to vote the shares in their account. To increase the number of shares employees can vote, companies have set up ESOPs so that the ESOP trustee has to vote the shares that have not yet been placed in the accounts of individual employees in a way that mirrors how the employees have voted. In other words, with a leveraged ESOP, a large number of shares can be placed in the employees' hands even though the ESOP loan has not been paid off.

In the late 1980s, the Polaroid Corporation placed more than 14 percent of its stock in an ESOP. It passed full voting rights through to the ESOP participants, and set up the trust so that the trustee had to vote the undistributed shares in the same way that the employees voted their shares. Because Polaroid was a Delaware corporation, the creation of this ESOP made a takeover all but impossible, given the feelings of the vast majority of Polaroid's employees that a takeover would not be in their best interests.

The group trying to take over Polaroid, the Shamrock Holding Company, sued Polaroid over the establishment of the ESOP, but Polaroid won the case. The Delaware judge ruled that the ESOP was legal because it was not established solely as a takeover defense. Polaroid had been considering an ESOP long before Shamrock Holding came along as a way to give its employees a significant incentive to help the company meet new competition in the technology arena. Because of the confidential voting by the employees and the mirror voting by the trustee, this was not simply a case of placing a lot of shares in a trust and then having management control the trustee. In other words, the judge ruled that an ESOP with pass through voting can be used as a successful takeover defense precisely because the employees vote the shares rather than the trustee.

The judge was also impressed with more than a decade of research showing that ESOPs can increase productivity if combined with a more participative management style. Polaroid had begun to implement new management procedures along with its ESOP. Finally, the judge found that the ESOP was funded with pay cuts and the elimination of other employee benefits, so it did not have a negative cost for the other shareholders. Polaroid also purchased stock on the open market to limit the dilutive effect on the other shareholders. Finally, the sale of stock to the ESOP was financed by a loan from an outside source, and this money provided new capital to the Polaroid Corporation (559 A.2d 257 (Del. Ch. 1989)).

The National Cash Register Company (NCR) was not successful in its attempt to use an ESOP as a takeover defense. This battle began in November 1990, when the American Telephone and Telegraph Company (AT&T) offered to purchase all of the NCR stock by exchanging it for AT&T stock. On December 5, 1990, the NCR board of directors announced that it had found AT&T's offer of $90 a share ($90 worth of AT&T stock in exchange for each share of NCR stock) to be inadequate. On December 6, 1990, AT&T bypassed the board of directors and offered to buy NCR shares directly from the shareholders at $90 a share.

NCR was not a Delaware company, but it had established a staggered 12-member board of directors. This meant that in any one year only one-third of the board members could be replaced at the stockholder's meeting. However, shareholders owning 25 percent of the shares could call a special meeting to replace the entire board. At this special meeting, a vote of 80 percent of the shares would be required to replace the entire board. On January 21, 1991, AT&T had the necessary votes from 25 percent of the stockholders and asked for the special meeting. That meeting was scheduled for March 28, 1991, along with the regular annual meeting of the stockholders. By the end of January, 1991, owners of 70 percent of NCR's stock had agreed to trade their shares to AT&T for shares of AT&T stock.

NCR had first considered an ESOP in 1986 but rejected it. In 1988 and 1989, it had considered an ESOP again but only as a possible takeover defense. There was never any consideration of the other uses of an ESOP, such as to improve employee productivity. On February 20, 1991, NCR's board of directors authorized the sale of 5½ million shares of convertible preferred shares to a newly created ESOP. The shares would be sold to the ESOP at $90.75 a share. Each share of convertible preferred could be converted into eight-tenths of a share of common stock (meaning that common stock would have to rise above $113 a share before it would make sense to convert the preferred shares into common stock). Also, each share of convertible preferred stock was entitled to one vote even though it was only convertible into eight-tenths of a share of common stock (the NCR board of directors called this "heavy voting" stock).

To begin the ESOP, NCR would place one share of this new convertible preferred stock in each of the individual accounts of 24,000 employees. This was called "seeding" the ESOP. The rest of the stock would be voted by the trustee based on the way these initial shares were voted by the employees (mirror voting). This, in effect, gave each of the 24,000 employees in the ESOP the power to vote 229 shares. While this was a leveraged ESOP, with all of the shares being issued at once, no outside loan was taken out to pay for this share purchase. Instead, the ESOP trustee gave NCR a note for $500 million, with the note to be paid off over time as NCR made payments into the ESOP trust. With the creation of this ESOP, 8 percent of the voting shares had been placed in the hands of the employees.

AT&T and NCR battled in a federal district court over the question of whether or not this ESOP would be allowed to be created and vote shares in the upcoming fight for control of the NCR board of directors (761 F. Supp. 475 (S.D. Ohio 1991)). The federal judge was disturbed by the fact that, unlike most leveraged ESOPs, which bring in new money to the enterprise, this ESOP did not. Also, unlike many ESOPs that either buy shares on the open market or receive wage and benefit reductions from the employees to lessen the effect on the other shareholders, this NCR ESOP did neither of these things.

The judge was also disturbed by the fact that NCR's own outside attorneys refused to certify that these new shares of convertible preferred stock had been "validly issued" because no actual money had been received in exchange for the stock. This might have made it impossible for the shares to be traded on the New York Stock Exchange or to refinance the ESOP debt in the future.

The new ESOP convertible preferred stock also had a provision that if the price of the common stock fell over the next 14 months, the conversion price would be moved lower to match the new lower price of common stock (a price reset feature). This meant that if the employees rejected AT&T's offer and the price of NCR common stock fell, as it was expected to do, the employees' convertible preferred stock would have a significantly lower conversion price than the initial $113. The judge found this to be "unprecedented."

The judge in the NCR case compared what NCR had done with what Polaroid had done. In the Polaroid case, the ESOP had been under consideration for a year before the takeover became a real possibility. The NCR ESOP was only seriously considered once NCR needed a takeover defense. The Polaroid ESOP was implemented to improve employee morale and also brought new capital into the company through a "real" loan. The shares purchased by the Polaroid ESOP did not involve heavy voting rights, a price floor, or a reset provision, and the Polaroid employees gave up something in exchange for the ESOP while the NCR employees did not. The judge concluded that the NCR ESOP was established simply to impede corporate democracy and to allow the current NCR management to maintain control. The ESOP was canceled.

At the meeting on March 28, 1991, AT&T failed to get the 80 percent vote it needed to replace NCR's entire board of directors. It did have enough votes to replace 4 of the 12 members at the regular stockholder's meeting that followed. AT&T was then faced with waiting a year to complete the deal or making a higher offer for the NCR stock. On May 7, 1991, the NCR board of directors accepted AT&T's new offer of $110 a share. All of NCR's stockholders received $110 worth of AT&T stock in exchange for each of their NCR shares.

Can an ESOP whose employees have full voting rights and whose trustee must vote the unallocated shares to reflect the way the employees vote their allocated shares provide some defense against a hostile takeover? Yes, but only if the ESOP has been set up before the wolf is at the door and it is clear that it was set up to perform some of the other functions judges and shareholders consider legitimate uses for ESOPs. Setting up an ESOP at the last minute is probably not going to be allowed when the group trying to accomplish the takeover goes to court to enforce its rights.

During the late 1980s, dozens of major companies used ESOPs as part of a takeover defense strategy. When Robert Maxwell tried to buy Harcourt Brace Jovanovich in 1987, the board of directors rejected his offer of $44 a share and leveraged the company instead, paying the stockholders a special cash dividend of $40 a share and newly issued preferred stock. It also sold convertible preferred stock to its ESOP, which it had created earlier with excess assets from a terminated pension plan. This move was challenged in court; however, the judge ruled that because the employees were free to vote their shares, the action was not an illegal attempt to entrench management (664 F. Supp. 1519 (S.D.N.Y. 1987)).

In 1990, Harold Simmons tried to buy Lockheed. As part of his effort, he attempted to buy 10 million shares from the company's ESOP. He apparently felt that he could not successfully buy out the company as long as that large block of stock was controlled by the employees. He failed in his efforts to buy the ESOP stock and ultimately gave up his attempt to buy Lockheed. Harold Simmons apparently thought that if the company were broken up and some of its assets sold off, the company would be worth significantly more than the current market price. The employees, for obvious reasons, had very little desire to see the company dismembered and sold off in this way.

The list of ESOPs used at least in part as a takeover defense at the end of the 1980s would be quite long. When Pennzoil announced that it would use most of the $2.6 billion it received from Texaco as settlement of its legal dispute to buy almost 9 percent of the stock of Chevron Corporation, Chevron announced that it would borrow $1 billion to place additional shares into the hands of employees through an ESOP. FMC paid a special cash dividend to shareholders and a special stock dividend to its employee benefit funds, increasing the employee ownership stake to about a fourth of the company's stock. Resorts International used an ESOP to buy stock held by the founder's estate to avoid having that stock sold to an unfriendly investor, while the Whitman Corporation, makers of the famous Whitman's sampler, used an ESOP to help avoid takeover by a group of Canadian investors.

The Effect of ESOPs on Share Prices

Research shows that when a public company announces that it has plans to adopt an ESOP, its stock price often goes up. Whenever a company makes an announcement of any type, this carries new information to the market and the market evaluates the likely impact of that information on the future earnings flow of the company. The "announcement effect" studies have shown that the market generally sees ESOPs as adding to the future earnings flow. This is a rational response because ESOPs can bring significant tax benefits as well as incentive and productivity benefits to a company, and it is possible to structure ESOP transactions with only a minimum of dilution of shareholders' interest in the company. Share prices respond by an average of three or four percentage points when ESOPs are adopted for nondefensive purposes. On the other hand, ESOPs adopted to defend against a possible takeover have been shown to lower the stock prices, primarily because they tend to take the company "out of play." When a company is being pursued by a prospective buyer, its stock price is increased to abnormally high levels. An "ESOP defense" makes it less likely that the offeror's bid will succeed, and this causes the share price to fall by 3 to 5 percent.

Professor Michael A. Conte
Center for Business and Economic Studies
University of Baltimore
Baltimore, Maryland

Labor Concessions: A Tale of Two Unions

During the 1980s, hundreds of companies in the United States came to the verge of bankruptcy because of outdated equipment and outmoded ways of organizing the work process. Many of these companies went to the labor unions representing their employees and asked for concessions ranging from reduced wages to drastic changes in work rules and job classifications. Two unions represented thousands of industrial workers during this period, the United Steel Workers of America (USWA) and a union that we shall call Union XYZ (it will be nameless to protect the innocent). The USWA worked to become acquainted with what ESOPs could and could not do and how they might be used by their members. Union XYZ did not. At the end of 1990, approximately 50,000 members of the USWA were participating in 23 employee ownership plans. Union XYZ had no employees participating in employee ownership plans even though a similar number of its members had been forced to reduce their wages and restructure their work rules. Which union did a better job of looking out for its members' interests? Let's examine what the USWA did to answer that question.

Most situations that resulted in USWA members agreeing to participate in employee ownership plans fell into two categories. The first category involved a company that was suffering a temporary cash flow problem. In this case, USWA engaged in "investment bargaining" to get the company to set up an ESOP that would give employees a minority interest in the company. In these cases, the employees gave up some of their current income in return for future income that would be derived from the ESOP. The employees received stock that would be worth significantly more once the temporary cash flow problem was resolved. The 1985–1986 negotiations marked the first significant use of ESOPs in this way. This was a particularly difficult period for the American steel industry. Employment had dropped from 452,000 workers in 1977 to fewer than 200,000 in 1985. Faced with foreign competition and a recession, the American steel industry was losing money in the mid-1980s.

In April 1986, USWA and LTV Steel Corporation signed a new three-year agreement. In exchange for wage concessions, the employees received promises of cash profit-sharing bonuses in the future and stock in a nonleveraged ESOP. Similar contracts were negotiated with Bethlehem Steel, Wheeling-Pittsburgh Steel, CF&I Steel, and Kaiser Aluminum. Several of these agreements also resulted in a union representative being placed on the board of directors. To the extent that these companies recover, the employees involved will have something to show for the concessions they were going to have to make anyway to save their jobs.

In more than a dozen cases, the issue was not seeing the company over a tough period but preventing a shutdown or bankruptcy. In these cases, the USWA negotiated an employee buyout of the company using a leveraged ESOP. So far, only one of these companies has gone bankrupt.

One of the most successful USWA-led employee buyouts occurred at Copper Range Company, a copper mine in Michigan's Upper Peninsula. In 1985, the mine had been closed for more than two years because of low copper prices and bad labor-management relations when the owners decided to turn off the pumps and flood the mine. The USWA and local management offered to buy the mine instead. The mine reopened employing 900 workers. Management owned 30 percent of the new company's stock; USWA members took a 33 percent pay cut in exchange for a 70 percent ownership stake. By 1989, copper prices were up and the company had become profitable. The union members decided to sell to a German mining company, with the result that a typical member received more than $50,000 for his ESOP shares (not bad for four years' work). The German buyer agreed to significant wage improvements and to create a new ESOP that would acquire 20 percent of the new company's stock.

In 1985, Bliss-Salem, Inc., a manufacturer of rolling mills in Ohio, was down to 37 USWA member employees; annual sales were down to $8 million a year; and the company was losing over $1 million a year. The employees used an ESOP to buy most of the company's stock. By 1990, the company had sales of $40 million and more than 350 employees.

The largest buyout occurred at the end of 1989 when 5,000 workers purchased the bar division of LTV Steel and turned it into Republic Engineered Steels. This new company required more than $400 million of investment in new equipment, and the employees, through their ESOP, were the only buyers willing to make that kind of long-term investment in the American steel business.

The members of XYZ union were not so lucky. Because their union did not know how to use ESOPs to save troubled companies, thousands of this union's members lost their jobs in the 1980s. We will never know if the creative use of ESOPs would have saved any of these companies.

Improve Corporate Performance

Research conducted throughout the 1980s demonstrated that firms with significant levels of employee ownership performed as well or better than did their competitors. A 1980 study by Thomas Marsh and Dale McAllister, reported in the Spring 1981 issue of the *Journal of Corporation Law*, showed that companies with ESOPs had a productivity growth rate twice that of their competitors during the five-year period from 1975 to 1979. A 1983 study by Corey Rosen and Katherine Klein, reported in the August 1982 issue of the *Monthly Labor Review*, showed that companies with more than 50 per cent employee ownership created three times more jobs than did comparable companies. A 1986 study by Michael Quarrey, reported in the September, 1987 issue of the *Harvard Business Review*, looked at 45 companies with ESOPs, examining their performance both before and after setting up the ESOP and comparing that performance with their competitors. This study found that the ESOP companies grew 3.7 percent faster than their competitors before setting up the ESOP and 6.3 percent faster after setting up the ESOP.

What these and a dozen other studies demonstrate is that, in most cases, companies with employee owners do at least as well as their competition and often do better. They can have greater productivity and faster employment growth. They are also more likely to stay in business when business turns down.

These and other studies also show that one other variable helps account for these results—the way the employees are treated. Companies with employees who are given an ownership stake in the company and who are also given more say in how their individual job is performed do better than their competitors. Companies that introduce quality circles, total quality management, or other forms of participatory management without also introducing employee ownership do not have a general record of improved performance. Likewise, companies that introduce employee ownership without making an effort to listen to employees more, communicate with employees more, and allow employees to have a greater impact on how their jobs are structured also do not improve performance beyond the industry norm.

Agenda Item: Karl in the Shop

As I was sitting, listening, during our monthly shop committee (now called the worker owner committee) meeting, I was pleased but also a little concerned about one of the agenda items that said merely: Karl in the shop. I knew I'd been remiss in not going into the shop more often. Trips, outside activities, my personal life were all taking time and energy, and my usual daily walks through the shop had decreased. Silently I considered how I could be more disciplined and return to my regular habit of walking through the shop. I thought how I might come in earlier, stay later, change my schedule to get into the shop more often. I was pleased that my presence in the shop was considered important by the employees who now owned stock through their ESOP.

Finally, this item came up. Phil, a longtime friend and worker owner, looked very serious. He started by saying, "Karl, will you stay out of the shop?" Ouch! He continued to explain that the worker owners felt that if they polished the molds for Boeing the way I wanted them to, Boeing would take their work elsewhere. The worker owners were acting on their feeling of empowerment and telling the boss he was not only wrong, but they felt it would hurt the company's bottom line.

Now I still go out into the shop; but when I do, I work hard to make *suggestions and recommendations* on how I think something needs to be done. The worker owners like it better that way and so do I.

Karl A. A. Reuther
Reuther Mold & Mfg. Co.
Cuyahoga Falls, Ohio

These results are what common sense would lead us to expect. Forms of management that try to make employees take more responsibility for the quality of their work without giving them any incentive to do so seem destined to fail. Making employees owners without treating them any differently could actually cause them to perform less well if they feel cheated by the process. Companies that make employees owners and encourage them to take more initiative and responsibility can reap the benefits of improved corporate performance.

Perhaps the most famous ESOP success story after Weirton Steel in West Virginia is Springfield Remanufacturing in Missouri. This small company that specialized in rebuilding engines was a not very profitable division of International Harvester when in 1982 it was bought by the managers and the employees with an ESOP. The company's turnaround has been so successful that it now sponsors monthly seminars to teach other executives how to combine employee ownership with participatory management techniques. The company trains every worker to read a financial statement and then gives them the financial statements of the company so the workers can keep track of the company's progress. The company teaches their employees that business is a game and making a profit is how you win the game. After the ESOP buyout, the company had an 89-to-1 debt-to-equity ratio. It went on to grow from 165 to 500 employees by the end of 1989 and to pay off its original ESOP loan ahead of schedule.

Privatization and Economic Development

While most Americans do not realize it, companies are privatized in the United States every day. This happens because a company originally formed as a nonprofit corporation wishes to become a profit-making company, or a nonprofit corporation wishes to spin off a division into a profit-making company. We saw in Chapter 12 that this was how AdGap became a new profit-making company by spinning itself off from Synanon. The AdGap privatization used an ESOP to place the shares into the hands of the employees.

This method of privatization is almost unique in American history. The usual pattern is for a small group of managers and board members to have the company valued as low as possible. They then take out a loan, using the new company's assets as collateral, and pay the money either to the charity that once had owned the division, or to a group of charities following the guidelines of the state attorney general. Once the loan is paid off, the small group of managers and former board members own the company. That is the pattern of privatization that many former Communist party officials who still control most of the state-owned companies in Eastern Europe would like to see followed. For obvious reasons, some leaders in these countries are resisting this pattern, hoping instead to set up a system that will allow employees to participate in ownership through the use of an ESOP.

One approach to privatization is simply to give all the citizens certificates that they can use to buy shares in the new companies. The new companies go from being owned by the state to being owned by private citizens. Many experts do not think this is the best way to privatize these companies. These companies were assets of the government, and that government is now in need of money to provide social services for the citizens. Why should the government simply give away these companies? Besides, once they are given away, is there any reason to think that the companies will succeed without any capital to buy modern machinery? Also, the employees of the newly private company will be expected to make sacrifices. Why should they?

If we were advising these governments, we might suggest that, instead of giving these companies away, they should be sold. The government social security administration might keep some the shares to use in the future to pay for social services. Some shares could be sold to the employees through an ESOP, while other shares are sold on the open market to anyone with money to buy them. Half of the money paid by the ESOP and the outside investors would go to the government to compensate it for the company it no longer owns, and half would go to provide expansion capital for the new company.

Where would the ESOP loans come from? In 1990, 40 Western countries joined together to form the European Bank for Reconstruction and Development, with more than $12 billion in assets to lend to newly privatized companies. If these loans were made to ESOPs, these new companies would have the money they need for expansion and the employees would have a real ownership stake in the companies they work for. What better way to help insure that the loan will actually be repaid so more money will be available to lend to other East European companies in the future?

Economic development is a concern in every country, even in the United States. How can governments use tax benefits, loans, and grants to entice companies into areas that are economically depressed? Here is another area where ESOPs could play a role.

Take the case of a city that gave millions of dollars to outside investors to help them renovate a once grand hotel in the center of the city. The city put up most of the money for the renovation. If the project fails, the city will be out a lot of money and the investors will be out a little money. If the project is a success, the outside investors will own a valuable hotel and the city will ultimately receive tax revenues from it.

Is this a good deal for the city and its citizens? If the city is going to put up most of the money, shouldn't it have some ownership in the business? If it does not want to be a co-owner, why not treat the grant as if it were an ESOP loan and place shares in employee accounts over the years? Better still, why shouldn't the city receive shares for its contribution and sell those shares to a leveraged ESOP once the project is a success?

When the United States government agreed to provide a guaranteed loan to the Chrysler Corporation, it demanded that an ESOP be created to provide employees with an incentive to help save the company. It worked so well that the employees voted a few years later to close down the ESOP and take the money. Would there be a Chrysler Corporation today if there had not been an ESOP? We will never know. We do know that states and cities across America make similar loans and grants every year and could provide their citizens with a real benefit if they considered the use of ESOPs in more situations.

Employee ownership has already been used as part of the privatization process in countries such as Mexico, Argentina, and Great Britain. In each country, the use of employee ownership has had its advantages and disadvantages. In Great Britain, mainly the higher paid employees benefited. In Argentina, only 10 percent of the stock went to the employees, which was too little and too late in many cases. We can hope that the other countries of the world will be able to learn from these experiences to limit the disadvantages and increase the advantages. By setting up a real ESOP, which both pays money to the selling government and provides new working capital for expansion, the enterprises would have a much greater chance of success. By allocating the stock over many years in the future, the workers will have a real incentive to make the new company successful.

15

The Problem with ESOPs

In the last few chapters we have focused on the advantages of employee stock ownership plans (ESOPs) and cooperatives (co-ops). Both have disadvantages as well. In some cases, a profit-sharing plan can provide some of the advantages of an ESOP without some of the disadvantages. In some cases, an ESOP can provide some of the advantages of a co-op without some of the disadvantages.

Simulating an ESOP with a Profit-Sharing Plan: Pros and Cons

Two major advantages of an ESOP are the rollover feature for shareholders of private companies selling stock to an ESOP and the ability of ESOPs to borrow money for the company. If the owners of a company are not interested in these advantages, they might consider using a profit-sharing plan instead of an ESOP to give ownership to their employees.

While ESOP have advantages, they also have disadvantages, at least from the point of view of some people. If the company's shares are not traded on a stock exchange, the company must hire someone to perform an annual evaluation of the company and its stock. While this is not that expensive, particularly after the first year, it is an expense.

Shares held by a profit-sharing plan are not required to have such an evaluation. Employees must be allowed to vote their shares on major issues, such as mergers, if the shares are held by an ESOP. This is not the case with a profit-sharing plan. Generally, the trustee of a profit-sharing plan votes the shares on all issues. Also, when participants in an ESOP reach age 55, they have a right to ask that their account be diversified into a large group of stocks. Profit-sharing plans have no such diversification requirement.

An ESOP is required to invest primarily in the stock of the company the beneficiaries work for. A profit-sharing plan, on the other hand, can be written to allow all or most of its assets to be invested in the company's own stock, or it can be written to allow it to invest all or most of its assets in other stocks and bonds. This allows a profit-sharing plan to be more flexible, buying company stock when it is down and perhaps selling it when it is overpriced. Of course, a profit-sharing plan cannot borrow money, with the loan guaranteed by the company, to make a large stock purchase when the price is low, as an ESOP can. Also, once an ESOP is leveraged, up to 25 percent of payroll may be used to repay principal on the loan. A profit-sharing plan is generally limited to having 15 percent of payroll placed in the profit-sharing accounts of the employees. Before the Tax Reform Act of 1986, companies could place funds in a profit-sharing plan only if the company actually made a profit. Since 1986, companies have been free to place funds in a profit-sharing plan without regard to whether or not they actually made a profit in a particular year.

Generally, ESOP participants are entitled to ask for a distribution of their account earlier than are participants in a profit-sharing plan. An ESOP must allow people who die, retire, or become disabled to begin receiving money the year after they stop working for the company. Also, ESOP participants are allowed to receive their account balance at the end of the sixth year after they leave the company unless the ESOP loan has not been paid off. A profit-sharing plan does not have to make this preretirement distribution.

A profit-sharing plan may pay out in any way the plan specifies, including a lump sum payment, annual payments for a period of years, or annual payments over the life expectancy of the retiring employee. An ESOP participant can demand the stock instead of cash unless the bylaws of the company require all stockholders to be active employees. A profit-sharing plan participant can not demand the stock and will not receive stock in most cases in the United States (in Great Britain employees get the stock, not cash, from profit-sharing plans).

One advantage of an ESOP is the fact that dividends are tax deductible for the company when paid on ESOP stock and either passed through to the employees or used to pay down the ESOP loan. Dividends paid on stock held by a profit-sharing plan are not tax deductible to the corporation.

If a company wants employees to have a significant ownership stake in the company without any voting rights and without the right to ask for stock instead of cash, a profit-sharing plan can accomplish this goal. However, a profit-sharing plan will not be able to perform most of the functions discussed in the last two chapters. For example, it cannot borrow money for expansion or to buy out a major shareholder. It will not be able to act as a takeover defense because the law will generally consider the trustee of a profit-sharing plan to be a captive of management rather than a "real" shareholder when it comes time to count votes (this may be avoided by allowing the profit-sharing plan participants to vote their shares, just like ESOP participants).

Which should a company create? A profit-sharing plan can be turned into an ESOP or an ESOP can be set up alongside a profit-sharing plan when the time comes to take advantage of the ESOP's special abilities, so it is not an either-or decision. Because both profit-sharing plans and ESOPs are defined-contribution plans, they should, at least in theory, be easier to terminate than regular pension plans. The employees are given the value of their individual accounts, and they can roll over that money into Individual Retirement Accounts (IRAs). Of course, because we are talking about the Internal Revenue Code, things are never as simple as they could be, but profit-sharing plans and ESOPs are more flexible than defined-benefit pension plans. They do not have to be insured as defined-benefit pension plans must be, and they are not subject to some of the regulations that have made defined-benefit pension plans a disappearing species on the American employment landscape.

For a variety of reasons, some of America's largest corporations have placed a significant amount of stock in their profit-sharing plans.

The Hallmark company, a company that is on everyone's list of the best companies to work for, is about one-third employee owned through its profit-sharing plan. Procter & Gamble, a company in the top 20 of the Fortune 500 list, has a profit-sharing plan that currently owns about one-fourth of the company's stock. Procter & Gamble allows employees to vote all of the shares they have in the company profit-sharing plan on all corporate issues. In 1984–1985, Quaker Oats Company changed its profit-sharing plan to allow employees to vote the shares in their accounts; the company also established an ESOP. In 1989, Quaker Oats decided the advantages of an ESOP outweighed the disadvantages, terminated its profit-sharing plan, and increased the annual contribution to the ESOP. The ESOP will hold mainly convertible preferred stock.

Simulating a Co-op with an ESOP: Pros and Cons

At the end of Chapter 11 we discussed briefly the possibility of simulating a co-op with an ESOP. Let's return to that discussion knowing what we now know about ESOPs. What are some of the problems with a co-op? Some people don't like the fact that everyone is equal. They think people who have been with the company longer should have more say in how the company is run. This can be done with an ESOP because the longer an employee is with the company, the more shares the employee will have in his or her individual account and the more votes at the shareholder's meetings.

Cooperatives, particularly very successful co-ops, face another problem. Outgoing members want to receive the true economic value of their share of the company, but a new member often does not have enough money to buy them out. Because the organization is a co-op, this share cannot be sold to a nonmember, causing a financial problem for everyone involved. With an ESOP, the outgoing member can sell all of his or her shares to the company or the ESOP for their true value, while the new employee acquires stock slowly over the years as stock is placed into the employee's individual ESOP account.

For those who want the buyout flexibility of an ESOP but the equal voting rights of a co-op, an ESOP can also oblige. An ESOP can be written so that every ESOP participant has one vote, regardless of the number of shares in the person's individual account, which would allow the ESOP to act as a co-op for the purposes of voting and an ESOP for the purposes of valuing the individual's financial stake in the company over the years.

One reason co-ops do not borrow money for expansion is because many lenders expect a seat on the board of directors when they make a large loan to a small company. In many countries, a co-op cannot oblige them. An ESOP company can. It can set up its board of directors to contain employee representatives, bank representatives, and outside directors from the community or other businesses. Also, unlike a co-op, an ESOP can borrow money and deduct the principal along with the interest payments. This ability to deduct principal payments and dividend payments made to the ESOP to pay off the ESOP loan makes an ESOP loan a better risk than most loans to small companies.

One of the problems with trying to structure a corporation to act like a co-op has been the problem of double taxation. A corporation must pay taxes before paying dividends. However, a corporation with an ESOP does not have this problem to the extent that all or most of the shares are held by an ESOP and passed through to the ESOP participants. This also avoids the payment of Social Security taxes, which are due on "wages" but not on dividends.

As noted in Part One, there are many attributes of ownership, and these attributes can be divided up using corporation and securities law. One company that took advantage of this was Republic Container. When the employees bought the company through an ESOP, their new company issued two kinds of stock. The first type of stock has full control over the corporation but no claim to earnings or assets. In other words, the first type of stock runs the company. Every employee is given one share of this type of stock and must surrender it upon leaving the company. The second type of stock, held by the ESOP, does not carry voting rights but does have a claim on the income and assets of the company. These shares are allocated to employees on the basis of pay; however, no employee gets an allocation for more than $20,000 a year in wages, which means most employees receive the same allocation each year.

Given all the things that can be done with an ESOP, every worker cooperative of any size in the United States should consider conversion to an ESOP company. Compared with a co-op, an ESOP is more expensive to create and manage, at least in terms of legal and plan management fees, but the advantages of an ESOP should soon outweigh these higher expenses.

The Problem with the Labor Department

In the United States, ESOPs are subject to regulation by both the Internal Revenue Service and the U.S. Department of Labor. This double regulation of pension and benefit plans is certainly one of the reasons why a company might think twice before setting up any pension or benefit plan. In some cases, in their desire to "protect" workers, the Labor Department has protected them right out of a chance to own shares in the company they work for. There have been two situations where this is a problem: when the ESOP is part of a leveraged buyout of a company, and when an ESOP buys a large block of stock using borrowed funds.

Section 3(18)(B) of the Employee Retirement Income Security Act (ERISA) says that an ESOP can only pay "adequate consideration" for the shares it purchases. This is defined to be the "fair market value" of the shares. But how do we decide the fair market value? If the shares are publicly traded, this is easy—the market sets the price. If the shares are not publicly traded, then the value should be based on the "unbiased judgment" of someone expert in this field.

Imagine a hypothetical leveraged buyout of a large company. Mr. Fatcat is planning to purchase 100 percent of the stock in the company and wants to pay as little as possible in cash. He finds he can borrow money from a variety of sources to purchase 60 percent of the company. If we suppose that the company costs $100 million, this means that the lenders will lend $60 million and Mr. Fatcat must come up with $40 million.

The employees, usually through their union, go to Mr. Fatcat and ask to participate in the buyout through an ESOP. Mr. Fatcat asks what the ESOP has to offer. The employees explain that because both principal and interest are tax deductible, the ESOP can borrow more money than would usually be the case. In this instance, the ESOP can borrow $70 million so that Mr. Fatcat has to put up only $30 million. Also, if the ESOP owns more than 50 percent of the stock, the interest rate will be lower. Again, this makes it possible to borrow more money or to pay off the loan quicker. Mr. Fatcat is intrigued. But the ESOP has to have controlling interest for this lower interest rate to work, which bothers Mr. Fatcat.

The employees explain that they are willing to allow Mr. Fatcat to elect a third of the members of the board of directors, the employees will elect a third through the ESOP, and the rest of the directors will be from the bank and other outside sources acceptable to both the employees and Mr. Fatcat. That seems fair to Mr. Fatcat. He figures the deductible principal, the lower interest rate, and higher employee morale are worth something. The employees are also willing to forgo a scheduled pay raise until the company meets a set of profitability criteria, which also adds value to their offer. But how much? The employees and their union believe that what they can offer is worth 51 percent of the stock and what Mr. Fatcat can offer—cold cash to the tune of $30 million—is worth 49 percent of the stock.

From Mr. Fatcat's point of view, the employees are driving a very hard bargain. They bring lower wage costs, higher employee morale, a lower interest rate on the loan, and a larger loan. They do not bring any cash to the table. Mr. Fatcat can get the loan without the ESOP, but the ESOP loan has some nice features. He also likes the rollover feature; if he keeps his shares in this private company for more than three years and then sells them to the ESOP, he can roll over the proceeds and delay paying income taxes on his gain. He doesn't think he will want to do this but it is a possibility. Mr. Fatcat agrees, but the Labor Department says no.

What is the Labor Department's objection? They say that the money the ESOP borrows, in this case $70 million, should be treated just like the cash Mr. Fatcat puts up. The ESOP should own 70 percent of the stock, and Mr. Fatcat should own 30 percent. Mr. Fatcat says no deal. He thought giving the ESOP 51 percent was too steep; besides, he can borrow most of that money without the ESOP. The deal is off, which is a shame.

The deal Mr. Fatcat was about to agree to was a real bargain for the employees. They were getting a large block of stock in the new company. Because of the lower interest rate and deductibility of principal, the newly leveraged company would have been more likely to stay out of bankruptcy court. Instead Mr. Fatcat went through with the deal without an ESOP, the company ran into a recession, and a third of the employees lost their jobs. The company went into bankruptcy, so the lender had to hire lawyers to get part of the money back that it had lent to Mr. Fatcat for the buyout. Mr. Fatcat had to fight to maintain his ownership stake in the company.

When the company was reorganized, the employees still did not have any ownership stake in the company but they did have lower wages (their union wage agreement was canceled by the bankruptcy judge), and many of their former co-workers were on unemployment. The small profit-sharing plan they did have was canceled because the company could not afford to make the payments. The Labor Department "protected" these workers right into the poorhouse.

A second example of the Labor Department's misguided "protection" surfaced in the summer of 1990, when the Labor Department sued the ESOP trustees for the Wardwell Braiding Machine Company (17 BNA Pension Reporter 1494 (D.R.I. 1990)). The Labor Department's complaint alleged that, in December 1985, the board of directors of the Wardwell Braiding Company agreed to set up an ESOP that would purchase 2,600 shares of common stock for $5,460,000. This was a leveraged ESOP with a 10-year loan. The Labor Department sued, arguing that the ESOP had paid more than "adequate consideration" for the shares. Why did the Labor Department think this? Because once the ESOP loan was taken out, the company became a highly leveraged company with a debt of more than $5 million (the debt taken on to allow the ESOP to buy the stock). As a consequence, the share value of the stock after the purchase was a great deal less than the purchase price. To which the defendants responded, "Of course it was."

To see why, imagine that you are buying a company worth $6 million, and the ESOP is borrowing $5 million to buy most of the shares of the company. The day before the deal the company is worth $6 million and has no debt. The day after the deal the company is worth $1 million ($6 million of value minus $5 million of debt). If our hypothetical ESOP paid $12 a share (using borrowed funds), the shares might be valued at $2 a share after the ESOP loan is taken out. Of course, over the years, as the loan is paid off, the share price will rise to reflect the lowering of the debt.

The same thing happens when a person buys a house. The buyer puts up $10,000 cash as a down payment and the bank lends $90,000 so the buyer can purchase a house worth $100,000. The homeowner has paid $100,000, but the house is worth only $10,000 when the debt is taken into consideration. But the buyer has not been cheated in this case. The individual put up $10,000 cash and has a house worth $10,000, but a house that will be worth much more when the loan is paid off.

In the Wardwell Braiding case, the ESOP put up no cash whatsoever. What the ESOP did (and it was a pretty neat trick) was to purchase a large block of stock with nothing! To do this, the company had to take on debt that reduced the value of the company, at least on its balance sheet, because assets minus debts equaled a lower amount for shareholder equity. As the loan is paid off, the stock will rise in value.

The Labor Department was eventually convinced to drop its complaint in the Wardwell Braiding case. What is worrisome about this case, however, is the Labor Department's apparent lack of understanding about how these transactions work. To return to the hypothetical $5 million loan discussed above, using the Labor Department's reasoning, the ESOP paid $12 a share for stock that was worth only $2 a share the next day. The correct analysis is that the ESOP paid $0 a share for stock that was worth $2 a share the next day and will be worth a great deal more in the years to come. This is not a stupid deal, it is a brilliant deal, a deal anyone in the world would kill for! We can only hope in the future that the Labor Department will allow employees to take part in these amazing deals and not "protect" them out of the potential gains that might come their way.

The Problems with ESOPs

A wide variety of critics have made a number of complaints about ESOPs during the 1980s. Let's take them one at a time.

1. *ESOPs are risky.* Critics point out that ESOPs buy stock in just one company, rather than in a large number of companies, and that this in inherently risky for the participants. This may be true theoretically, but look at the financial reality of most ESOPs. The company would not have an employee benefit plan if it could not have an ESOP. The employees have shares that may be risky, but they would have nothing without the ESOP. Also, the employees have not put up their own hard-earned money to buy the stock. Instead, they have done what rich people have been doing for centuries—borrowed money to buy the stock. ESOP participants have the best deal in history: they haven't had to put up even a down payment, and they are not personally liable to pay off the debt.

2. *ESOPs don't build enough wealth for employees.* If Congress has given ESOPs all of these advantages, why don't ESOPs own hundreds of billions of dollars worth of stock? The answer is, Give it time. When pension and benefit funds began to expand during World War II, they also didn't own much stock after only a few years of existence. By the 1990s, they owned trillions of dollars worth of stocks, bonds, and real estate and will have a controlling interest in most large U.S. companies by the end of the decade. While ESOPs will not match this growth record, as ESOP loans are paid off and as ESOP companies grow, ESOPs will come to own hundreds of billions of dollars worth of stock by the turn of the century. In many cases, this is stock that the participating employees would never have been able to afford to buy any other way.

3. *ESOPs don't make companies more productive.* One of the reasons that Congress gave ESOPs the advantages they have was the belief that if employees owned stock in the companies for which they worked, they would work harder and smarter. Research throughout the 1980s demonstrated that this was true only if the ESOP was combined with a real plan to give employees more input in how their particular job was done. This makes sense when you think about it. Imagine a company president telling a group of employees that they are now owners of a significant share of the company's stock and ending the speech with, "All right, now shut up and get back to work!" That has happened

in some cases. If productivity is the desired result, ownership alone is not enough. That ownership has to be combined with a real effort to allow those new owners to contribute their ideas. Participatory management has paid off in hundreds of ESOP companies across America.

Connor Springs Company based in California is one example. The Japanese companies that it supplies no longer test Connor Springs parts because Connor Springs has demonstrated a consistent ability to deliver quality products. How does it do that? Part of the quality assurance program is to give every employee the power to shut down the assembly line that he or she is working on if there is a problem. Employees do just that from time to time. As one Connor Springs executive put it, "I wouldn't be willing to give that power to people who were not also owners."

4. *ESOP employees are not full owners because they don't vote.* Critics charge that ESOP participants are not real owners because they do not always have full voting rights. If the company is a public company, ESOP employees vote their shares just like any other shareholder. If it is a private company, ESOP employees can be given full voting rights or be limited to voting only on major issues such as whether or not the company should merge. Let's put this into perspective. American workers will soon own a controlling interest in a majority of America's largest corporations. Those workers will have absolutely no say in how those companies behave. They own those shares through pension and benefit funds whose trustees vote the shares without consulting the employees, who are the beneficiaries of the fund. Employees in ESOPs have far more voting rights that these other workers. Second, in cases where ESOP employees have not been given full voting rights, the company probably would not have set up an ESOP if that had been a requirement. Surely partial voting rights and ownership of shares the employees would not otherwise have owned are better than no shares at all.

5. *ESOPs cost the taxpayers too much.* ESOPs enjoy tax advantages. Most of these advantages are also enjoyed by other plans, such as profit-sharing plans, and are not unique to ESOPs. About the only tax advantage that is unique to ESOPs is the ability to

borrow money at a lower interest rate because the lender can exclude from income taxes half of the interest income. This advantage has never cost the United States government more than $1 billion a year; in most years, it has been significantly less than that. A more legitimate complaint would be the more than $40 billion a year the government spends to subsidize the purchase of mansions by its wealthiest citizens! Under current rules, this special interest rate is available only if the ESOP owns more than 50 percent of the stock and the employees vote their stock. Because of these restrictions, these low-interest-rate ESOP loans are usually found in situations where the company would be a candidate for bankruptcy without the help of an ESOP loan. More than half of these "troubled" ESOP companies are still in business, paying taxes and keeping their employees off unemployment and welfare. It is difficult to add up the numbers, but government is saving a significant amount by keeping these companies in business. To the extent that these once-troubled companies grow and become real competitors on the world market, as Chrysler did after its bailout, this is a good investment for U.S. taxpayers.

APPENDIX

ESOPs and Profit-Sharing Plans in Great Britain

Since 1978, British companies have been able to set up profit-sharing plans to purchase their own shares and ultimately to distribute those

This appendix was written by the author, based in part on information furnished by the ESOP Center in London and the law firm of Clifford Chance, also based in London. While I wish to thank them for the information supplied, I am responsible for any errors this appendix may contain. British law is still changing rapidly in this area, and this short summary is meant to point out the basic similarities and differences between British and American ESOPs, not to serve as a legal guide. Anyone considering setting up an ESOP under British law should contact a law firm or the ESOP Center in London for the most up-to-date information.

shares to the employees. A trust is set up and the company makes contributions to the trust for employees. These contributions are tax deductible for the company if the rules of Inland Revenue (the British equivalent of the U.S. Internal Revenue Service) are met. Shares are purchased with the money and placed in the individual accounts of the employees. While a trust participant, the employee can vote the shares in his or her account just like any other shareholder. Employees may have an amount equal to 10 percent of annual salary (up to a maximum of £6,000 a year) placed in their individual account. Employees who make less than £20,000 a year may have up to £2,000 placed in their account each year regardless of their actual salary. Funds must be allocated on "similar terms" to all employees based on a percentage of salary or length of service (or, presumably, an equal amount for each employee if that amount is £2,000 a year or less).

Why would employees want to have money placed in such a fund instead of receiving it as wages? The tax advantages are significant. First, the money placed in the trust is not subject to the income and social security taxes that wages are subject to. Second, after the shares have been in the trust for five years, they are distributed to the employees. While the shares are in the trust, the dividends on the shares are passed through to the employees. When the employees sell shares, they only pay capital gains taxes on any increase in value over the price originally paid for the shares. Because everyone in Great Britain can receive up to £5,500 of capital gains a year tax free, most employees will not pay any tax on this increase in share value. These shares are also subject to indexation relief, meaning any increase in value due to inflation is not counted as taxable gain.

Since the mid-1980s, Britain has been moving toward developing an employee stock ownership plan similar in many respects to the U.S. version. The major difference between a profit-sharing plan and an ESOP in both Great Britain and the United States is the ESOP's ability to borrow money to purchase a large block of shares. As in the United States, a British company sets up a trust, which borrows money (with the loan guaranteed by the company) and buys a large number of the company's shares (either from the company or on the open market). In Great Britain, most companies set up two trusts, an ESOP trust to borrow the money and buy a large block of shares, and a profit-sharing trust to accept contributions from the company each year. This contributed money is used to buy shares from the ESOP trust and place them in the employee's individual accounts. The ESOP trust uses these contributions and any dividends it receives on the shares it owns to pay off the loan it took out to purchase the shares in the first place. As with any British profit-sharing plan, the employees receive the shares after they have been held by the plan for five years; employees do not pay any income tax until those shares are sold.

The early ESOPs in Great Britain were set up without specific legislation and are commonly called "case law" ESOPs. In the Finance Act of 1989, ESOPs were recognized in British statute law for the first time. Also, after the Finance Act of 1990, owners of stock in private British companies can now enjoy the "rollover" feature similar to that available for American ESOPs, providing the companies use a statutory ESOP (the ESOP must end up owning at least 10 percent of the company's stock). This ability to roll over the proceeds of the sale of stock to an ESOP and avoid capital gains taxes until the replacement securities are sold should encourage wider use of statutory ESOPs in Great Britain in the future.

Whether case law or statutory, a British ESOP can do most of the things an American ESOP can do: buy out a retiring owner, provide a market for shares in a private company, provide employees with a stake in a leveraged buyout, provide a tax-efficient way to raise new capital, and provide employees with a long-term financial stake in the company they work for.

There are differences between the British and American ESOP. In the United States, ESOPs must benefit a large group of employees. In Great Britain, an ESOP can be set up to benefit only top management (although if it is paired with an approved profit-sharing plan, the rules that apply to profit-sharing plans must also be followed). In the United States, an ESOP trust is generally exempt from taxes on its income and capital gains. In Great Britain, an ESOP trust may be subject to such taxes. In the United States, ESOPs can be set up without share-holder approval in most cases. In Great Britain, the U.K. Stock Exchange requires that all employee share-ownership schemes (including stock options and ESOPs) that are adopted by listed companies and that involve the issuing of new shares be approved by shareholders.

Groups representing large institutional investors such as the Association of British Insurers and the National Association of Pension Funds
have adopted guidelines concerning when they will agree, as shareholders, to employee share-ownership schemes. Basically, these guidelines limit the issuance of new shares to employees to 10 percent of
issued common stock over any 10-year period. For stock option plans
for top executives, that amount is limited to 5 percent over a 10-year
period. If an ESOP purchases existing shares (which is usually the
case, unless the ESOP is being used to borrow additional capital in a
tax-advantaged way), these guidelines would not apply.

Changes in British law due to the Finance Act of 1990 make it clear
that an ESOP can borrow money from an outside source, such as a
bank, and have the company guarantee the loan. While there is no
special interest rate tax break available in Great Britain similar to the
interest income exclusion that can be available in the United States,
there is one way a British ESOP can save money. If the shares purchased with the ESOP loan are "owned" by the bank, the bank can
receive tax-free dividend income on those shares. This can be used to
reduce the interest payments paid by the ESOP, with the ESOP buying
the shares at an agreed price from the bank as the loan is paid off. The
ESOP then sells the shares to the company's profit-sharing plan for
allocation to employees.

The creation of statutory ESOPs did not bring about the formation
of very many ESOPs in Great Britain because of the strict rules that
apply to the creation and operation of a statutory ESOP. For example,
a majority of the trustees of the statutory ESOP must be elected by
the employees. If such a rule had been in force in the United States,
few ESOPs would probably have been created. Also, a statutory ESOP
must allocate shares to a large group of employees, while many case
law ESOPs have been set up to benefit only top management.

By the end of 1991, less than 100 ESOPs had been created in
Great Britain. If we count only ESOPs designed to benefit most of a
company's employees, rather than just top management, only a few
dozen were in existence by the end of 1991, and several of those were
created as part of the privatization of British companies in the 1980s.
As the retiring owners of private companies learn about the rollover
feature, we can expect this number to increase greatly in the 1990s.

16

The Future of
Ownership Sharing

People who try to predict the future by using something other than a crystal ball usually begin, "If trends continue." We will not be an exception. If trends continue, U.S. pension and benefit funds will own a controlling interest in most of America's 1,000 largest corporations by the end of the 1990s. If trends continue, the employees of those companies, as a group, will be the largest single stockholder in more than half of those 1,000 corporations. Employees will have a significant ownership stake in 20,000 other American corporations, ranging in size from J.C. Penney, with its 175,000 employees, to companies with a few dozen employees.

The United States will be the first modern industrial society to be "really" owned by its workers. That ownership will be structured in an amazing variety of ways. American workers will own stock in companies they do not work for mainly through pension plans, thrift plans, profit-sharing plans, and private after-tax investments in mutual funds. American workers will own stock in the companies they do work for through stock option and stock purchase plans, payment in the form of regular and restricted stock, employee stock ownership plans (ESOPs), pension funds, thrift plans, and profit-sharing plans.

In Trusts We Trust

All U.S. currency is imprinted with the motto In God We Trust. It should say In Trusts We Trust. What began as a way to get around the wage-control laws imposed during World War II has become the greatest engine for private investment and wealth creation in history. While the United States government has gone deeper and deeper into debt during the 1980s, American pension and benefit trust funds have become more and more powerful as players on the world economic stage. These trusts have just begun to invest in companies outside the United States. This trend will continue as these trusts seek to diversify their holdings not only by buying stock in a large number of companies, but also by buying the stock of companies centered in a large number of countries. In the twenty-first century, the real test of whether or not a developing country has "made it" will be whether or not U.S. and other pension and employee benefit funds feel they can invest in the stock of that country's companies without taking an unreasonable risk.

When many of the leaders in these developing countries think of the "threat" of outside investors, they usually conjure up pictures of mysterious millionaires from London or executives from giant Japanese conglomerates coming to rape the local countryside and exploit the local population. More and more during the twenty-first century these outside investors will be trusts representing workers in the United States and other countries investing for their retirement. These trusts will not want to rape anything or exploit anyone. They will want a reasonable return on the money they invest. They will demand political stability and laws governing corporate governance and the sale of securities that assure them a voice in the companies they invest in (in other words, they will not be investing in Peru as long as the Shining Path Movement controls the countryside or in Japan as long as major stockholders can be kept off the board of directors). They will want a chance to reap a windfall if a takeover artist comes knocking, so they will be loath to invest in companies incorporated in states such as Delaware, Georgia, Illinois, Kansas, Pennsylvania, Massachusetts, New York, New Jersey, or South Dakota, where special statutes make it difficult for takeover artists to engineer a buyout.

These pension and benefit funds will be familiar with the idea that ownership should be shared with the employees, not as a gift but as a reward for work done and as part of the regular compensation plan. They will want to know how the countries they might invest in intend to bring this about. They will also want to know what the countries they might invest in are doing to encourage their citizens in general to own shares in local companies both through pension and benefit plans and directly through incentives to make stock purchases. They will avoid investing in Austria or Australia until the citizens of those countries significantly increase the breadth and depth of their investment in their own economies.

Other factors will be looked at in judging the potential for long-term economic growth in various countries. The ratio of the national government's debt to the nation's gross national product will be one measure. Just as a company with debts equal to or greater than the stockholder's equity are not generally considered to be good investments, so countries that owe more than the entire economy can produce in a year will be struck off the list. Canada and the United States, with national debts fast approaching this level, may soon find that their own pension and benefit funds will no longer invest in the stocks and bonds issued by their own corporations.

More and more these funds will be looking to invest in growth companies. This will be another reason not to invest in Japan. During the 1970s and 1980s, a new automobile company emerged in Japan, Honda. Because of the closed nature of the Japanese economy, this excellent company had to essentially become an American company to grow.

Some critics argue that benefit and pension funds do little to help the economy because simply buying stock that is publicly traded on stock exchanges does not really create new investment. Nothing could be further from the truth. Venture capitalists are willing to take risks with their money by investing in start-up companies only because they know there will be a market for their shares if the company does grow and become successful. The same is true of employees who accept stock and stock options in the hope the company will eventually "go public" and their stock worth pennies when first acquired will be worth dollars when sold.

Exhibit 16.1   Investing for Retirement Based on Annual
Contribution of $4,000 from 1971 through 1991

Instrument	Annual Average Return	Accumulated Savings*
Treasury bills	7.74%	$191,627
Corporate bonds	9.45	235,614
Stocks (S&P 500)	11.83	316,022

Source: Terence P. Pare, "How Good a Deal Is Your 401(k)?" *Fortune*, 15 June 1992, 45–46.
* Assume investment compounded at average annual rate.

Thinking of Retirement

What should someone planing for retirement do to help insure a secure retirement? First, the retiree will have Social Security. Social Security is a defined-benefit pension fund guaranteed by the federal government and indexed to increase payments with inflation. This is the only kind of defined-benefit pension fund most people should have, if given a choice. The defined-benefit pension funds offered by government employers are also indexed for inflation and guaranteed by a government with the ability to raise taxes if necessary to make the payments to its retired workers.

In the private sector in the United States, defined-benefit pension funds have not been a very good deal in most cases. First, they do not adjust for inflation. Second, more and more pension plans are "integrated" with Social Security, meaning the payment to the retired worker will be reduced by the amount paid by Social Security. In other words, as Social Security payments go up to keep pace with inflation, the defined-benefit pension payment will simply go down and the retired worker will not really be keeping up with inflation after all.

If possible, a private sector worker should have two defined-contribution benefit funds. The first should be a profit-sharing plan or a thrift plan that takes pretax dollars and invests in a wide variety of growth stocks. The value of these investments will rise with inflation and as the economy grows. Exhibit 16.1 shows the average return on three basic types of investments during the 1970s and 1980s and the amount someone who invested $4,000 a year in a 401(k) plan would have at the end of 20 years if the person had invested in each of the three basic types of investments. Nothing beats stock in the long run. That has been true throughout the twentieth century, even including the Great Depression years of the 1930s.

The second defined-contribution plan should be a leveraged ESOP. The leveraged ESOP allows the employer to place 25 percent of payroll in a combination of an ESOP and a defined-contribution fund. This allows for the maximum use of tax-free dollars for investment for the future. While the ESOP investment will in some ways be riskier, in other ways it will be safer. By buying stock with borrowed money, the employees have the best chance of getting the stock while the value is low and selling it decades later when the value is high. As we have seen in earlier chapters, the stock price will go up in most cases simply as a factor of having the ESOP loan paid off, if for no other reason.

While ESOP participants will have many of their eggs in one basket, they will have the comfort of knowing that so do their fellow employees, which gives everyone a real incentive to see to it that their company is successful. During the 1980s, many financially healthy companies were bought using a leveraged buyout (LBO). Many of these ended up in bankruptcy court during the recession of 1990–1992. However, none of the healthy company LBOs that used an ESOP loan ended up in bankruptcy. This suggests that if a company is going to be leveraged, the ESOP is a safer way to go in most cases.

Of course, anyone planning for retirement will want to own a paid-for home when they retire and have their debts paid off. Money from Social Security and the profit-sharing or thrift plan will provide basic living expenses. The money from the ESOP, if the company was successful, will make the difference between getting by and having a great time.

The Tax Man Cometh Again

We began this book by looking at what history will say was one of the great inventions of modern government, the tax incentive. It was also one of the worst inventions because it became a license for politicians to put in thousands of special tax loopholes for wealthy campaign contributors. If anyone asked us what we would do to rationalize the

American personal income tax system, we might answer by saying that there should be a few special tax incentives for individuals, and that's all. If government wants to do other things, those other things should be done by paying out direct subsidies. Let's suppose the personal income tax system in the United States began with the basic tax brackets of 15 percent for those making below an annual adjusted gross income of $25,000, 30 percent for those with incomes between $25,000 and $100,000, and 40 percent for those with incomes above $100,000.

There would be a $6,000-a-year personal income tax exemption. No one can live on less that $6,000 a year, so this seems reasonable. There would be up to a $6,000-a-year deduction for dependents. There would be a $6,000-a-year deduction for taxpayers who own their own home, regardless of the size or existence of a mortgage. This would encourage everyone to buy a home, particularly those low-income people who are not encouraged by the current system of mortgage interest deductions, which currently costs more than $40 billion in lost tax revenue and mainly goes to the richest 20 percent of Americans. There would be up to a $6,000-a-year deduction for contributions to charities. This is the other big tax loophole for America's richest citizens, who have the privilege of putting their money into private trust funds instead of paying it over as taxes (that is what President Bush did with most of his income while he was president). The average person does not get to do this and neither should rich people. Finally, the first $6,000 of dividend income received from U.S. corporations would be tax free. A person who took advantage of these five exemptions and deductions would earn almost $55,000 before having to move into the 30 percent tax bracket.

If we take into account the fact that lower-income taxpayers are paying more than 15 percent in Social Security taxes a year and that those earning more than $55,000 a year are not, we would really have a flat tax of about 30 percent for 95 percent of the U.S. population.

What about capital gains? We heard a lot about capital gains during the 1992 presidential campaign. Why should capital gains get a tax break? The major reason is to encourage investment in the U.S. economy. All right, let's make half of all capital gains tax free if the gain is from buying and selling common stock in U.S. companies and the stock is held for at least five years. To qualify as a U.S. company, the company would have to be incorporated in the United States (not be controlled by a foreign company) and spend more than half of its payroll in the United States.

What about capital gains that come from buying and selling everything else, from paintings to antique furniture? Why should the tax system encourage rich people to do this with their money when we need them to invest in American companies? If you insist, then let's let everyone have up to $6,000 a year of capital gains of that sort tax free (they would have to hold the object at least five years). This makes it fair for the middle class rather than just a tax break for the rich. Americans already receive a tax break when they get old enough and sell their big homes to buy smaller retirement homes, so we don't need to plan for that in the capital gains section of the tax code.

If this new tax system were put in place, we could expect the average price of stock in U.S. companies to increase between 20 and 25 percent. While this would make the rich richer, it would make the pension, benefit, and mutual funds that own more than half of the common stock of U.S. corporations richer as well. It would greatly reduce the chances that the Pension Benefit Guarantee Corporation would have to bail out private defined-benefit pension funds in the decades to come.

Why should we raise taxes on the rich to 40 percent and then give them a tax break if they invest in American companies? Because the current system does not give them much incentive to take the risks involved in buying stock. Studies of America's richest individuals suggest that most of their wealth is invested currently in very safe bonds. Even if we gave them a capital gains tax break, if they are subject to only about a 30 percent income tax rate, a break on capital gains taxes might not stimulate them to buy stock. By raising their taxes to 40 percent and then giving them a tax break for investing in U.S. companies, we can expect a great deal more investment.

Economic Development in the 1990s

When we look at the countries that developed successfully during the last two centuries, we see that they did it in one of two ways (or a combination of the two). They either encouraged foreigners with money to invest in their economies, or they encouraged their own citizens to invest. During the 1970s and 1980s, a group of developing counties tried a third approach, borrowing large sums of money from foreign banks. This turned out to be a disaster that will haunt them into the next century.

How do countries encourage foreigners to make investments in the local economy? They stabilize the political system and create a stable and active stock market where local citizens can buy and sell stock. How do they encourage their own citizens to invest? Japan taxed the interest on savings at a much lower rate. This provided the funds needed to rebuild the Japanese economy after World War II. It also left Japan with an economy in which a handful of families actually "own" most of the economy. A developing country that wished to learn from the past might kill two birds with one stone. By encouraging citizens to invest in local corporations through tax incentives that encourage them to buy stock, they would both create and stimulate a local stock market and encourage local citizens to invest in their own economies.

The easiest way to do this would be to allow citizens to invest pretax dollars up to some maximum a year in the restricted stock of local companies. This stock could not be sold for a period of years, let's say five. When sold, the income would be taxed at a special capital gains tax rate, not as regular income. The combination of being able to invest with pretax dollars and paying lower taxes when the stock is finally sold should be enough.

Of course, for this to be an incentive, there must be a personal income tax and that tax rate must be high. The average American pays 15 percent Social Security taxes and another 15 percent in other income taxes. This would be enough. A country such as Ireland, with a 50 percent tax bracket for most income and a relatively sophisticated citizenry, might find a tremendous increase in local investment. The key would be to require those stock purchases to be in local companies. No developing country should follow the example of Canada and provide tax incentives for investing in the stock of another country's companies. That has helped the U.S. stock market to stay strong but it has not done anything for Canada.

Many countries with a large foreign debt also have many state-owned enterprises in need of privatization. One way that U.S. companies in bankruptcy get out of bankruptcy is to turn debt into equity. Banks and others who once held bonds and other forms of debt are given stock in exchange. If the new company with less debt is successful, the shareholders eventually get their money back when they sell their shares. The same thing could be done using stock and an ESOP. A country with a lot of foreign debt could privatize its state-owned enterprises and give banks holding the debt stock in the companies in exchange for part of the debt. The rest of the debt would be transferred to the companies in the form of an ESOP loan. As the loans are paid off, the rest of the stock would be distributed to the employees. The country would no longer be in debt, and the newly privatized enterprises would have a real chance to succeed.

In many parts of the world, a visitor is struck by the contrast between the wealth of the region in the form of natural resources and the poverty of the people who live there. This is usually the case because the wealth is owned by people who do not live in the region. The profits from the exploitation of those natural resources are shipped to another region to be spent or invested.

This picture is not universal. In some areas, the local region is rich and so are the people who live there. This invariably means that the owners live in the area. If those owners are also spread out among the general population, investing and spending the money they have earned in the area, then the best kind of economic development has taken place. By encouraging workers to become owners, local companies can be anchored in the community (worker-owners seldom vote to move the factory to another country), and the greatest economic benefit can be achieved from every dollar earned by the sale of local products. The Mondragon region in Spain is a testament to what can happen when profits are spent and invested in the local area instead of being shipped to another region.

The Legacy of President Reagan

During the 1980s, President Ronald Reagan set out to accomplish, and did accomplish, three things: make the rich richer by lowering their taxes, create 20 million new low-paying jobs, and win the Cold War. He also violated the fundamental principles of macroeconomics, which resulted in a weakened U.S. infrastructure and a $4 trillion national debt.

The fundamental principles of macroeconomics tell us that during a recession or a depression the national government can be the employer and borrower of last resort. If the private sector cannot employ everyone, government can hire the unemployed to work on public works projects that improve the society's infrastructure. If interest rates are low and capital still goes begging, government can borrow that money and use it to improve the society.

President Reagan paid $150 billion a year to people without asking them to do anything. He called it welfare. What a waste of public funds! He borrowed $3 trillion even though interest rates were very high, leaving later generations to pay off those high-interest-rate bonds for decades to come.

Government Policy and Stock Prices

By the mid-1990s, a third of all the common stock in U.S. corporations will be owned by American pension and benefit plans; a third will be owned by mutual funds, institutions, and small investors; and a third will be owned by rich people. For the first time in American history, government policy will focus on improving share prices to help average Americans increase their wealth. There are basically two ways that government can improve share prices: by helping to increase the price/ earnings ratio, and by helping to increase corporate earnings.

The United States government can increase price/earnings ratios by reducing interest rates. During 1992, everyone talked about low interest rates in the United States, but these rates applied only to short-term borrowing. Long-term interest rates remained high. The only way for government to reduce long-term interest rates is to stop borrowing so much money, which means reducing the size of the national deficit. With low inflation, low deficits, and low long-term interest rates, price/earnings ratios will go up and so will share prices.

How could the United States government help companies increase earnings? By helping to reduce the expenses that are currently taking so much money out of corporate earnings. These expenses include the cost of health care, worker's compensation, product liability insurance, and environmental protection. What if the United States government had one agency to deal with Social Security, health care, consumer and worker disability insurance, and environmental protection. What if this system was funded in part by sales taxes on products based on the estimated cost of paying the medical, disability, and environmental costs caused by making and consuming those products; and what if a company could receive a percentage of those funds if it could prove that its products did not cause injury to workers, consumers, or the environment, regardless of what country that company happened to be in? Such a system would put American companies on a more equal footing with product producers in other countries and would give every company a real incentive to produce safe products safely and with the least harm to the environment.

In Search of Ownership

In the early 1980s, Thomas J. Peters and Robert H. Waterman wrote a very popular book called *In Search of Excellence* (Harper & Row, 1982). This book still makes fascinating reading a decade after its first publication. Many of the companies listed as excellent in the early 1980s were not doing so well by the early 1990s. The list includes General Motors, IBM, Wang, Digital, and Texas Instruments, to name just a few.

Business books and seminars in the 1980s were required to provide the reader or listener with a few simple platitudes to help them make immediate changes in their companies. In this case, the eight platitudes were: (1) a bias for action; (2) closeness to the customer; (3) autonomy and entrepreneurship; (4) productivity through people; (5) hands-on, value driven; (6) stick to the knitting; (7) simple form, lean staff; and (8) simultaneous loose-tight properties. Looking back a decade later, it seems that these platitudes helped some companies and not others.

When you read the entire book, you discover that what the authors are really impressed by are rank-and-file employees who go out of their way to provide better service or force a large company to take a chance on their ideas. Throughout the book, the authors tell the story of "product champions," employees who have the courage to take an idea for a new product through to success.

Peters and Waterman talk about all of the studies that show that the best way to get workers to make real progress is to give them "a modicum of apparent control over his or her destiny" (p. xxiii). They tell us that companies have to really believe "people are our most important asset" (p. 16). They point out that quality control generated on the shop floor is much better than inspector-generated quality control (p. 29). They claim that the fastest way to success is to get employees to have a "personal identification with the company's success" (p. 39). They say that an excellent company has excellent customer relations and that "customer relations simply mirror employee relations" (p. 166).

They tell us that excellent companies encourage the "entrepreneurial spirit" in all of their employees (p. 201) and that excellent companies have a great deal of informal communication (p. 218). They say that companies have to "trust" their employees, the employees have to trust management (p. 236), and that excellent companies do not keep "secrets" from their employees (p. 241). They quote David Packard, who said that an excellent company has "innovative people at all levels in the organization" (p. 286). They then discuss all the gimmicks, such as quality circles and job enlargement, that have come and gone and failed to turn companies into excellent companies. In the early 1990s, the gimmicks included total quality management and the belief that attending a one-day seminar would somehow make bad managers into good managers. It does not.

How do we make average companies into excellent companies? How do we get employees to have an entrepreneurial spirit, and how do we get managers to trust their employees? If we look back at the excellent companies that were excellent in 1982 and are still considered excellent in 1993, we find that many of them emphasize employee ownership. Procter & Gamble has always had a high level of employee ownership. Hewlett-Packard and Delta Airlines also have a high level of employee ownership.

If we look at the technology companies that are still successful in the 1990s and those that are not, we find that California's Silicon Valley beat out Boston. Is that because the climate in Silicon Valley is more conducive to success, or is it because many of the Silicon Valley companies had to introduce a variety of ways to share ownership with employees from the beginning in order to lure quality employees out to California in the 1950s, and they continue to maintain those programs?

Getting employees to trust the company and really give it their best effort requires more than just the latest gimmick. Getting managers to really share information with employees requires more than a seminar leader telling them that this is a good idea. When employees know that they actually have a significant amount of their personal wealth tied up in the company, they have a very real incentive to go the extra mile to make something work. When managers are told that employees, as a group, are the largest single stockholder in the company, they begin to trust them and tell them more. Participatory management is the key, but it takes two to tango. The employee has to be willing to actually participate more in controlling his or her work environment and the managers have to be willing to let them.

There are hundreds of pertinent stories. Take, for example, the company that introduced a leveraged ESOP and explained to the employees that if they could just reduce waste from the current level of 7 percent to 5 percent, that alone would pay the interest on the ESOP loan. Two months later the waste level was below 4 percent. There were no quality circles, special waste-abatement teams, or high-priced waste elimination consultants, just an ESOP combined with a good one-hour lecture on what an ESOP is and how it works.

Weirton Steel Company has an advertisement that asks if you would like to deal with a company that has 7,942 customer service representatives, 7,942 quality control engineers, 7,942 steel production specialists—you get the point. Weirton turned every employee into each of these things by making the employees owners. Avis, Polaroid, and thousands of other American companies have done the same thing.

During the early 1990s, we heard a lot about empowerment. If we could just empower people in America's ghettos, all of our problems would be over. H. Ross Perot, after the Los Angeles riots of 1992, said that what the ghetto needs is "capital and credit." But these catch words miss the point. How do you empower people? How do you provide them with capital and credit? You make them owners. We have to wonder what race relations in the United States would be like today if the federal government had really given every former slave family 40 acres and a mule and provided them with a basic education instead of filling the South with carpetbaggers after the Civil War.

During the 1980s, the media told the stories of people in Wall Street who got very rich very quickly. The reality is that, for most working people, the only way to get rich quick is to do something illegal. (It turns out that that was how many of the people on Wall Street managed it also.) Is there a way for average working people to get rich without becoming criminals?

Take the case of a gentleman we shall call Bill (to protect his privacy). Bill lives in Los Angeles. On returning from World War II, Bill bought a house in what was then a working-class neighborhood. He used a 30-year mortgage. He also went to work for Nabisco at the bottom of the ladder. Over the next 40 years, Bill did his job. He likes to tell the story of how he would call his wife from a pay phone and let it ring twice and hang up. That way he saved the dime and his wife knew he was coming home for lunch.

Bill did his job well and invested a little in Nabisco stock each month through the company's stock purchase plan. In the late 1980s, Nabisco was bought out twice by buyout artists, and Bill ended up with over half a million dollars. He got rich by doing a good job and investing in his company. Oh, by the way, Bill's house was recently valued at more than $350,000 because he and his neighbors made their neighborhood an attractive place in which to live.

In the 1980s, more than 2,000 Microsoft employees became millionaires almost overnight because they had stock options and stock in the company. A gentleman told me that every month he waited to go to work for H. Ross Perot's company, EDS, cost him a million dollars in the long run because of the value of the stock options and other ownership incentives.

When my ancestors left Scotland for the United States, they came for ownership. When my great grandfather left Tennessee for West Texas in the 1880s, he went because the government promised him two square miles of land. All he had to do was to make the desert bloom, fight the bandits, plant some trees, and get in a cash crop. That's all! Those two square miles still produce the best cotton in the world. Is there anything short of the promise of ownership that would have gotten him to make that move and make that farm a success?

Investing with Employee Owners

During 1992, a new mutual fund appeared on the scene. It promised to invest in companies that treated their employees well. That is a good beginning, but why stop there? Why not invest in companies that have employee-owners? Exhibit 16.2 provides a list of the largest U.S. companies in which the employees own more than 10 percent of the company's stock. Of course, as an investor, you would still want to consider other factors. Employees own a lot of stock in Sears, but no one in their right mind would actually buy stock in Sears today. It certainly takes more than "just" a reasonable level of employee ownership to make a company a good investment. However, all things being equal, companies that do have a reasonable level of employee ownership, and combine that with real efforts at participatory management, have been good investments in the past and will probably continue to be good investments in the future.

When Chrysler introduced an ESOP for the rank and file and hired a CEO who was willing to work for only stock options, I bought stock. When the CEO wanted a salary and the employees wanted out of the ESOP, I sold. It was just that simple.

The time has arrived when an investor can make the decision to invest only in companies in which the employees and the executives are both committed to long-term growth through personal stock ownership. Joseph Blasi and Douglas Kruse of Rutgers University and Michael Conte of the University of Baltimore have introduced the Employee Ownership Index and the Employee Ownership Investors Index to allow investors to track the performance of public companies whose employees own more than 10 percent of the company's stock. These indexes currently include 205 companies with 10 percent employee ownership and more than $50 million in market value. The Employee Ownership Index reflects how a mutual fund that invested

Exhibit 16.2 Major Public U.S. Companies with More Than
10 Percent Employee Ownership at End of 1990
(listed in descending order of size)

Of Fortune 500's Largest Industrial Companies

Ford	FMC	Hartmarx
Texaco	Owens-Corning	McCormick
Chevron	Armstrong	Ball
Procter & Gamble	Rohm & Haas	Wheeling-Pittsburgh
Xerox	Quantum	Pentair
McDonnell Douglas	Olin	Savannah
Phillips Petroleum	Corning	ITT Rayonier
Allied Signal	Tribune	Aristech Chemical
Sara Lee	Knight-Rider	Consolidated Papers
Unocal	Westvaco	Interlake
Lockheed	USG	Intergraph
Anheuser-Busch	Sherwin-Williams	Cooper Tire
Coastal	Diamond Shamrock	Crystal Brands
Ashland Oil	Louisiana Pacific	Dennison
Textron	Gencorp	SPX
TRW	Stanley Works	Avondale
James River	Cabot	Imperial Holly
PPG	Polaroid	Toro
Northrop	Willamette	Lukens
Colgate-Palmolive	Cyprus Minerals	Reynolds
Boise Cascade	Harcourt Brace	Tyler
Inland Steel	Jovanovich	Kimball International
Whitman	E-Systems	Chemed
Johnson Controls	Clark Equipment	Butler Manufacturing
Grumman	Weirton Steel	Allied Products
Cummins Engine	Data General	

Of Fortune 50's Retailing and Transportation Companies

Retailing	*Transportation*
Sears	Delta Air
Kroger	TWA
J.C. Penney	Pan Am
May Department Store	Federal Express
Carter Hawley Hale	Consolidated Freightways
Tandy	Yellow Freight
Lowe's	Roadway Services
Long's Drugs	America West

Source: Joseph Blasi and Douglas Kruse, *The New Owners: Mass Emergence of Employee Ownership*
(New York: Harper Business, 1991).

equally in the stock of these 205 companies might perform. The Employee Ownership Investors Index is market-capitalization weighted, meaning it reflects how a mutual fund that invested more heavily in the larger companies might perform. Stock indexes such as the Dow Jones Industrial Average and the S&P 500 are weighted in this way.

During 1991, the Dow Jones Industrial Average rose 20.3 percent and the S&P 500 rose 26.3 percent. The Employee Ownership Investors Index rose 25.6 percent during that year. The Employee Ownership Index (which is not capitalization weighted) rose 35.9 percent during 1991. The difference between the two employee ownership indexes reflects the fact that small companies did better than big companies in 1991. The professors have also looked at how 626 publicly traded companies with more than 4 percent employee ownership did in 1991. Again, this group outperformed the Dow Jones Industrial Average and the S&P 500 Index. These results suggest that the level of employee ownership is a factor that investors should begin to consider (results reported in the Summer 1992 issue of the *Journal of Employee Ownership Law and Finance*).

We know from a great many research studies conducted in the 1980s that employee ownership has its greatest effect when it is combined with participatory management techniques. Investors should become more interested in which companies actually employ these techniques. A list of large companies with significant levels of employee ownership and participatory management styles would include America West Airlines, Lowe's, Herman Miller, PepsiCo, Polaroid, Federal Express, Apple Computer, E-Systems, Kroger, Oregon Steel, J.C. Penney, Procter & Gamble, Tandycrafts, Crown Crafts, Preston Trucking, Michael Baker Company, and Weirton Steel.

When considering investments around the world, many American investors are only just beginning to realize that in many European countries the workers elect representatives to the board of directors even though they have no ownership stake in the company. In the 1990s and beyond, workers are going to have more and more of a say in how companies are run. That being the case, do you want to invest in companies in which the workers have that element of control and no ownership of their own to provide them with an incentive to be concerned with the long-term growth of share value, or would you prefer them to have the same financial stake in the enterprise that you, the outside stockholder, has?

Tomorrow

The hope is that in the twenty-first century countries will compete economically, not militarily. This is a dream every world leader should be working to realize. Over the last two centuries we have found that countries in which the average citizen has a say in the political system (we call that democracy) are less prone to revolution and make better allies in times of war. We have also seen that when the average citizen has an ownership stake in the local economy by owning a home and having some ownership in the local companies, the local economy is more stable and a safer investment.

Many leaders in developing countries think that no one would want to invest in their economy when they could invest in Japan. Quite the contrary. Why would anyone want to invest in Japan? The lesson of the last four decades is that the time to invest in Japan was "then" not "now." Investors around the world are looking for the "next" Japan. Will it be Poland, Hungary, or the Ukraine? Will it be Mexico, Argentina, or Bolivia? Will it be Botswana, Angola, or South Africa? If these countries are willing to create incentives for their citizens to literally "buy into" the local economy, the effect of that local saving, combined with foreign investment, could be significant economic growth in the century ahead.

What about the United States? The United States will continue to be a good investment in the decades ahead. In many cities across America, entrepreneurs, armed with technical know-how, smart legal advice, venture capital, and talented employees, are creating the IBMs and General Motors of the twenty-first century. A few are even rebuilding formerly dying companies such as Xerox and Polaroid. America may be down, but it is a long way from out.

Of the world's seven most developed economies (the United States, Canada, Japan, Great Britain, France, Germany, and Italy), the United States has the greatest potential to produce growth companies in the 1990s. Canada is in danger of breaking up; Japan and Germany have no growth companies; Italy cannot control the Mafia; and France cannot control its students or its farmers. Great Britain has spent two decades preparing for the capitalist revolution, but that revolution cannot begin until investors, workers, and managers begin to think of British workers as potential partners rather than lower-class hooligans drawing a wage because it pays better than the dole.

The United States looks like a good bet for the decades ahead. It would be an even better bet if the high cost of national defense and health care could be brought under control. Both have been a major drag on the U.S. economy throughout the 1980s and early 1990s. It would also be a better bet if race relations could be improved.

Everyone is looking for the magic bullet, the special gimmick, the real McCoy that will make a difference in either their company, their neighborhood, or their country. Management styles emerge and fade. Circles, squares, and triangles are drawn on blackboards. Catchwords come and go; seminars come and go; books come and go. The problems remain.

The truth is that, no matter what the problem, ownership must be a big part of the solution. While it is not the whole answer, it is a start. It is the one factor that has made a real difference through the decades across countries, companies, and neighborhoods. It cannot do the job alone. A neighborhood of homeowners without adequate police protection is not a safe neighborhood. A country with unstable politics is not a safe investment environment. A company with a thousand "one-minute managers" and no real idea of where it is going or how it is going to get there is not a good place to work or invest in even if all of those managers own stock. Ownership is part of the solution. But imagine the possibilities.

Imagine a community where recession means everyone works a few hours less until times get better, but no one is fired or loses their home. Imagine a laid off worker who can get by on the income from his investments until he finds another job or begins a company of his own. Imagine a community where the residents own their own homes and most of the mortgages have been paid off. Imagine a company that really does know how to succeed in a fast-changing world because every employee really does have an entrepreneurial spirit. The possibilities are limited only by our imagination.

Index